المدخل إلى علم النحو

A FUNDAMENTAL PRIMER OF NAHW

Compiled by
Muawiyah ibn Mufti Abdussamad Ahmed

British Library Cataloguing in Publication Data
A catalogue record for this book is available from the British Library.

Published & Distributed by:
Jamiatul Ilm Wal Huda
30 Moss Street
Blackburn
Lancashire, U.K.
BB1 5JT
T: 01254 673105
W: www.jamiah.co.uk
E: info@jamiah.co.uk

Compiled by: Muawiyah ibn Mufti Abdussamad Ahmed
E: muawiyahahmed@hotmail.co.uk

Edited by: Umm 'Abdurrahman & Yusuf Dalal

ISBN: 978-1-910967-19-5

Printed by: Imak Ofset, Turkey

بسم الله الرحمن الرحيم

In the name of Allah, the most Merciful, the ever Kind

قَالَ حَمَّادُ بْنُ سَلَمَةَ

"مَثَلُ الَّذِيْ يَطْلُبُ الْحَدِيْثَ وَلَا يَعْرِفُ النَّحْوَ كَمَثَلِ الْحِمَارِ عَلَيْهِ مِخْلَاةٌ لَا شَعِيْرَ فِيْهَا"

[المستطرف في كلّ فنّ مستظرف]

Hammad ibn Salamah mentions:

The person who studies Hadeeth without knowing Nahw is like the donkey that carries the feed bag without any barley within it.

[al-Mustatraf]

Contents

Introduction

In the name of Allah, the most Merciful, the ever Kind. All praise and thanks belong to Allah, Lord of the universe and Master of our fortunes, and may the choicest of peace and blessings be showered upon our beloved Prophet Muhammad ﷺ, his companions and upon all who follow their example.

To achieve a deep and coherent understanding of any language, it is of imperative importance that an individual grasps the fundamental and foundational rules; thereafter, they must work to increase their vocabulary within that language. This is no different when studying Arabic: as a student embarks on the journey of creating proficiency in the Arabic language with the aim of furthering their ability to study and benefit from the canonical texts of Islam, i.e. the Holy Qur'an and the Prophetic Traditions, many sciences and disciplines need to be studied. The prominent historian Ibn Khaldoon pens in the preface of his famed book on history,

علوم اللسان العربي أركانه أربعة وهي اللغة والنحو والبيان والأدب ومعرفته ضروريّة على أهل الشريعة

The core modules of the Arabic language are four: lexicology, syntax, rhetoric and literature. A deep understanding of the language is imperative for the students of the religion.

Ibn Khaldoon then ranks each of the core modules according to their order of importance; he emphasises the significance of syntax by giving it the highest ranking from the four. Furthermore, ibn Qutaybah attributes a proverb to the second Caliph Umar RA in his book, *Gareebul Hadeeth*:

تعلّموا السنن والفرائض واللحن كما تعلّموا القرآن

Study the Prophetic Traditions, the obligatory acts and the ability to discern errors in the Arabic language (syntax and language) just as you study the Qur'an.

The Pre-Islamic Arabs learnt Arabic as their mother tongue and could easily understand the language without the need to formally study grammar rules; similar to how many people learn their own mother tongue. However, once Islam was revealed and the Arabic language was used for the Holy scripture, the importance of Arabic was no longer restricted to just the Arabs. As Islam was a religion for all people, to understand Arabic would now become important for Arabs and non-Arabs alike. Hence, for the ease of the non-Arabs, during the caliphate of 'Ali R.A., under the guidance and instruction of the Caliph, Abu al-Aswad ad-Duwali embarked on the challenge of formally formulating the Arabic grammar rules. These rules were then developed further and refined in the later centuries by many grammarians and scholars. May Almighty Allah reward all those that made the language easier for us. Ameen

This is a primer in Arabic syntax, which should be studied in the first year of Arabic studies. Thereafter, students should study an intermediate text of Arabic syntax – this will further consolidate their understanding of Arabic syntax and also fill in any gaps (as some challenging and less important discussions have intentionally been left out of this primer). One intermediate book for Arabic syntax can be Hidayatun Nahw. Alhamdulillah, with the Grace of Almighty Allah, Hidayatun Nahw has been published by Jamiatul Ilm Wal Huda with more than 800 questions and answers in English, with the permission of Almighty Allah, this will be a good book to study after completing this primer in Arabic syntax.

It is only with the infinite grace and the divine ability showered by Almighty Allah that my attempts at compiling these notes on Arabic syntax have come together as the work before you. I embarked on this task with the intention of making the Arabic language more accessible for the students of Arabic, thus allowing them to benefit from the Holy Qur'an and the Prophetic Traditions with a greater degree of rigour and accuracy. This compilation includes an introduction to Arabic syntax along with the key terms found in the classical and contemporary works. The book is divided into more than 40 lessons for the ease of students. The recommended timeframe to study this compilation would be 6-9 months, that includes memorising all the important terms with understanding and completing all the activities. The compilation can actually be studied quicker; however, this could lead to the student forgetting the science and terms. Therefore, it would be ideal to cover 2/3 lessons a week properly and use any extra time for revision or using a suitable Arabic text to highlight any rules and terms learnt thus far. In the penultimate lesson of this primer, over fifty Arabic sentences are provided with tables to fill in the grammatical breakdown *(tarkeeb)* detail – this will enable students to consolidate their understanding of Arabic syntax in a practical manner. Also, the final lesson of this primer comprises of flow charts for Arabic syntax – students should use these for routine revisions of the subject and should also annotate around the flow charts with the keyword reminders.

Despite this small effort of mine amalgamated with the divine ability granted to me by Almighty Allah, I accept the weakness within myself and concede that there may be mistakes. Therefore, I request all readers to email me, without hesitation, regarding any corrections or suggestions that may enhance future prints and works.

Finally, I conclude with an expression of my gratitude and appreciation. Primarily, I express my praise and thanks to the Creator, Almighty Allah, for granting me the ability to understand, comprehend and try to present the science of Arabic syntax in a simplified manner. There is no doubt, without this blessed favour of the Almighty Allah, one would be incapable of completing even the minutest of tasks. I then wish to extend a special sense of gratitude to my dear father and respected teacher, Mufti Abdussamad Ahmed. His teachings, spiritual upbringing, advice and guidance have always been instrumental for me in all my endeavours. Neither can I forget all those friends of mine who assisted me in the completion of this work; I pray that Almighty Allah reward them with abundant success in both worlds and makes this effort a means of salvation for them on the day of Judgement and a means of entry into Paradise.

It would be a challenge to give exclusive mention to all these friends by name; however, I feel obliged to express gratitude to my beloved wife, Umm 'Abdurrahaman, for her editing, continued support and love. I must also express gratitude to my dear friend, Yusuf Dalal, for editing the complete primer along with contributing invaluable suggestions. I pray Almighty Allah rewards both of them abundantly and accepts this effort as a service for His religion. May He reward us for every individual who derives any benefit from this compilation and may He make us benefit from the accepted supplications and prayers of all, especially the pious. I conclude with a prayer that Almighty Allah enters every one of us into the highest ranks of Jannah without any reckoning, may He allow us to gain His pleasure, and may He grant us the companionship of Prophet Muhammad ﷺ and the righteous and pious souls. Ameen

Muawiyah ibn Mufti Abdussamad Ahmed

LESSON 1: INTRODUCTION

The definition and purpose of Nahw (Arabic Syntax):

1) To learn the grammatical state of each word.

   For example, the first word of Surah Fatihah is read as اَلْحَمْدُ (with a dhammah on the last letter), so why is it not اَلْحَمْدَ (with a fathah on the last letter) or اَلْحَمْدِ (with a kasrah on the last letter)?

2) To learn the method of joining words to make a meaningful sentence.

3) To save oneself from making mistakes when reading, writing and speaking Arabic.

Important terminologies:

Below are some important terminologies that should be learnt before advancing further, although some terms will become embedded later after frequent usage of the terms.

	Term	Meaning
1	اِسْم	A noun
2	فِعْل	A verb
3	حَرْف	A particle
4	ضَمَّة	*Dhammah* is the name given to this sign ـُ (above a letter)
5	مَضْمُوْم	This is the name given to a letter that is in a *dhammah* (ending) state.
6	فَتْحَة	*Fathah* is the name given to this sign ـَ (above a letter)
7	مَفْتُوْح	This is the name given to a letter that is in a *fathah* (ending) state.
8	كَسْرَة	*Kasrah* is the name given to this sign ـِ (below a letter)
9	مَكْسُوْر	This is the name given to a letter that is in a *kasrah* (ending) state.

10	سُكُوْن/جَزْم	*Sukoon/Jazm* is the name given to this sign ـْـ (above a letter)
11	حَرَكَة	This is the collective name of *dhammah, fathah* and *kasrah.*
12	مُتَحَرِّك	This is the name of the letter with a dhammah, fathah or a kasrah.
13	سَاكِنْ	This is the name for a letter which has a *sukoon* upon it.
14	تَنْوِيْن	*Tanween* is the name given to the following: ـٌـ (the double *dhammah),* ـًـ (the double *fathah),* ـٍـ (the double *kasrah).*
15	تَشْدِيْد	*Tashdeed* is the name given to this sign ـّـ (above a letter). This sign appears when two same letters appear together; they are merged (and written as one) and the *tashdeed* sign is placed upon it. E.g., رَبْبَ - notice the second and third letters are the same. Hence, they will be merged and become رَبّ (written as one letter).
16	مُشَدَّد	This is the name for a letter which has a *tashdeed* upon it.
17	وَاحِد	This refers to singular form. E.g. نَصَرَ (*He* (*one man*) helped.)
18	تَثْنِيَة	This refers to dual form. E.g. نَصَرَا (*They* (*two men*) helped.) Note: In the English language, there is no separate scale for dual, rather it is 'singular' or 'plural'. However, in Arabic, there is the 'dual' form and thereafter the 'plural' form.
19	جَمْع	This refers to plural form. E.g. نَصَرُوْا (*They* (*three or more men*) helped.)
20	مُذَكَّر	This is the masculine form. E.g. نَصَرَ (*He* (one man) helped.)
21	مُؤَنَّث	This is the feminine form. E.g. نَصَرَتْ (*She* (one woman) helped.)
22	كَلِمَة	This is a singular word.
23	كَلَام	This is a sentence/phrase.

LESSON 2: MEANINGFUL UTTERANCES

Any human utterance in Arabic is called a لَفْظ.

A لَفْظ (utterance) has two types:

1) لَفْظ مَوْضُوْع – meaningful utterance,
2) لَفْظ مُهْمَل – meaningless utterance.

	Term	Meaning
1	لَفْظ	Any utterance from a person's mouth; whether meaningful or meaningless. Example: The word 'door' (بَابٌ) if uttered by a person is an **utterance;** hence, called a لفظ .
2	لَفْظ مَوْضُوْع	Any **meaningful utterance** that comes from a person's mouth. Example: The word 'door' (بَابٌ) if uttered by a person is a **meaningful utterance;** hence, called a لفظ مَوْضُوْع .
3	لَفْظ مُهْمَل	Any **meaningless utterance** that comes from a person's mouth. Example: The word 'repap' (the reverse of the word 'paper') if uttered by a person is a **meaningless utterance;** hence, called a لفظ مُهْمَل .

Note: A **meaningless utterance** holds no purpose, hence no rules, in grammar; therefore, it will no longer be discussed in this book.

ACTIVITY: 1

Write, with reason, if the following Arabic words are لفظ موضوع or لفظ مهمل . The meaning of the different words is given in brackets if the word has a meaning.

Word	Type	Reason
قَلَم (pen)	meaningful utterance	
نَصَرَ (he helped)	meaningful utterance	
دَيْز	meaningless utterance	
سَيَّارَة (car)	لفظ موضوع	It is a meaningful utterance
لَبِحَسُط	meaningless utterance	
كِتَابٌ (book)	لفظ	

Types of لَفْظ مَوْضُوْع :

The لَفْظ مَوْضُوْع has two types:

1) مُفْرَد (also called كَلِمَة) – a single word,
2) مُرَكَّب (also called كَلَام) – a phrase/sentence, also referred to as a 'compound'.

	Term	Meaning
1	مُفْرَد / كَلِمَة	A **single word** which is meaningful.
		Example: The word 'window' (نَافِذَة) if uttered by a person is a **single word** which is meaningful; hence called a مفرد or كلمة .
2	مُرَكَّب / كَلَام	**Two (or more) words** joined together in a meaningful manner – this could be a meaningful **sentence** or a meaningful **phrase**.
		Example: The words 'Muhammad is present' (مُحَمَّدٌ حَاضِرٌ) is formed of two (or more) words joined together, creating an overall meaningful sentence. Hence, it is called a مُرَكَّب or كَلَام .

ACTIVITY: 2

Write, with reasoning, if the following are مُفْرَد or مُرَكَّب .

The meaning of any difficult words is given in the footnotes.[1]

Word/Phrase	Type	Reason
دَفْتَرُ خَالِدٍ	مركب	
اَلْبَابُ مُغْلَقٌ	MURAKKAB	
اَلطَّعَام		
سَيَّارَة	مفرد	It is a single word
طَالِبٌ طَوِيْل		
اَلْكِتَابُ عَلَى الْمَكْتَبِ		
اَلطَّعَامُ لَذِيْذٌ		
اَلْمَاء		

1

دَفْتَر	Notebook
اَلْبَاب	The door
مُغْلَق	Locked
اَلطَّعَام	The food
سَيَّارة	Car

طَالِب	Student
طَوِيْل	Tall
اَلْكِتَاب	The book
عَلَى	Upon
اَلْمَكْتَب	The desk

لَذِيْذ	Delicious
اَلْمَاء	The water

LESSON 3: SINGLE WORDS

A single word (مُفْرَد / كَلِمَة) is divided into three types:

1) اِسْم – noun,
2) فِعْل – verb,
3) حَرْف – particle.

	Term	Meaning
1	اِسْم	This is a **noun** – a word that names something, e.g a person, place or thing. Nouns are not limited to time.
		Example: The word 'pen' (قَلَم), is the name of a thing, hence a **noun.**
2	فِعْل	This is a **verb** – an action. Verbs are limited to time, i.e. past, present or future tense.
		Example: 'He wrote' (كَتَبَ), is an 'action' word, hence a **verb.** This is an example of a past tense verb.
3	حَرْف	This is a **particle** – usually a 1- or 2-lettered word used to 'join' between two nouns or a verb and a noun.
		Example: The word 'in' (فِيْ); this is a 2-lettered particle. The word فِيْ could be used in sentence like: دَخَلَ مُحَمَّدٌ فِيْ الْمَسْجِدِ (Muhammad entered **in** the Masjid).

ACTIVITY: 3

Based on the meanings, write whether the following words are اسم , فعل or حرف.

Word	Type	Reason
فَتَحَ (he opened)	Verb	Because he did Something
شَايٌ (tea)	Noun	It is a Liquid .
هَاتِفٌ (phone)	Noun	An electrical Device
سَيَّارَةٌ (car)	اسم	It is a name of a thing, hence a **noun.**
مِنْ (from)	Noun	Area
يَنْصُرُ (he is helping)	Verb	doing Something
مَكْتَبٌ (desk)		
وَ (and)		

Signs of single words

The aforementioned three types have some unique **signs (عَلَامَات)** which distinguish them from each other.

At this stage, only some of the most basic signs will be mentioned.

Signs of a noun (عَلَامَات الْإِسْم):

	Sign with example
1	It has an (ال) at the beginning of the word. Any word with (ال), which means 'the', at the beginning of it will be a noun.
	Example: The words أَلْقَلَم (the pen), أَلْكِتَاب (the book), أَلْبَاب (the door); all of these words are **nouns** as they have an أَلْ before it.
2	It has a particle of *jarr* (حَرْف الجرّ) before it. If a word has a particle of *jarr* (حرف الجرّ) before it then that word itself will be a noun. More detail regarding the particle of *jarr* will be studied later.
	Example: The word كِتَاب in فِيْ كِتَابٍ is a noun as it has a particle of *jarr* before it.
3	It has a *tanween* on the last letter of the word. Any word which has a *tanween* on the last letter would indicate that the word is a noun. A *tanween* is a ـٌ , ـً or ـٍ (i.e the double *harakah).*
	Example: The word كِتَابٌ (book) is a noun as it has a *tanween* on the last letter. The word طَالِبٌ (student) is a noun as it has a *tanween* on the last letter.

Signs of a verb (عَلَامَات الْفِعْل):

	Sign with example
1	It has the word قَدْ (verily) before it. Any word with قَدْ before it would indicate that the word itself is a verb.
	Example: The word سَمِعَ (he heard) in قَدْ سَمِعَ is a verb as it has the word قَدْ before it.
2	It has the particle سَـ (very soon) before it. Any word with سَـ before it would indicate that the word itself is a verb.
	Example: The word يَنْصُرُ (he is helping) in سَيَنْصُرُ (very soon he is helping) is a verb as it has the word سَـ before it.
3	It has the word سَوْفَ (soon) before it. Any word with سَوْفَ before it would indicate that the word itself is a verb.
	Example: The word تَعْلَمُ (you will know) in سَوْفَ تَعْلَمُ is a verb as it has the word سَوْفَ before it.

Signs of a particle (عَلَامَاتُ الْحَرْفِ):

	Sign with example
1	1- lettered or 2-lettered words are usually particles. Sometimes particles may be 3-lettered.
	Example: The word مِنْ (from) is a particle – it is 2-lettered. The word بِـ (with) is a particle – it is 1-lettered.
2	Joining/connecting between two nouns or between a noun and a verb.
	Example: The word عَلَى (upon) in the sentence جَلَسَ **عَلَى** الْكُرْسِيِّ (He sat **upon** a chair) is a particle as it joins between the verb جَلَسَ (he sat) and the noun الْكُرْسِيّ (chair).
3	Generally, if the word cannot be identified as a noun or a verb, then it will be a particle. So, for each word, check if it is a noun or a verb; if it is neither then it will be a particle.
	Example: The word مِنْ (from) cannot be identified as a noun or a verb, hence it will be identified as a particle.

ACTIVITY: 4

Write, with reasoning, if the underlined words are اسم , فعل or حرف .

The meaning of any difficult words is given in the footnotes.[2]

Phrase	Type of word		Reason
رَبِّ الْعَالَمِيْنَ			
سَوْفَ أَنْصُرُ			
قَدْ قَامَ			
أَنْعَمَ عَلَى الْمُؤْمِنِيْنَ	حرف		It is joining between a verb and a noun
كِتَابٌ كَبِيْرٌ			
دَخَلَ مُعَلِّمٌ			
سَافَرَ مِنْ مَكَّةَ			
سَيَقُوْلُ			

2

رَبّ	Lord
الْعَالَمِيْن	The worlds
سَوْفَ	Very soon
أَنْصُرُ	I will help
قَدْ	Verily

قَامَ	He stood
أَنْعَمَ	He blessed
عَلَى	Upon
الْمُؤْمِنِيْن	The believers
كِتَابٌ	A book

كَبِيْرٌ	Big
دَخَلَ	He entered
مُعَلِّمٌ	A teacher
سَافَرَ	He travelled
يَقُوْلُ	He will say

LESSON 4: COMPOUND PHRASES/SENTENCES

Complete Sentence

A single word (مُرَكَّب / كَلَام) is divided into two types:

1) الْمُرَكَّبُ الْمُفِيْد – a complete compound,
2) الْمُرَكَّب غَيْرُ الْمُفِيْد – an incomplete compound.

	Term	Meaning
1	الْمُرَكَّبُ الْمُفِيْد	This is a **complete compound** – i.e. after the speaker completes his speech, some complete information or a request, etc. is known. In other words, it is a **complete sentence.**
		Example: The sentence دَخَلَ مُحَمَّدٌ فِيْ الْمَسْجِدِ (Muhammad entered in the Masjid) is a المركّب المفيد as it is a complete sentence from which complete information is known.
2	الْمُرَكَّبُ غَيْرُ الْمُفِيْد	This is an **incomplete compound** – i.e. after the speaker completes his speech, complete information such as news or a request, etc. is **not fully known.** In other words, it is an **incomplete sentence.**
		Example: The phrase قَلَمُ طَالِبٍ (a student's pen) is a المركّب غير المفيد as it is an incomplete sentence from which complete information is unknown. One may question, what about the student's pen?

ACTIVITY: 5

Write whether the following compounds are المركّب المفيد or المركّب غير المفيد ?[3]

Compound	Type	Reason
طَعَامٌ لَذِيْذٌ		
اِنْكَسَرَ الْقَلَمُ		
حَفِظْتُ الْقُرْآنَ		
نَصَرَ مُحَمَّدٌ عُمَرَ	المركب المفيد	Complete set of information becomes known.
رَجُلٌ صَالِحٌ		
بَيْتٌ جَدِيْدٌ		
ذَهَبَ الرَّجُلُ		

3

طَعَام	Food
لَذِيْذ	Delicious
اِنْكَسَرَ	Broke
اَلْقَلَم	The pen
حَفِظْتُ	I memorised

اَلْقُرْآن	The Qur'an
نَصَرَ	He helped
رَجُلٌ	A man
صَالِحٌ	Pious
بَيْتٌ	A house

جَدِيْدٌ	New
ذَهَبَ	He went
الرَّجُلُ	The man

Further discussion on الْمُرَكَّب الْمُفِيْد :

A **complete compound** is called الْمُرَكَّب الْمُفِيْد. This is also called جُمْلَة (**sentence**).

The جُمْلَة (sentence) is of two types:

1) الْجُمْلَة الْخَبَرِيَّة – informative sentence,
2) الْجُمْلَة الْإِنْشَائِيَّة – non-informative sentence,

	Term	Meaning
1	الْجُمْلَة الْخَبَرِيَّة	This is such a sentence that **has the possibility of being true or false.**
		Example: The sentence مَحَمَّدٌ جَالِسٌ (Muhammad is sat) is an **informative sentence** as the statement is either **true** or **false.**
2	الْجُمْلَة الْإِنْشَائِيَّة	This is such a sentence that **does not** have the possibility of being true or false.
		Example: The sentence اِيْتِ بِالْمَاءِ (bring the water) is a **non-informative sentence** as the statement cannot be regarded as either **true** or **false.**

Types of الْجُمْلَة الْخَبَرِيَّة :

The جُمْلَة خَبَرِيَّة (informative sentence) is of two types:

1) الْجُمْلَة الْاِسْمِيَّة – nominal sentence,
2) الْجُمْلَة الْفِعْلِيَّة – verbal sentence,

	Term	Meaning
1	الْجُمْلَة الْاِسْمِيَّة	This is such a sentence which starts with a **noun.**
		Example: The sentence مَحَمَّدٌ جَالِسٌ (Muhammad is sat) is an informative sentence which starts with the **noun** مُحَمَّدٌ .
2	الْجُمْلَة الْفِعْلِيَّة	This is such a sentence which starts with a **verb.**
		Example: The sentence جَلَسَ مُحَمَّدٌ (Muhammad is sat) is an informative sentence which starts with the **verb** جَلَسَ **.**

Types of الْجُمْلَة الْإِنْشَائِيَّة :

The جُمْلَة إِنْشَائِيَّة (non-informative sentence) is of many types, including the following:

1) الْأَمْر – imperative (positive command),
2) النَّهْي – prohibition (negative command),
3) الْإِسْتِفْهَام – interrogative,
4) التَّرَجِّي – hope,
5) النِّدَاء – exclamation,

	Term	Meaning
1	الْأَمْر	This is an **imperative** sentence (one giving a **positive command**).
		Example: The sentence اِيْتِ بِالْمَاء (bring the water) is a non-informative **imperative** sentence as it includes a positive command.
2	النَّهْي	This is a **prohibitive** sentence (one giving a **negative command**).
		Example: The sentence لَا تَجْلِسْ هُنَا (don't sit here) is a non-informative **prohibitive** sentence as it includes a negative command.
3	الْإِسْتِفْهَام	This is an **interrogative** sentence (one which includes a **question**).
		Example: The sentence هَلْ أَتَى مُحَمَّدٌ؟ (Has Muhammad come?) is a non-informative **interrogative** sentence as it includes a question.
4	التَّرَجِّي	This is a sentence with a **hope** (expressed by the speaker).
		Example: The sentence لَعَلَّ الْإِمْتِحَانَ سَهْلٌ (Hopefully the exam will be easy) is a non-informative sentence as it includes a **hope** (wish).
5	النِّدَاء	This is an **exclamative** sentence (one which includes an exclamation mark or **calling someone**).
		Example: The sentence يَا مُحَمَّدُ! (O Muhammad!) is a non-informative **exclamative** sentence as it involves calling someone.

Note: There are other types of جُمْلَة إِنْشَائِيَّة (non-informative sentences) which can be studied in more advanced books of grammar.

ACTIVITY: 6

Determine whether the following sentences are جملة خبريّة or جملة إنشائيّة .

Sentence	English	Type	Reason
السَّيَّارَةُ كَبِيْرَةٌ	The car is big.	خبرية	The sentence can be true or False
لَا تَضْرِبْ أَحَدًا	Don't hit anyone.	جملة انشائية	The sentence cannot be true or False
اِفْتَحِ الْكِتَابَ	Open the book.	جملة انشائية	The sentence cannot be true or False
الدَّرْسُ سَهْلٌ	The lesson is easy.	جملة خبريّة	This is such a sentence which has the possibility of being **true** or **false.**
الْمَاءُ بَارِدٌ	The water is cold.	جملة خبرية	Sentence can be T or F
لَا تُغْلِقِ الْبَابَ	Don't lock the door.	جملة انشائية	Sentence cannot be T or F

ACTIVITY: 7

Write whether the following sentences are جملة اسميّة or جملة فعليّة .

Sentence	English	Type	Reason
السَّيَّارَةُ كَبِيْرَةٌ	The car is big.	جملة اسمية	Starts with noun
وَسِعَ الْكُرْسِيّ	The chair was wide.	جملة فعلية	Starts with noun
الْكِتَابُ جَدِيْدٌ	The book is new.	جملة اسمية	Starts with noun
الدَّرْسُ سَهْلٌ	The lesson is easy.	جملة اسميّة	The informative sentence starts with a **noun.**
الْمَاءُ بَارِدٌ	The water is cold.	جملة اسمية	Starts with noun
اِنْكَسَرَ الْقَلَمُ	The pen broke.	جملة اسمية	Starts with noun

ACTIVITY: 8

Decide which type of جملة إنشائيّة the following sentences are:

Sentence	English	Type	Reason
لَعَلَّ الكِتَاب جَدِيْدٌ	Hopefully, the book is new.	4	Hopeful sentence
يَا عَبْدَ الرَّحْمَن!	O Abdurrahman!	5	exclamation
لَا تَضْرِبْ أَحَدًا	Don't hit anyone.	2	Prohibition
اِفْتَحِ الْكِتَابَ	Open the book.	الأمر	This is an **imperative** sentence.
هَلْ جَاءَ الْأُسْتَاذُ؟	Has the teacher come?	3	Interrogative
اِيْتِ بِالْمَاءِ	Bring the water.	1	Imperative

Further discussion on الْمُرَكَّب غَيْرُ الْمُفِيْد :

The الْمُرَكَّب غَيْرُ الْمُفِيْد has many types, from amongst them are:

1) الْمُرَكَّب الْإِضَافِيّ – possessive phrase,
2) الْمُرَكَّب التَّوْصِيْفِيّ – descriptive phrase,

	Term	Meaning
1	الْمُرَكَّب الْإِضَافِيّ	This is a phrase that is made up of (at least) two words – the possession and the possessor.
		Example: The phrase قَلَمُ مُحَمَّدٍ (Muhammad's pen) is a possessive phrase as it consists of a possessed item (the pen, قَلَم) and the possessor (Muhammad, مُحَمَّدٍ).
2	الْمُرَكَّب التَّوْصِيْفِيّ	This is a phrase that is made up of (at least) two words – the described and the description/adjective.
		Example: The phrase كِتَابٌ صَغِيْرٌ (small book) is a descriptive phrase as it consists of a described item (the book, كِتَابٌ) and the description/adjective (small, صَغِيْرٌ).

Note: There are other type of المركّب غير المفيد which are studied in more advanced books of grammar.

ACTIVITY: 9

Write whether the following phrases are المركّب الإضافيّ or المركّب التوصيفيّ .

Sentence	English	Type	Reason
رَجُلٌ طَوِيْلٌ	Tall man	التوصيفي	It in a descriptive phrase
بَيْتُ عُثْمَانَ	Uthman's house	التوصيفي	Possessive phras
مَاءٌ حَارٌّ	Hot water	توصيفي	Descriptive phras
كِتَابُ يُوْسُفَ	Yusuf's book	المركّب الإضافيّ	It is a possessive phrase – the book is the possession and Yusuf is the possessor.
سَيَّارَةُ الْمُدِيْرِ	Principal's car	الإضافي	Possessive phras

ACTIVITY: 10

Annotate the following flowchart by giving the definition and example for each word.

Flow chart for لفظ and its types:

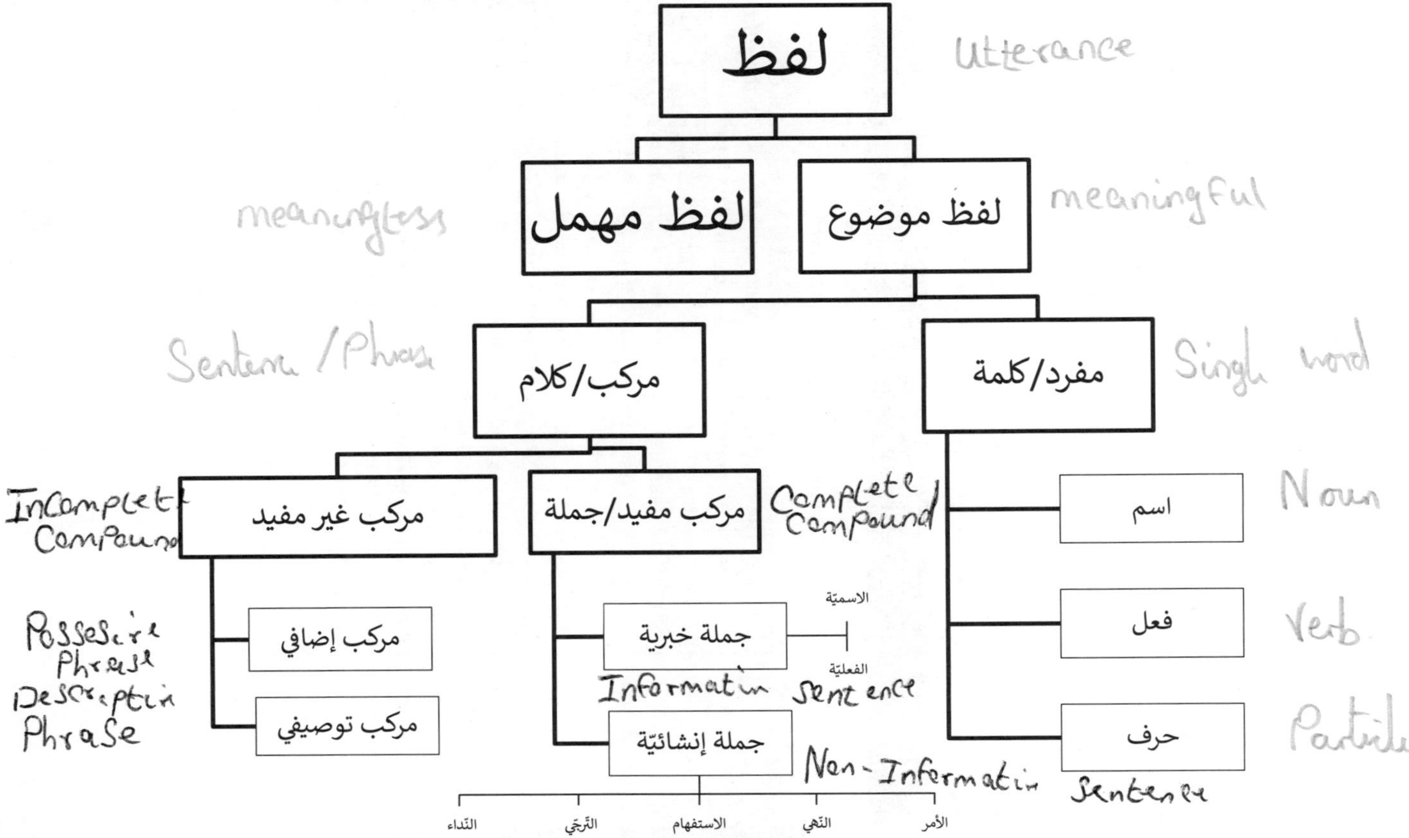

LESSON 5: DIFFERENT GRAMMATICAL STATES

As we have learnt, in the Arabic language words are of **three** types: اسم (nouns), فعل (verbs) and حرف (particles).

Some of these types of words follow specific **grammatical states (حَالَاتٌ)** in sentence structures. In this chapter, a brief explanation will be given regarding the grammatical states for different types of words; once more chapters of grammar are studied, a more detailed discussion on grammatical states will be given.

Grammatical states of اسم (noun):

The اسم (noun) has **three** grammatical states. These are:

	State	Meaning
1	حَالَةُ الرَّفْعِ	This is when the word is in the *rafa'* state (حالة الرفع). In **basic Arabic words**, this will be seen by the *dhammah* (ـُ) added onto the last letter (single harakah or tanween).
		Example: The word اَلْحَمْدُ in the sentence اَلْحَمْدُ لِلّٰهِ is in the ***rafa'* state,** therefore a ***dhammah*** can be seen on the last letter.
2	حَالَةُ النَّصْبِ	This is when the word is in the *nasab* state (حالة النصب). In **basic Arabic words**, this will be seen by the *fathah* (ـَ) added onto the last letter (single harakah or tanween).
		Example: The word الصِّرَاطَ in the sentence اِهْدِنَا الصِّرَاطَ is in the ***nasab* state,** therefore a ***fathah*** can be seen on the last letter.
3	حَالَةُ الجَرِّ	This is when the word is in the *jarr* state (حالة الجر). In **basic Arabic words**, this will be seen by the *kasrah* (ـِ) added onto the last letter (single harakah or tanween).
		Example: The word الْمَغْضُوْبِ in the phrase غَيْرِ الْمَغْضُوْبِ is in the ***jarr* state,** therefore a ***kasrah*** can be seen on the last letter.

Note: Not all nouns in the *rafa'* state will have *dhammah,* not all nouns in the *nasab* state will have *fathah,* nor will all nouns in the *jarr* state have *kasrah;* rather, a more detailed explanation will be given when advanced types of nouns are studied. Only basic nouns are indicated in the table above.

Grammatical states of فعل (verb):

Certain types of فعل (verb) have **three** grammatical states.[4] These are:

	State	Meaning
1	حَالَةُ الرَّفْعِ	This is when the word is in the *rafa'* state (حالة الرفع). In **basic Arabic words**, this will be seen by the *dhammah* (ـُ) added onto the last letter.
		Example: The word نَعْبُدُ in the sentence إِيَّاكَ نَعْبُدُ is in the ***rafa'* state,** therefore the ***dhammah*** can be seen on the last letter.
2	حَالَةُ النَّصْبِ	This is when the word is in the *nasab* state (حالة النصب). In **basic Arabic words**, this will be seen by the *fathah* (ـَ) added onto the last letter.
		Example: The word تَفْعَلَ in the sentence لَنْ تَفْعَلَ is in the ***nasab* state,** therefore the ***fathah*** can be seen on the last letter.
3	حَالَةُ الجَزْمِ	This is when the word is in the *jazm* state (حالة الجزم). In **basic Arabic words**, this will be seen by the *sukoon* (ـْ) added onto the last letter.
		Example: The word تُنْذِرْ in the sentence لَمْ تُنْذِرْهُمْ is in the ***jazm* state,** therefore the ***sukoon*** can be seen on the last letter.

Note: Not all verbs in the *rafa'* state will have *dhammah,* not all the verbs in the *nasab* state will have *fathah,* nor will all verbs in the *jazm* state have a *sukoon;* rather when the advanced types of verbs are studied a more detailed explanation will be given. At this stage, only the basic level words are indicated to in the above table.

Grammatical states of حَرْف (particles):

The حُرُوْف (particles)[5] are not considered to have any grammatical states, rather they are called مَبْنِي (indeclinable), or for easier understanding they can be referred to as **'stubborn'** or **'inflexible'** words. This will be studied in more detail later.

[4] The three grammatical states are for the فعل مضارع (present/future tense verb). Further discussion regarding verbs will come later in the book and is studied in more detail in the books of *sarf* (morphology).

[5] The word حُرُوْف (particles) is the plural of حَرْف (particle).

ACTIVITY: 11

Fill in the table below with either a tick (✓) or a cross (✗).

	GRAMMATICAL STATES			
1	حالة الرفع	2 حالة النصب	3 حالة الجرّ	4 حالة الجزم
اسم	✓	✓	✓	✓
فعل	✓	✓	✓	✗
حرف	✗	✗	✗	✗

ACTIVITY: 12

Decide whether the following words are nouns or verbs. Then, write the grammatical state of each word with basic reasoning.

Word	Meaning	Noun/Verb	State	Reason
كِتَابٌ	Book	Noun	الرفع 1	Because it ends with Dhammah
يَسْمَعَ	He is hearing	Verb	النصب 2	Because it ends in with FatHAH
تَلِدُ	She is giving birth	Verb	3 1	Because it ends in DHAMMAH
يَنْصُرُ	He is helping	Verb	حالة الرفع	It is an action word = verb. It has a *dhammah* on the last letter = *rafa'* state.
قُرْآنٌ	(Holy) Qur'an	Noun	4	
قَلَمًا[6]	Pen	Noun	1	
سَيَّارَةٌ	Car	Noun	2	
سَاعَةٍ	Watch	Noun	2	
يَفْتَحْ	He is opening	Verb	4	
أَعُوْذُ	I am seeking refuge	verb	1	

[6] In most cases when the noun ends with a *tanween fathah,* it will add on an alif at the end. This is not always the case, for example if the last letter is a round *taa,* then an *alif* will not be added on.

LESSON 6: NUMBER

When indicating towards number (عَدَد), in many languages there is a singular and plural form. However, in the Arabic language, we have **three** forms:

1) وَاحِد – singular form,
2) تَثْنِيَة – dual form,
3) جمع – plural form.

	Number	Meaning
1	وَاحِد	This is when the word indicates towards **one** person/thing – hence, **singular.**
		Example: The word قَلَم means **one** pen, hence **singular**.
2	تَثْنِيَة	This is when the word indicates towards **two** people/things – hence, **dual.**
		Example: The word قَلَمَان means **two** pens, hence **dual**.
3	جَمْع	This is when the word indicates towards **more than two** people/things – hence, **plural.**
		Example: The word أَقْلَام means **three** pens, hence **plural**.

The method of making a 'dual' form:

The method of making the **dual form** from the singular form is by adding the following letters at the **end** of the singular word:

	Dual form	Rule
1	ـَانِ	Add the form (ـَانِ) at the **end** of the singular word.
		Example: The word قَلَمَانِ means 'two pens', it is made from the singular word قَلَم by adding the letters (ـَانِ) – that is a *fathah* on the last letter of the singular and then adding an *alif* and a *noon.*
2	ـَيْنِ	Add the form (ـَيْنِ) at the **end** of the singular word.
		Example: The word قَلَمَيْنِ means 'two pens', it is made from the singular word قَلَم by adding the letters (ـَيْنِ) – that is a *fathah* on the last letter of the singular and then adding an *yaa* and a *noon.*

Note: In حالة الرفع the form (ـَانِ) is added, and in حالة النصب and in حالة الجرّ the form (ـَيْنِ) is added. This will be studied in more detail later.

Further examples of 'dual form':

The following table mentions further examples of the 'dual form', it includes examples for masculine form and for feminine form.

	Singular	ـَـانِ added	ـَـيْنِ added
Masculine	رَجُل Man	رَجُلَانِ (**two** men)	رَجُلَيْنِ (**two** men)
Feminine	اِمْرَأَة **Women**	اِمْرَأَتَانِ (**two** women)	اِمْرَأَتَيْنِ (**two** women)

Note: The round *taa* (ة) in the singular feminine will be changed to a flat *taa* (ت) when converted to dual form.

Types of plurals:

In Arabic, the plural form can be divided into **two** types:

1) جَمْع مُكَسَّر – broken plural,
2) جَمْع سَالِم – sound plural.

	Number	Meaning
1	جَمْع مُكَسَّر	This is when the layout of the letters from the **singular** format of the word is **broken** and changed.
		Example: The plural word رِجَال is made from the singular word رَجُل – notice the singular word had the letters *raa, jeem* and *laam* in that order; however in the plural, an *alif* was inserted between the *jeem* and the *laam.* Hence, the singular structure and layout of the letters has been **broken,** so it is a 'broken plural'.
2	جَمْع سَالِم	This is when the layout of the letters from the **singular** format of the word is **sound** and **not** changed.
		Example: The plural word مُسْلِمُوْنَ is made from the singular word مُسْلِم – notice the singular word had the letters *meem, seen, laam* and *meem in that order;* in the plural word, these first four letters have remained the same and in the same order. Hence the singular structure and layout of the letters has remained **sound/safe**, so it is a 'sound plural'.

Types of جمع سالم (sound plural):

In Arabic, the plural form can be divided into **two** types:

1) جَمْع مُذَكَّر سَالِم – sound masculine plural,
2) جَمْع مُؤَنَّث سَالِم – sound feminine plural.

	Number	Meaning
1	جَمْع مُذَكَّر سَالِم	This is when the layout of the letters from the singular form is **sound** and unchanged, and the plural identifies something **masculine.**
		Example: The plural for the masculine singular word مُسْلِم is مُسْلِمُوْن .
2	جَمْع مُؤَنَّث سَالِم	This is when the layout of the letters from the singular form is sound and unchanged, and the plural identifies something **feminine.**
		Example: The plural for the feminine singular word مُسْلِمَة is مُسْلِمَات .

The method of making 'sound plural' form:

The method of making a **sound masculine plural** from the singular form is adding the following letters at the **end** of the singular word:

	Sound masculine form	Rule
1	ـُوْنَ	Add the form (ـُوْنَ) at the **end** of the singular word.
		Example: The word مُسْلِمُوْنَ is made from the singular word مُسْلِمٌ by adding the letters (ـُوْنَ) – that is a *dhammah* on the last letter of the singular word and then adding a *waaw* and a *noon* with a *fathah.*
2	ـِيْنَ	Add the form (ـِيْنَ) at the **end** of the singular word.
		Example: The word مُسْلِمِيْنَ is made from the singular word مُسْلِمٌ by adding the letters (ـِيْنَ) – that is a *kasrah* on the last letter of the singular and then adding a *yaa* and a *noon* with a *fathah.*

Note: In حالة الرفع the form (ـُوْنَ) is added, and in حالة النصب and in حالة الجرّ the form (ـِيْنَ) is added. This will be studied in more detail later.

The method of making a **sound feminine plural** from the singular form is adding the following letters at the **end** of the singular word:

	Sound feminine form	Rule
1	ـَـاتٌ	Add the form (ـَـاتٌ) at the **end** of the singular word **after** removing the round *taa* from the singular.
		Example: The word مُسْلِمَاتٌ is made from the singular word مُسْلِمَةٌ by adding the word (ـَـاتٌ) – that is a *fathah* on the last letter of the singular after removing the round *taa,* and then adding an *alif* and flat *taa* with a *dhammah.*
2	ـَـاتٍ	Add the form (ـَـاتٍ) at the **end** of the singular word **after** removing the round *taa* from the singular.
		Example: The word مُسْلِمَاتٍ is made from the singular word مُسْلِمَةٌ by adding the word (ـَـاتٍ) – that is a *fathah* on the last letter of the singular after removing the round *taa,* and then adding an *alif* and flat *taa* with a *kasrah.*

Note: In حالة الرفع the form (ـَـاتٌ) is added, and in حالة النصب and in حالة الجرّ the form (ـَـاتٍ) is added. This will be studied in more detail later.

ACTIVITY: 13

Mention, with reason, whether the following words are singular (واحد), dual (تثنية) or plural (جمع).

Word	English	Type	Reason
خَاشِعَاتٌ	God-fearing women	Plural	More than 2
كُتُبٌ	Books	Singular	Indicates less than 2
هَاتِفَيْنِ	Two phones	Dual	2 of something
مُفْلِحُوْنَ	Successful men	جمع	It indicates upon more than two and it has an ending of ـُوْنَ which is a sign of a type of plural.
صُلَحَاء	Pious individuals	Dual	Indicates 2 types
قَلَنْسُوَةٌ	Hat	Singular	Indicates less than 2
حُرُوْف	Letters/particles	Plural	Indicates more than 2
دَفْتَرَانِ	Two notebooks	Dual	2 of something
اِسْم	Name	Singular	only 1 of each person

ACTIVITY: 14

Mention, with reason, the type of plural (جمع) for the following words.

Plural word	English	Type	Reason
خَاشِعَاتٌ	God-fearing women		Women are mentioned
نَاصِرُوْنَ	Helping men	مكسّر	It is masculine
مُعَلِّمَاتٍ	Female teachers		It is Feminine
مُفْلِحُوْنَ	Successful men	جمع مذكّر سالم	It has an ending of ـوْنَ which is a sign for sound masculine plural (جمع مذكّر سالم).
صُلَحَاء	Pious individuals	مذكر	
كُتُبٌ	Books		

ACTIVITY: 15

Annotate the following flowchart by given the definition and example for each word.

Flowchart for the chapter of 'number' (عَدَد):

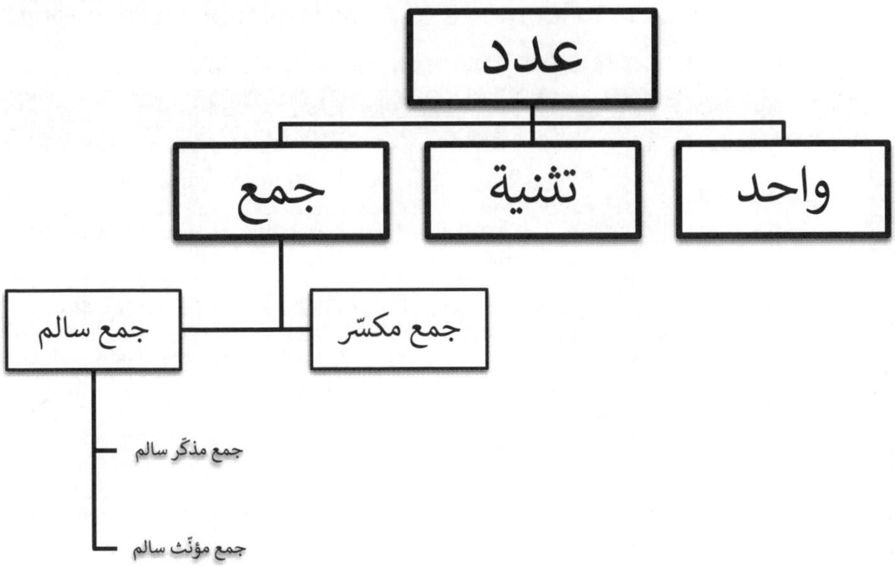

LESSON 7: GENDER

Based on the two genders (جِنْس), the Arabic language has some rules. The two genders are referred to as:

1) مُذَكَّر – masculine,
2) مُؤَنَّث – feminine.

	Gender	Meaning
1	مُذَكَّر	This is when the word indicates upon a **masculine** thing.
		Example: The word كِتَاب (book) is regarded as masculine in the Arabic language, as it does **not** have any signs for being feminine.
2	مُؤَنَّث	This is when the word indicates upon a **feminine** thing.
		Example: The word سَاعَة (watch) is regarded as feminine in the Arabic language, as it **does** have a sign for being feminine.

Common signs for feminine gender:

In Arabic, all words will be considered masculine by default, unless there is a sign or reason to identify a word as feminine. From amongst some of the common signs for the feminine gender are:

	Gender	Meaning
1	**Round *taa* (ة)**	When a word ends in a round *taa,* it will be feminine.
		Example: The word سَاعَة (watch) is feminine. The sign is that it ends with a round *taa.*
2	**Shortened *Alif* (ألف مقصورة)**	When a word ends in a shortened *alif,* then it will be feminine.
		Example: The word صُغْرَى (very small) is feminine. The sign is that it ends with a shortened *alif* (which is written as a *yaa* with a *fathah* before it).
3	**Prolonged *Alif* (ألف ممدودة)**	When a word ends in prolonged *alif,* then it will be feminine.
		Example: The word بَيْضَاء (white) is feminine. The sign is that it ends with a prolonged *alif* (one that is normally written with a *madd).*
4		When a name is used which is specific for a female, then that will also be feminine.

	Female name	**Example:** The name مَرْيَم (Maryam) will be feminine as it is a female name, although other signs of femininity are not present in the word itself.
5	**Words specific for females**	When a word is specifically used for a female, then that will also be feminine.
		Example: The word أُمّ (mother) is feminine as it is a word specific for a female.
6	**Name of cities/towns**	The names of countries, cities, towns and villages are regarded as feminine in the Arabic language.
		Example: The word شَام (Syria) is regarded as feminine as it is a name of a place.
7	**Name of tribes**	The names of tribes are regarded as feminine in the Arabic language.
		Example: The word قُرَيْش (Quraysh) is regarded as feminine as it is a name of a tribe.
8	**Double body parts**	**Double body parts** are generally regarded as feminine, however, there are some exceptions to this.
		Example: The word يَد (hand) is feminine as it is a double body part.

ACTIVITY: 16

Mention, with reason, whether the following words are masculine (مذكّر) or feminine (مؤنّث). 2

Word	English	Type	Reason
أُخْت	Sister	2	Words specific for females.
كِتَاب	Book	1	None of the signs of feminine
ابْن	Son	1	Word specific for males
عَيْن	Eye	مؤنّث	Eyes are 'double body parts' – a sign of feminine form.
نَاقَة	She-camel	2	Words specific for female
لَنْدَن	London	2	Name of place
قَلَم	Pen	1	has none of them signs
مِرْفَق	Elbow	2	Double parts body

Types of feminine form (مُؤَنَّث) based on the 'signs':

Based on the **signs** for the feminine form, the feminine form can be divided into **two types:**

1) مُؤَنَّث لَفْظِي – feminine by signs in the word,
2) مُؤَنَّث مَعْنَوِيّ – feminine by meaning,.

Note:

1) مُؤَنَّث لَفْظِي is also called مُؤَنَّث قِيَاسِيّ ,
2) مُؤَنَّث مَعْنَوِيّ is also called مُؤَنَّث سَمَاعِيّ ,

	Type of feminine based on sign		
1	مُؤَنَّث لَفْظِي/قِيَاسِيّ	This is when **signs** of the 'feminine form' are **visibly present** in the actual words. Example: The word سَاعَة (watch) is مؤنث لفظي as the round *taa* at the end indicates upon feminine form.
2	مُؤَنَّث مَعْنَوِيّ/سَمَاعِيّ	This is when **signs** of the 'feminine form' are **not visibly** present in the actual words, rather they are assumed as feminine by meaning. Example: The word يَد (hand) is مُؤنّث معنوي as there is nothing in the actual word which indicates it is feminine, rather it is the meaning (being a double body part) which indicates it is feminine.

The following table categorises the signs of feminine form mentioned above.

مؤنث لفظي/قياسيّ
Round *taa* (ة)
Shortened *Alif* (ألف مقصورة)
Prolonged *Alif* (ألف ممدودة)

مؤنّث معنويّ/سماعيّ
Female name
Words specifically used for females
Name of cities/towns
Name of tribes
Double body parts

Note: Some words are regarded as feminine without any signs being present, they are simply **passed on through generations** as feminine words in the Arabic language. For example, the word شَمْس is regarded as feminine despite it not having any signs for it to be considered a feminine word.

ACTIVITY: 17

Mention, with reason, whether the following words are مؤنث لفظي or مؤنث معنوي.

Word	English	Type	Reason
مِصْر	Egypt		
خَدّ	Cheek		
كُبْرَى	Very big		
عَيْن	Eye	مؤنث معنوي	Eyes are 'double body parts' – a sign of feminine form, but not from the words (مؤنث معنوي).
فَاطِمَة	Fatimah		

ACTIVITY: 18

Annotate the following flowchart by giving the definition and an example for each word.

Flowchart for the chapter of 'gender' (جنس):

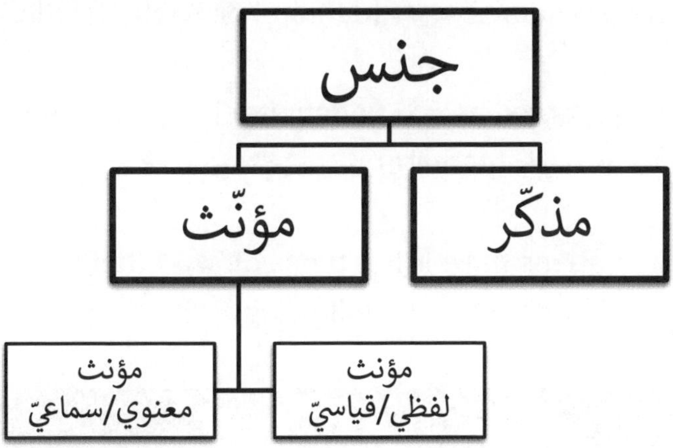

LESSON 8: DEFINITENESS

Based on the definiteness (تَخْصِيْص)of a **noun,** there are two types:

1) مَعْرِفَة – definite noun,
2) نَكِرَة – indefinite noun.

	Definiteness	Meaning
1	مَعْرِفَة	This is when the word is referring to a **specific** person/thing.
		Example: The word اَلرَّجُل (**the** man) is definite – as it is talking about a **specific** man.
2	نَكِرَة	This is when the word is referring to a **common** person/thing.
		Example: The word رَجُلٌ (**a** man) is indefinite – as it is talking about a **common** man (any man).

Types of definite nouns (مَعْرِفَة):

In the Arabic language, grammarians have mentioned a few methods to identify whether a noun is مَعْرِفَة (definite) or نَكِرَة (indefinite).

All words will be regarded as نَكِرَة (indefinite) by default, unless they can be proven to be مَعْرِفَة (definite).

Hence, the grammarians have listed types of مَعْرِفَة (definite). Among the types of مَعْرِفَة (definite) are the following:

	Definite noun	Meaning
1	ضَمِيْر	This refers to **pronouns**. All pronouns are considered definite.
		Example: The pronoun إِيَّاكَ (you) in إِيَّاكَ نَعْبُدُ (we worship **you**) is definite – as all pronouns are definite.
2	عَلَم	This refers to **proper nouns** (i.e. names of people/things). All proper nouns are considered definite.
		Example: The proper noun مُحَمَّدٌ in ذَهَبَ مُحَمَّدٌ (Muhammad went) is definite – as all proper nouns are considered as definite.

3	اِسْم الْإِشَارَة	These refer to **demonstrative pronouns** (i.e. 'this', 'that', 'those', etc.). All demonstrative pronouns are considered definite. Example: The demonstrative pronoun هَذَا **(this)** in هَذَا قَلَمٌ (**This** is a pen.) is definite – as all demonstrative pronouns are considered definite.
4	الإِسْم الْمَوْصُوْل	These refer to **relative pronouns** (i.e. 'who', 'which', 'that', 'where', etc.). All relative pronouns are considered definite. Example: The relative pronoun اَلَّذِيْ **(who)** in جَاءَنِيْ الرَّجُلُ الَّذِيْ حَفِظَ الْقُرْآنَ (The man came to me **who** memorised the Qur'an) is definite – as all relative pronouns are considered as definite.
5	اَلْمُعَرَّف بِ(ال)	This refers to a noun prefixed with "ال". All nouns prefixed with "ال" are considered definite. Example: The word اَلرَّجُلُ (**the** man) is definite as it is prefixed with "ال".
6	اَلمُضَافُ لِمَعْرِفَة	When a noun is in a possessive structure, then the noun for the possession (owned item) will be considered **definite** if the possessor it refers to is also **definite.** Otherwise, the 'possession noun' will be **indefinite.** Example: The word قَلَمُ (pen) in the phrase قَلَمُ زَيْدٍ (Zayd's pen) is **definite;** this is since the word قَلَم is the 'possessed' item, so it will follow the 'possessor' (in this case, Zayd) in terms of being definite or not. As the word Zayd is a definite noun, the word قَلَم will also be a definite noun.
7	اَلْمُعَرَّف بِ(النِّدَاء)	This is referring to a noun which has a **vocative particle** before it. Example: The word رَجُلُ (man) in يَا رَجُلُ is definite as it is preceded by a vocative particle (يَا).

Note: All these types will be studied in more detail later in relevant chapters.

ACTIVITY: 19

Mention, with reason, whether the following words are definite (معرفة) or indefinite (نكرة). [The words in **bold**].

Bold words	English	Type	Reason
مِصْر	Egypt		
خَدٌّ	Cheek		
الْكِتَابُ	The book		
عَيْنٌ	Eye	نكرة	There is no sign for it to be definite – hence, it is indefinite.
فَاطِمَة	Fatimah		
يَا أُسْتَاذُ	O teacher!		

مِفْتَاحُ السَّيَّارَةِ	The car's key		
مِفْتَاحُ بَابٍ	Door's key		
الَّتِيْ	Who		
ذَٰلِكَ	That		
هُمْ	Them		
الْمُفْلِحُوْنَ	The successful ones		
يُوْسُفُ	Yusuf		

ACTIVITY: 20

Annotate the following flowchart with definitions and examples for each word.

<u>Flowchart for the chapter of 'definiteness' (تخصيص)</u>:

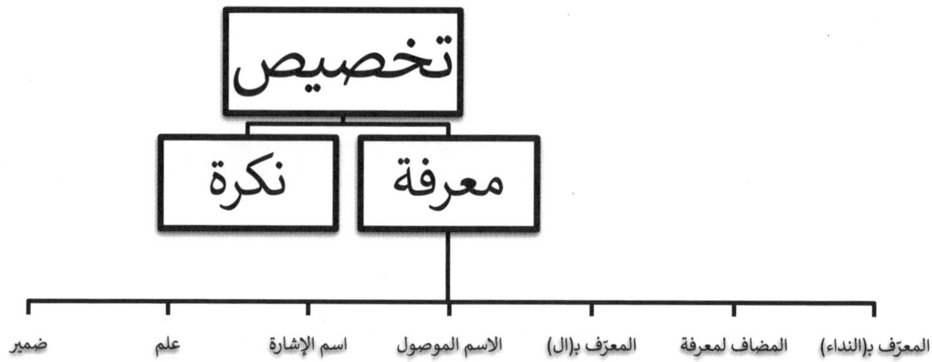

LESSON 9: DIMINUTIVE NOUN

In many languages including Arabic, there is a certain form to show that somebody or something is **small**; this is called a **diminutive noun** (إسْم التَّصْغِيْر).

For example, in the English language:

- a small kitchen is referred to as a kitchenette (with the suffix 'ette'),
- a small hill is called a hillock (with the suffix 'ock'),
- a small wave is called a wavelet (with the suffix 'let').

So, different suffixes are added to words to create their diminutive form in the English language.

Similarly, Arabic also has some unique scales for showing that a word is in diminutive (تصغير) form. The scale of the diminutive form is dependent upon the number of letters in the original word.

Number of letters	Scale	Examples		
		Original word		Diminutive form
3	فُعَيْلٌ	رَجُلٌ Man	→	رُجَيْلٌ Small man
4	فُعَيْلِلٌ	مُسْرِفٌ One who is extravagant	→	مُسَيْرِفٌ One who is slightly extravagant
5 (a)	فُعَيْلِلٌ With the last letter dropped	سَفَرْجَلٌ Quince (fruit)	→	سُفَيْرِجٌ Small quince (fruit)
5 (b)	فُعَيْلِيْلٌ	قِرْطَاسٌ Paper	→	قُرَيْطِيْسٌ Small paper

Note:

1) Generally, nouns have 3, 4 or 5 letters in each word, hence the grammarians usually only mention the diminutive form for these nouns.
2) If the 5-lettered word does not have any alif, waaw or yaa in the fourth letter position, then it will follow the **5 (a) scale**, however, if it does have an alif, waaw or yaa in the fourth letter position, then it will follow the **5 (b) scale**.

Purpose of diminutive nouns (اِسْم التَّصْغِيْر)

The diminutive noun serves a few purposes, including:

	Purpose	Meaning
1	مَحَبَّة Love	This is to show the meaning of **love** for the person/thing being addressed. Example: The word رَجُلٌ means 'man', whereas the word رُجَيْلٌ could (possibly) mean **'beloved man'**.
2	تَحْقِيْر To degrade	This is to show the meaning of **degrading** the person/thing being addressed. Example: The word رَجُلٌ means 'man', whereas the word رُجَيْلٌ could (possibly) mean **'degraded (useless) man'**.
3	تَقْلِيْل To show less	This is to show/create the meaning of **less** (in quantity) for the person/thing being addressed. Example: The word دِرْهَم means 'dirham' (a currency), whereas the word دُرَيْهِم means **'a few dirhams'**.
4	تَصْغِيْر To show smallness	This is to show/create the meaning of **smallnes** for the person/thing being addressed. Example: The word كِتَاب means 'book', whereas the word كُتَيِّب means **'a small book'**.
5	تَقْرِيْب To show closeness	This is to show/create the meaning of **closeness** for the person/thing being addressed. Example: The word قَبْلَ means 'before', whereas the word قُبَيْلَ means **'shortly before'**.

Note: In some words, the meaning created by the diminutive form is obvious; however, in some words, it is possible that more than one of the diminutive meanings could be intended. In such a case, the correct meaning must be inferred from the context or by asking the speaker.

ACTIVITY: 21

Write the diminutive form (اسم التصغير) for the following words with meaning.

Word	English	Diminutive noun	English (indicating to purpose)
وَلَدٌ	Child	1	
عُصْفُوْر	Sparrow	3	
مَطْعَمٌ	Restaurant	4	
فَرَزْدَق	Loaf of bread	فُرَيْزِدٌ	Small loaf of bread (creates meaning of 'smallness')
قَلَمٌ	Pen	4/5	

LESSON 10: RELATIVE NOUN

When **linking** a person or an object to a specific place or subject, etc. it is given a special name in the Arabic language, الْإِسْمُ الْمَنْسُوْبُ . This will be referred to as a **'relative noun'** – where a noun is recognised as being related or connected to another.

Method of making الاسم المنسوب:

The الاسم المنسوب is made by:

1) adding the letter *yaa* with *tashdeed* (يَاءٌ مُشَدَّدَة) at the end of the word, and
2) giving a Kasrah to the last original letter.

When there are tashdeed and the sign is underneath it is a kasra

Some examples are mentioned below:

Word	English	Relative noun form	English
مَكَّة	Makkah	مَكِّيٌّ	Person/item from Makkah
لَنْدَن	London	لَنْدَنِيٌّ	Person/item from London
نَحْو	Nahw (Arabic grammar)	نَحْوِيٌّ	Someone strongly associated/expert in Nahw

Note: If a word has a round *taa* (ة) at the end of it, the round *taa* will drop when making the الاسم المنسوب form, as seen above in the example of مَكَّة .

ACTIVITY: 22

Write the relative noun (الاسم المنسوب) for the following words with meaning.

Word	English	Relative noun form	English
بَغْدَاد	Baghdad	[illegible]	Baghdaydun
هَاشِم	Hashim (name of a family tribe)		Hashiemun
بَلَاكْبَرْن	Blackburn (town in England)	بَلَاكْبَرْنِيٌّ	Person/item from Blackburn
صَرْف	Sarf (Arabic morphology)		SHRFiun

LESSON 11: DECLINABLE & INDECLINABLE WORDS

In the Arabic language, one of the most important purposes of studying Arabic grammar is to understand the end case of each word. For example, the first word of Surah Fatihah is read as اَلْحَمْدُ (with a dhammah on the last letter), so why is it not اَلْحَمْدَ (with a fathah on the last letter) or اَلْحَمْدِ (with a kasrah on the last letter)?

Almost all the different lessons and chapters within Arabic grammar books are focussed directly or indirectly on allowing a student of Arabic to understand the end cases.

Before discussing this further, it would be useful to revisit the different grammatical states (حالات) of Arabic words.

There are **four** grammatical states in Arabic:

	State	Meaning
1	حَالَة الرَّفْعِ	This is when the word is in the *rafa'* state (حالة الرفع). In **basic Arabic words**, this will be seen by the *dhammah* (ـُـ) added onto the last letter (as a single harakah or tanween).
		This state occurs in **nouns (اسم)** and in **verbs(فعل)**.
2	حَالَة النَّصْب	This is when the word is in the *nasab* state (حالة النصب). In **basic Arabic words**, this will be seen by the *fathah* (ـَـ) added onto the last letter (as a single harakah or tanween).
		This state occurs in **nouns (اسم)** and in **verbs(فعل)**.
3	حَالَة الجَرّ	This is when the word is in the *jarr* state (حالة الجر). In **basic Arabic words**, this will be seen by the *kasrah* (ـِـ) added onto the last letter (as a single harakah or tanween).
		This state occurs **only** in **nouns(اسم).**
4	حَالَة الجَزْم	This is when the word is in the *jazm* state (حالة الجزم). In **basic Arabic words**, this will be seen by the *sukoon* (ـْـ) added onto the last letter.
		This state occurs **only** in **verbs(فعل)**.

Note: As the focus in Arabic grammar is mostly on nouns (اسم), only the grammatical states of nouns will be discussed from now onwards. As for verbs (فعل) and particles (حرف), they will have dedicated chapters towards the end of the book.

Declinable and indeclinable nouns:

The end-case of each noun is very important in the Arabic language. The end-case of each noun is referred to as the *i'raab* (إِعْرَاب) of the word. However, the *i'raab* does **not** change for ***all*** nouns; some nouns are 'stubborn' and are not ready to change their end case.

The following flow chart indicates the different types of nouns based on whether the end-case of the noun changes or not.

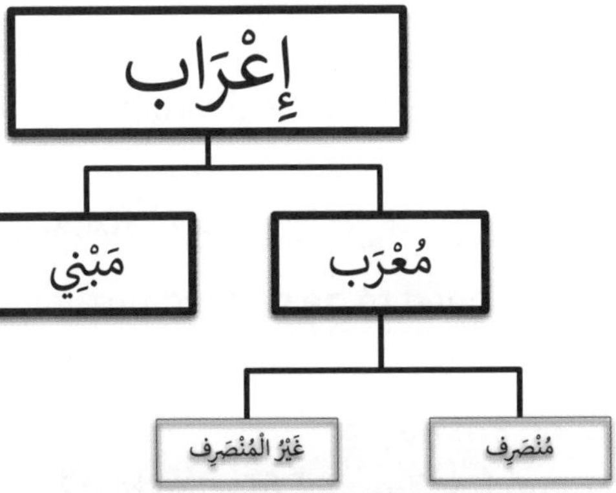

There are **two** types of nouns based on *i'raab* (end-case):

	Type	Another name	Meaning
1	الْإِسْمُ الْمُعْرَب **Declinable noun**	الْإِسْمُ الْمُتَمَكِّن	This is when the word is **declinable** and **flexible** - allowing the end-case of the noun to change. Example: The word كِتَابٌ (book) is such that it accepts changes to the end-case depending on the grammatical situation – it is a 'declinable' word.
2	الْإِسْمُ الْمَبْنِيّ **Indeclinable noun**	الْإِسْمُ غَيْرُ الْمُتَمَكِّن	This is when the word is **indeclinable** and **stubborn** - **not** allowing the end-case of the noun to change. Example: The word هَذَا (this) is such a word that does **not** accept changes to the end-case, irrespective of the grammatical situation – it is an 'indeclinable' word.

There are **two** types of declinable (مُعْرَب) nouns:

	Type	Meaning
1	مُنْصَرِف **Triptote**	This is a **fully flexible** noun – hence, in all **three** grammatical states, it allows a change. Example: The word كِتَابٌ (book) is such that it accepts changes to the end-case in all **three** grammatical states – it is a مُنْصَرِف word.
2	غَيْرُ الْمُنْصَرِف **Diptote**	This is a **semi-flexible** noun – hence, it only allows change in **two** of the grammatical states. Example: The word مَسَاجِدُ (plural of Masjid) is such that it accepts changes to the end-case in **two** grammatical states, not all three cases – it is a غَيْرُ الْمُنْصَرِف word.

Key points to note:

1) By default, all nouns will be declinable (مُعْرَب) and fully flexible (مُنْصَرِف).
2) So, only the nouns that are semi-flexible (غَيْرُ الْمُنْصَرِف) or indeclinable (مَبْنِي) need to be studied further.

Some questions to be answered:

1) When will a noun be 'flexible' (declinable)?
2) When will a noun be 'fully flexible' (triptote)?
3) When will a noun be 'semi-flexible' (diptote)?
4) Which grammatical state does the 'semi-flexible' (diptote) noun not change in?
5) When will a noun be 'stubborn' (indeclinable)?

These questions will be answered in the following chapters, where each of the above terms will be explained in more detail.

LESSON 12: DECLINABLE, TRIPTOTE AND DIPTOTE NOUNS

Nouns have **three** grammatical states. The state of each noun will dictate the end-case of the noun **depending on its form.** Some of the forms have been studied previously (mentioned in the table below), and the remaining forms will still be discussed in the remaining chapters of the book.

	States of nouns	Different forms			
		Basic word form	Dual form	Masculine plural form	Feminine plural form
1	حَالَةُ الرَّفْعِ	الرَّجُلُ or رَجُلٌ	رَجُلَانِ	مُسْلِمُوْنَ	مُسْلِمَاتٌ
		ends with a ـُ or ـٌ	ends with a ـَانِ	ends with ـُوْنَ	ends with ـَاتٌ
2	حَالَةُ النَّصْبِ	الرَّجُلَ or رَجُلًا	رَجُلَيْنِ	مُسْلِمِيْنَ	مُسْلِمَاتٍ
		ends with a ـَ or ـً	ends with a ـَيْنِ	ends with ـِيْنَ	ends with ـَاتٍ
3	حَالَةُ الجَرِّ	الرَّجُلِ or رَجُلٍ	رَجُلَيْنِ	مُسْلِمِيْنَ	مُسْلِمَاتٍ
		ends with a ـِ or ـٍ	ends with a ـَيْنِ	ends with ـِيْنَ	ends with ـَاتٍ

Note: Please refer to earlier relevant chapters for quick revision with further examples.

The declinable nouns (الْإِسْمُ الْمُعْرَبُ) or (الْإِسْمُ الْمُتَمَكِّنُ) has **two** types:

	Type	Meaning
1	مُنْصَرِف Triptote	This is a **fully flexible** noun – hence, in all **three** grammatical states, it allows a change.
		Example: The word كِتَابٌ (book) is such that it accepts changes to the end-case in all **three** grammatical states – it is a مُنْصَرِف word.
2	غَيْرُ الْمُنْصَرِف Diptote	This is a **semi-flexible** noun – hence, it only allows change in **two** of the grammatical states.
		Example: The word مَسَاجِدُ (plural of Masjid) is such that it accepts changes to the end-case in **two** grammatical states, not all three cases – it is a غَيْرُ الْمُنْصَرِف word.

The مُنْصَرِف nouns:

The default for all **nouns** is to be **declinable (مُعْرَب) and fully flexible (مُنْصَرِف).**

A **fully flexible (مُنْصَرِف)** noun is a noun which accepts:

- changes in all **three** grammatical states,
- *tanween* (ـٌ or ـً or ـٍ).

<u>Examples</u>: The following **basic words** are مُنْصَرِف (triptote/fully flexible)

	States of nouns	Different words			
		قَلَمٌ (pen)	الْقَلَمُ (the pen)	مُحَمَّدٌ (Muhammad)	سَيَّارَةٌ (car)
1	حَالَة الرَّفْعِ	قَلَمٌ	الْقَلَمُ	مُحَمَّدٌ	سَيَّارَةٌ
		ends with a ـٌ or ـُ	ends with a ـٌ or ـُ	ends with a ـٌ or ـُ	ends with a ـٌ or ـُ
2	حَالَة النَّصْب	قَلَمًا	الْقَلَمَ	مُحَمَّدًا	سَيَّارَةً
		ends with a ـً or ـَ	ends with a ـً or ـَ	ends with a ـً or ـَ	ends with a ـً or ـَ
3	حَالَة الجَرّ	قَلَمٍ	الْقَلَمِ	مُحَمَّدٍ	سَيَّارَةٍ
		ends with a ـٍ or ـِ	ends with a ـٍ or ـِ	ends with a ـٍ or ـِ	ends with a ـٍ or ـِ

So, it is noticeable of the above **basic words** that the ending of each word is changing in **all three** grammatical states, specifically:

- *dhammah* (ـٌ or ـُ) in حالة الرفع ,
- *fathah* (ـً or ـَ) in حالة النصب ,
- *kasrah* (ـٍ or ـِ) in حالة الجرّ .

Also, the words could accept a *tanween* if (ال) is not present at the beginning.

This shows that these words are **مُنْصَرِف (triptote/fully flexible).**

The غَيْرُ الْمُنْصَرِف nouns:

Some nouns, despite being declinable/flexible (مُعْرَب), they are only semi-flexible/diptote (غَيْرُ الْمُنْصَرِف).

A **semi-flexible (غَيْرُ الْمُنْصَرِف)** noun:

- changes in only **two** grammatical states (not all three),
- does not accept *tanween* (ـٌ or ـً or ـٍ).

Examples: The following **words** are غَيْرُ الْمُنْصَرِف (diptote/semi-flexible)

	States of nouns	Different words			
		يُوْسُفُ (Yusuf)	وِلْيَمُ (William)	مَسَاجِدُ (Masjids)	غَضْبَانُ (Angry)
1	حَالَةُ الرَّفْعِ	يُوْسُفُ ends with a ـُ	وِلْيَمُ ends with a ـُ	مَسَاجِدُ ends with a ـُ	غَضْبَانُ ends with a ـُ
2	حَالَةُ النَّصْب	يُوْسُفَ ends with a ـَ	وِلْيَمَ ends with a ـَ	مَسَاجِدَ ends with a ـَ	غَضْبَانَ ends with a ـَ
3	حَالَةُ الجَرّ	يُوْسُفَ ends with a ـَ	وِلْيَمَ ends with a ـَ	مَسَاجِدَ ends with a ـَ	غَضْبَانَ ends with a ـَ

So, it is noticeable for the above words that the ending of each word is changing in only **two** grammatical states:

- *dhammah* (ـُ) in حالة الرفع ,
- *fathah* (ـَ) in حالة النصب ,

Also, the words do **not** accept a *tanween.*

This shows that these words were **غَيْرُ الْمُنْصَرِف (diptote/semi-flexible).**

> Golden rule:
> The غَيْرُ الْمُنْصَرِف (diptote/semi-flexible) word will be given a ***fathah*** **(ـَ) in حَالَةُ الجَرّ** (as can be seen in the examples above).

LESSON 13: DIPTOTE NOUNS

The **diptote/semi-flexible (غَيْرُ الْمُنْصَرِف)** nouns do **not** accept *kasrah* in حالة الجرّ , rather they take the *fathah* even in حالة الجرّ.

What are the causes that make a noun into a غَيْرُ الْمُنْصَرِف?

There are **nine causes** that make a basic noun into a غَيْرُ الْمُنْصَرِفِ (semi-flexible) word. These causes are called أَسْبَابُ غَيْرِ الْمُنْصَرِفِ .

The **nine** أَسْبَابُ غَيْرِ الْمُنْصَرِفِ (causes of making a noun into semi-flexible) are:

	أَسْبَابُ غَيْرِ الْمُنْصَرِفِ	
	Causes	**Explanation & Example**
1	عَدْل 'changed'	This is when the original format of the noun has been **changed** to another format. Generally, this would only be known through common Arabic usage, hence, would be 'picked-up' from wider reading and dictionary usage. Example: The name عُمَرُ was originally عَامِرٌ (according to some grammarians). As the original format has been changed, عَدْل has occurred.
2	وَصْف 'description'	This is when the noun is a **description/quality**. Example: The word أَسْوَدُ (black) or the word عَطْشَانُ (thirsty) are examples of descriptions.
3	تَأْنِيْث 'feminine'	This is when the noun is referencing a **feminine** object or it has a round *taa* (ة) at the end of the word. Example: The name زَيْنَبُ - this name refers to a female. Example: The name طَلْحَةُ – despite this name referring to a male, as it has a round *taa* at the end, it will be considered to have the cause of تَأْنِيْث (for this chapter).
4	عَلَم 'proper noun (name)'	This is when the noun is a **proper noun**. This could be the name of a person, animal, place, etc. Example: The name زَيْنَبُ (a female name) or the name لَنْدَنُ (London – name of a city).
5	عُجْمَة 'non-Arabic'	This is when a noun is **non-Arabic.** Example: The name وِلْيَمُ (William – a **non-Arabic** name).

6	جَمْع '(certain) plurals'	This is when a noun is on the plural scale of مَفَاعِل or مَفَاعِيْل .
		Example: The word مَسَاجِد (plural of Masjid) is on the scale of مَفَاعِل . The word مَفَاتِيْح (keys) is on the scale of مَفَاعِيْل .
7	تَرْكِيْب 'joining words'	This is when **two nouns** are made into **one (new) noun.**
		Example: The word بَعْلَبَكّ is the name of a city; it is one word which was originally made from two words: بَعْل (name of an idol) and بَكّ (name of a king).
8	أَلِف وَنُوْن زَائِدَتَانِ 'extra (ان)'	This is when the noun ends with ***alif* and *noon*** (انِ) and the *alif* and *noon* are not part of the 'main letters'.[7]
		Example: The word عُثْمَان (Uthman) ends in an **extra** *alif* and *noon.*
9	وَزْنُ فِعْلٍ 'scale of verb'	This is when a **noun** is on the scale of a **verb.**[8]
		Example: The word أَحْمَدُ (Ahmed) is a noun on the scale of a verb.

Some overall rules for غَيْرُ الْمُنْصَرِف nouns:

1) A noun will **only** become غَيْرُ الْمُنْصَرِف if **two** of the causes (from the nine causes) are found. If only **one** cause is found, then generally that is not a strong enough reason to make the word غَيْرُ الْمُنْصَرِف .
2) However, if the **only** cause found is that it is on the plural scale of مَفَاعِل or مَفَاعِيْل (reason number 6 above), then that **single** cause alone is strong enough to make the word into a غَيْرُ الْمُنْصَرِف.
3) Once a word is accepted as غَيْرُ الْمُنْصِرِف , it will normally **not** accept a *kasrah* at the end of the word, rather in حالة الجرّ it will have a *fathah.*

   For example: إِلَى مَسَاجِدَ - in this phrase, the word مَسَاجِد is occurring in the حالة الجرّ , hence it should have a *kasrah;* however, as it is غير المنصرف it has a *fathah* in this example.

[7] The discussion of the 'main letters' (الحروف الأصليّة) and the 'extra letters' (الحروف الزائدة), one should consult the Sarf book.
[8] The scales of verbs can be studied in the Sarf book.

4) However, if the word has an *alif-laam* (ال) at the beginning or the word is a possessive noun [9](مضاف), then it will accept a *kasrah*. For example: **إِلَى الْمَسَاجِدِ** - the word مَسَاجِد occurs as غير المنصرف, so it would have a *fathah* at the end (in حالة الجرّ); however, as it has *alif-laam* (ال), it will now accept a *kasrah* in حالة الجرّ .

ACTIVITY: 23

The following words are غَيْر الْمُنْصَرِف . Write the two causes (or one cause if the cause is number 6 from above) that make them غَيْر الْمُنْصَرِف.

Word	English	Cause one	Cause two
فَاطِمَة	Fatimah (name)		
أَحْمَر	Red		
مَصَابِيْح	Lamp	On the scale of مفاعيل	'cause one is the equivalent of 2 causes'
عِمْرَان	'Imran (name)		
نُيُوْيُوْرك	New York		

ACTIVITY: 24

The following words are غَيْر الْمُنْصَرِف . Write the end-case *(harakah)* for each word in the different grammatical states (*haalaat*).

Word	حالة الرفع	حالة النصب	حالة الجرّ
أَحْمَر			
الْأَحْمَر			
الْمَسَاجِد	ـُـ	ـَـ	ـِـ (as it has an ال at the beginning of the word)
نُيُوْيُوْرك			
الْقَاهِرَة (Cairo)			

[9] The possessive structures and the term مضاف will be explained later in the book.

LESSON 14: INDECLINABLE NOUNS

As mentioned, Arabic nouns maybe declinable (مُعْرَب) or maybe indeclinable (مَبْنِيّ).

An indeclinable (مَبْنِيّ) noun is a noun that is **stubborn - not** allowing the end-case of the noun to change.

Example: The word هَذَا (this) is such a word that does **not** accept changes to the end-case, irrespective of the grammatical situation – it is an 'indeclinable' word.

The main discussions regarding declinable (مُعْرَب) nouns have been mentioned. Now, some detail regarding indeclinable (مَبْنِيّ) nouns will be mentioned.

In detailed grammar books, many types of indeclinable (مَبْنِيّ) nouns are mentioned. However, in this book, only **three** very common indeclinable (مَبْنِيّ) nouns will be mentioned.

Among the indeclinable (مَبْنِيّ) nouns are:

	Type of مَبْنِيّ	Meaning
1	ضَمِيْر **Pronoun**	These are special nouns used to refer to something which has already been mentioned earlier. Example: The noun إِيَّاكَ (you) in the statement إِيَّاكَ نَعْبُدُ (we worship **you** (O Allah)) is regarded as a pronoun – it is referring to Allah who has already been mentioned earlier.
2	اِسْمُ الْإِشَارَة **Demonstrative pronoun**	These are also referred to as the **indicating** nouns. They are nouns used when 'indicating/pointing' to something. Example: The noun ذَلِكَ (that) in the sentence ذَلِكَ الْكِتَابُ (**that** book) is a demonstrative/indicating noun as it indicates to the book being discussed.
3	الْإِسْمُ الْمَوْصُوْل **Relative pronoun**	These are special nouns used to attach sentences/phrases together where the second sentence is a relative clause for the first sentence – the second clause is giving some further information for the first clause. Example: The noun الَّذِيْ in جَاءَنِيْ زَيْدُ **الَّذِيْ** نَجَحَ فِيْ الْإِمْتِحَانِ (Zaid came to me **who** was successful in the exam) is a relative noun – it connects 'was successful in the exam' to 'Zaid' that came.

LESSON 15: PRONOUNS

The ضَمِيْر (plural: ضَمِائِر) are **pronouns** and are a type of the indeclinable (مَبْنِيّ) nouns.

In Arabic, the ضَمَائِر (pronouns) are divided into **five** categories.

	Type of ضَمَائِر	Meaning
1	ضَمِيْر مَرْفُوْع مُتَّصِل	This is a pronoun that is in **حالة الرفع** ***(rafa' state)*** and is **attached** to the word before it. Example: The pronoun تَ in the word أَنْعَمْتَ (**you** have bestowed) is a ضَمِيْر مَرْفُوْع مُتَّصِل as 'you' is in the *rafa'* state (as will be learned later) and the pronoun is **attached** with the word أَنْعَمْ .
2	ضَمِيْر مَرْفُوْع مُنْفَصِل	This is a pronoun that is in **حالة الرفع** ***(rafa' state)*** and is **detached** from the word before it. Example: The pronoun هُمْ (they) in the phrase هُمُ الْمُفْلِحُوْنَ (**they** are successful) is a ضَمِيْر مَرْفُوْع مُنْفَصِل as 'they' is in the *rafa'* state (as will be learned later) and the pronoun is **detached** (not connected to a word before it).
3	ضَمِيْر مَنْصُوْب مُتَّصِل	This is a pronoun that is in **حالة النصب** ***(nasab state)*** and is **attached** to the word before it. Example: The pronoun هُمْ (they/them) in the phrase رَزَقْنَاهُمْ (we provided food for **them**) is a ضَمِيْر مَنْصُوْب مُتَّصِل as the 'them' is in the *nasab* state (as will be learned later) and the pronoun is **attached** with the word رَزَقْنَا .
4	ضَمِيْر مَنْصُوْب مُنْفَصِل	This is a pronoun that is in **حالة النصب** ***(nasab state)*** and is **detached** from the word before it. Example: The pronoun إِيَّاكَ (you) in the phrase إِيَّاكَ نَعْبُدُ (we worship **you**) is a ضَمِيْر مَنْصُوْب مُنْفَصِل as the 'you' is in the *nasab* state (as will be learned later) and the pronoun is **detached** (not connected to a word before it).
5	ضَمِيْر مَجْرُوْر مُتَّصِل	This is a pronoun that is in **حالة الجرّ** ***(jarr state)*** and is **attached** to the word before it. Example: The pronoun كَ (you) in the phrase بِمَا أُنْزِلَ إِلَيْكَ (that which is revealed upon **you**) is a ضَمِيْر مَجْرُوْر مُتَّصِل as the 'you' is in the *jarr* state (as will be learned later) and the pronoun is **attached** with the word إِلَى before it.

All the aforementioned categories have **fourteen** pronouns based on number, gender and grammatical person (1st person, 2nd person, 3rd person).[10]

The following table mentions all the different categories with the fourteen forms. It is very important to learn them fluently, in order.

الضمير المجرور المتّصل	الضمير المنصوب المنفصل	الضمير المنصوب المتصل	الضمير المرفوع المنفصل	الضمير المرفوع المتّصل	DIFFERENT FORMS (صِيغَة)	
كِتَابُهُ	إِيَّاهُ	كَتَبَهُ	هُوَ	كَتَبَ	Singular male 3rd person	واحد مذكرغائب
كِتَابُهُمَا	إِيَّاهُمَا	كَتَبَهُمَا	هُمَا	كَتَبَا	Dual male 3rd person	تثنية مذكر غائب
كِتَابُهُمْ	إِيَّاهُمْ	كَتَبَهُمْ	هُمْ	كَتَبُوْا	Plural male 3rd person	جمع مذكر غائب
كِتَابُهَا	إِيَّاهَا	كَتَبَهَا	هِيَ	كَتَبَتْ	Singular female 3rd person	واحد مؤنث غائب
كِتَابُهُمَا	إِيَّاهُمَا	كَتَبَهُمَا	هُمَا	كَتَبَتَا	Dual female 3rd person	تثنية مؤنث غائب
كِتَابُهُنَّ	إِيَّاهُنَّ	كَتَبَهُنَّ	هُنَّ	كَتَبْنَ	Plural female 3rd person	جمع مؤنث غائب
كِتَابُكَ	إِيَّاكَ	كَتَبَكَ	أَنْتَ	كَتَبْتَ	Singular male 2nd person	واحد مذكر حاضر
كِتَابُكُمَا	إِيَّاكُمَا	كَتَبَكُمَا	أَنْتُمَا	كَتَبْتُمَا	Dual male 2nd person	تثنية مذكر حاضر
كِتَابُكُمْ	إِيَّاكُمْ	كَتَبَكُمْ	أَنْتُمْ	كَتَبْتُمْ	Plural male 2nd person	جمع مذكر حاضر
كِتَابُكِ	إِيَّاكِ	كَتَبَكِ	أَنْتِ	كَتَبْتِ	Singular female 2nd person	واحد مؤنث حاضر
كِتَابُكُمَا	إِيَّاكُمَا	كَتَبَكُمَا	أَنْتُمَا	كَتَبْتُمَا	Dual female 2nd person	تثنية مؤنث حاضر
كِتَابُكُنَّ	إِيَّاكُنَّ	كَتَبَكُنَّ	أَنْتُنَّ	كَتَبْتُنَّ	Plural female 2nd person	جمع مؤنث حاضر
كِتَابِيْ	إِيَّايَ	كَتَبَنِيْ	أَنَا	كَتَبْتُ	Singular 1st person	واحد متكلم
كِتَابُنَا	إِيَّانَا	كَتَبَنَا	نَحْنُ	كَتَبْنَا	Dual/plural 1st person	جمع متكلّم

Note:

- In the مُتَّصِل (attached) pronouns, only the underlined part is the pronoun.
- The هُمْ pronoun is sometimes هِمْ in the *jarr* state. More reading will make this clear.

[10] The discussion of the different fourteen forms based on number, gender and persons is discussed in the sarf book (A comprehensive study of Arabic morphology), volume 1. Please refer to the Sarf book for further explanation on this.

- There are no ضَمِيْر مَجْرُور مُنْفَصِل (**detached** pronouns in the *jarr* state) in the Arabic language.

ACTIVITY: 25

The following are verses from the Holy Qur'an, some of the pronouns (ضمائر) are highlighted and then noted in the box below. For these pronouns, write down the **type** of the pronoun and the **form** of the pronoun.

الٓمّٓ ١ ٣ اَلْبَقَرَة ٢

اُولٰٓئِكَ عَلٰى هُدًى مِّنْ رَّبِّهِمْ ۗ وَاُولٰٓئِكَ هُمُ الْمُفْلِحُوْنَ ۝٥

اِنَّ الَّذِيْنَ كَفَرُوْا سَوَآءٌ عَلَيْهِمْ ءَاَنْذَرْتَهُمْ اَمْ لَمْ

تُنْذِرْهُمْ لَا يُؤْمِنُوْنَ ۝٦ خَتَمَ اللّٰهُ عَلٰى قُلُوْبِهِمْ وَعَلٰى

سَمْعِهِمْ ؕ وَعَلٰٓى اَبْصَارِهِمْ غِشَاوَةٌ ۫ وَّلَهُمْ عَذَابٌ

عَظِيْمٌ ۝٧ وَمِنَ النَّاسِ مَنْ يَّقُوْلُ اٰمَنَّا بِاللّٰهِ وَ

بِالْيَوْمِ الْاٰخِرِ وَمَا هُمْ بِمُؤْمِنِيْنَ ۝٨ يُخٰدِعُوْنَ اللّٰهَ

وَالَّذِيْنَ اٰمَنُوْا ۚ وَمَا يَخْدَعُوْنَ اِلَّاۤ اَنْفُسَهُمْ وَمَا يَشْعُرُوْنَ ۝٩

فِيْ قُلُوْبِهِمْ مَّرَضٌ ۙ فَزَادَهُمُ اللّٰهُ مَرَضًا ۚ وَلَهُمْ عَذَابٌ

اَلِيْمٌ ۢ بِمَا كَانُوْا يَكْذِبُوْنَ ۝١٠ وَاِذَا قِيْلَ لَهُمْ لَا

تُفْسِدُوْا فِي الْاَرْضِ ۙ قَالُوْٓا اِنَّمَا نَحْنُ مُصْلِحُوْنَ ۝١١

ع ٣ وقف لازم

Write the detail for the pronoun **underlined**:

The grammatical state of the pronouns is mentioned (as that is not studied yet).

ضمير	Meaning	حالة	قسم (Type)	صِيغة (Form)
رَبِّهِمْ	Their lord	مجرور		
أَنْذَرْتَهُمْ	You warned them	مرفوع	ضمير مرفوع متصل	واحد مذكّر حاضر
تُنْذِرْهُمْ	You warn them	منصوب		
أَبْصَارِهِمْ	Their sight	مجرور		
آمَنَّا	We believe	مرفوع		
مَا هُمْ بِمُؤْمِنِيْنَ	They are not believers	مرفوع		
آمَنُوْا	They brought belief	مرفوع		
وَلَهُمْ	And for them	مجرور		
إِنَّمَا نَحْنُ مُصْلِحُوْنَ	Only we are rectifiers	مرفوع		

ACTIVITY: 26

From the above verses of the Holy Qur'an, pick any other five pronouns (ضمائر) which were not selected earlier, and fill in the detail for them below. Do not worry about mistakes regarding the grammatical states at this stage as this has not been studied properly yet.

ضمير	Meaning	حالة	قسم (Type)	صِيغة (Form)

LESSON 16: DEMONSTRATIVE PRONOUNS

The اِسْم الْإِشَارَة (demonstrative pronoun) is a noun used when 'indicating/pointing' to something. It is also called an 'indicating' noun.

Example: The noun ذَلِكَ (that) in the sentence ذَلِكَ الْكِتَابُ (that book) is a demonstrative/indicating noun as it indicates to the book.

In all languages, there are demonstrative pronouns. For example, in the English language:

- 'this' (used for singular near); e.g. '**this** is a book' (used if it is only one book and it is near),
- 'that' (used for singular far); e.g. '**that** is a book' (used if it is only one book and it is far),
- 'these' (used for plural near); e.g. '**these** are books' (used if it is many books and they are near),
- 'those' (used for plural far); e.g. '**those** are books' (used if it is many books and they are far),

So, the demonstrative pronoun is chosen depending on singular or plural and also depending on location (near or far).

Also, the location being 'near' or 'far' is decided by the imagination of the speaker; there is no fixed distance for when something is considered 'near' or 'far'.

In Arabic, as we also have a separate form for dual/two (تَثْنِيَة), there are additional demonstrative pronouns for 'dual near' and 'dual far'.

Further, in Arabic, there are separate demonstrative pronouns for masculine (مُذَكَّر) and feminine (مُؤَنَّث).

The following table mentions the different demonstrative pronouns in Arabic based on number, location and gender.

اِسْمُ الْإِشَارَةِ لِلْبَعِيْدِ Demonstrative pronoun 'far'			اِسْمُ الْإِشَارَةِ لِلْقَرِيْبِ Demonstrative pronoun 'close/near'			
جمع Plural	تثنية Dual	واحد Singular	جمع Plural	تثنية Dual	واحد Singular	
أُوْلَئِكَ	ذَانِكَ ذَيْنِكَ	ذَلِكَ	هَؤُلَاءِ	هَذَانِ هَذَيْنِ	هَذَا	مُذَكَّر Masculine
Them many (M)	Them two (M)	That (M)	These many (M)	These two (M)	This (M)	
أُوْلَئِكَ	تَانِكَ تَيْنِكَ	تِلْكَ	هَؤُلَاءِ	هَاتَانِ هَاتَيْنِ	هَذِهِ	مُؤَنَّث Feminine
Them many (F)	Them two (F)	That (F)	These many (F)	These two (F)	This (F)	

<u>Note</u>:

1) Some of the demonstrative pronouns in Arabic are pronounced slightly different to how they are written, hence, it would be advisable to first listen to them from a tutor. Sometimes, the writing rules differ from the pronunciation rules.
   <u>Example</u>: The demonstrative pronoun هَذَا is actually pronounced as هَاذَا with an *alif* after the letter *haa;* however, in writing, it is not normally written.
2) The dual category above has two options, that are based on the grammatical states. So هَذَانِ is used in *rafa'* case, and هَذَيْنِ is used in the other two grammatical states.
3) The demonstrative pronoun for the plurals is the same for both genders
4) Before moving further, students should learn the demonstrative pronouns properly.

Sentence structure of اِسْمُ الْإِشَارَة (demonstrative pronouns):

The اِسْمُ الْإِشَارَة (demonstrative pronoun) has a basic grammar structure.

	Keywords	Meaning
1	اِسْمُ الْإِشَارَة	This is the demonstrative pronoun that is used for indicating a person/thing.
		Example: The word هَذَا (this) in هَذَا مَسْجِد (**this** is a masjid) is the اسم الإشارة (demonstrative noun) as it is used to indicate to something (in this case, to the masjid).
2	الْمُشَارُ إِلَيْهِ	This is the person/thing the demonstrative noun is indicating to.
		Example: The word مَسْجِد (masjid) in هَذَا **مَسْجِد** (this is **a masjid**) is the المشار إليه as it is indicated upon (by the demonstrative noun).

Further example:

ذَلِكَ قَلَمٌ (that is a pen)	
قَلَمٌ	ذَلِكَ
المشار إليه	اسم الإشارة

ACTIVITY: 27

In the following phrases, identify the demonstrative pronoun and mention which category it is from. Also, state the اسم الإشارة and the المشار إليه for each.

Phrase	Meaning	Category	اسم الإشارة	المشار إليه
هَاتَانِ سَاعَتَانِ	These two are watches.			
هَؤُلَاءِ مُسْلِمُوْنَ	These people are Muslims.			
هَذَا رَجُلٌ	This is a man.	واحد مذكّر قريب	هذا	رجل
ذَلِكَ كِتَابٌ	That is a book.			
أُوْلَئِكَ مُفْلِحُوْنَ	Those people are successful.			
تِلْكَ نَافِذَةٌ	That is a window.			
أُوْلَئِكَ نِسَاءٌ	Those people are women.			

LESSON 17: RELATIVE PRONOUNS

The الْإِسْم الْمَوْصُوْل (relative pronoun) is a noun used to introduce a relative clause - this is a dependant clause which modifies the noun or clause prior to the relative pronoun.

Example: The noun الَّذِيْ (who) in the sentence جَاءَنِيْ الرَّجُلُ **الَّذِيْ** نَصَرَ الْقَوْمَ (that person came to me **who** helped the people) is a relative pronoun as it introduces the relative clause نَصَرَ الْقَوْمَ to the earlier clause.

In all languages, there are relative pronouns. For example, in the English language:

- 'who' (used for humans); e.g. 'The person came to me **who** helped the people',
- 'why' (used for reasons); e.g. 'I don't know **why** you made me do this.',
- 'where' (used for places); e.g. 'Place your bags **where** the coats are kept.',
- 'when' (used for time); e.g. 'Let's put maximum effort **when** the examination begins.'.

In Arabic, the relative pronouns change based on 'number' (singular, dual and plural forms) and 'gender' (masculine and feminine).

The following table mentions the different relative pronouns in Arabic based on number and gender.

اَلْإِسْمُ الْمَوْصُوْلُ Relative pronoun			
جمع Plural	تثنية Dual	واحد Singular	
اَلَّذِيْنَ	اَلَّذَانِ / اَلَّذَيْنِ	اَلَّذِيْ	مُذَكَّر Masculine
(those many) who (M)	(those two) who (M)	(the one) who (M)	
اَللَّاتِيْ / اَللَّوَاتِيْ	اَللَّتَانِ / اَللَّتَيْنِ	اَلَّتِيْ	مُؤَنَّث Feminine
(those many) who (F)	(those two) who (F)	(the one) who (F)	

Note:

1) The aforementioned 'relative pronouns' are the common relative pronouns in Arabic; hence they should be learnt well before advancing onto other relative pronouns. There are some other relative pronouns as well; many of them will be studied in more advanced books. However, the following table will add some other common relative pronouns to the above table.

اَلْإِسْمُ الْمَوْصُوْلُ Relative pronoun						
واحد/تثنية/جمع Singular/dual/plural	واحد/تثنية/جمع Singular/dual/plural	واحد/تثنية/جمع Singular/dual/plural	جمع Plural	تثنية Dual	واحد Singular	
مَا	مَنْ	أَيٌّ	اَلَّذِيْنَ	اَلَّذَانِ / اَلَّذَيْنِ	اَلَّذِيْ	مُذَكَّر Masculine
		Which (M)	(those many) who (M)	(those two) who (M)	(the one) who (M)	
		أَيَّةٌ	اَللَّاتِيْ / اَللَّوَاتِيْ	اَللَّتَانِ / اَللَّتَيْنِ	اَلَّتِيْ	مُؤَنَّث Feminine
Which (M/F)	Who (M/F)	Which (F)	(those many) who (F)	(those two) who (F)	(the one) who (F)	

The following table mentions the different relative pronouns discussed with examples.

Relative pronoun	Example	Meaning
اَلَّذِيْ	جَاءَنِيْ الرَّجُلُ **الَّذِيْ** نَصَرَ الْقَوْمَ	The man came to me **who** helped the people.
اَلَّذَانِ	جَاءَنِيْ الرَّجُلَانِ **الَّذَانِ** نَصَرَا الْقَوْمَ	The two men came to me **who** helped the people.
اَلَّذِيْنَ	جَاءَنِيْ الرِّجَالُ **الَّذِيْنَ** نَصَرُوْا الْقَوْمَ	Them many men came to me **who** helped the people.
اَلَّتِيْ	جَاءَتْنِيْ الْمَرْأَةُ **الَّتِيْ** نَصَرَتِ الْقَوْمَ	The woman came to me **who** helped the people.
اَللَّتَانِ	جَاءَتْنِيْ الْمَرْأَتَانِ **اللَّتَانِ** نَصَرَتَا الْقَوْمَ	The two women came to me **who** helped the people.
اَللَّاتِيْ	جَاءَتْنِيْ النِّسَاءُ **اللَّاتِيْ** نَصَرْنَ الْقَوْمَ	Them many women came to me **who** helped the people.

أَيٌّ	يُفْلِحُ الرَّجُلُ **أَيٌّ** مُجْتَهِدٌ	That man will be successful **who** is hardworking.
أَيَّةٌ	تُفْلِحُ الْمَرْأَةُ **أَيَّةٌ** مُجْتَهِدَةٌ	That woman will be successful **who** is hardworking.
مَنْ	نَجَحَ الرَّجُلُ **مَنِ** اجْتَهَدَ	That man will be successful **who** is hardworking.
مَا	اِرْكَبْ **مَا** شِئْتَ مِنَ الْخَيْلِ	Travel, O man, on **whichever** horse you wish to ride.

The relative clause is called the صِلَة in Arabic. The following table mentions the الاسم الموصول and the صَلَة in each sentence.

Example	Relative pronoun (الاسم الموصول)	Relative clause (صِلَة)
جَاءَنِيْ الرَّجُلَانِ **الَّذَانِ** نَصَرَا الْقَوْمَ	اَلَّذَانِ	نَصَرَا الْقَوْمَ
جَاءَنِيْ الرِّجَالُ **الَّذِيْنَ** نَصَرُوْا الْقَوْمَ	اَلَّذِيْنَ	نَصَرُوْا الْقَوْمَ
جَاءَتْنِيْ الْمَرْأَتَانِ **اللَّتَانِ** نَصَرَتَا الْقَوْمَ	اَللَّتَانِ	نَصَرَتَا الْقَوْمَ
جَاءَتْنِيْ النِّسَاءُ **اللَّاتِيْ** نَصَرْنَ الْقَوْمَ	اَللَّاتِيْ	نَصَرْنَ الْقَوْمَ
يُفْلِحُ الرَّجُلُ **أَيٌّ** مُجْتَهِدٌ	أَيٌّ	مُجْتَهِدٌ
اِرْكَبْ **مَا** شِئْتَ مِنَ الْخَيْلِ	مَا	شِئْتَ مِنَ الْخَيْلِ

ACTIVITY: 28

In the following phrases, identify the relative pronoun (الاسم الموصول) and the relative clause (صلة). Also, mention the category of the relative pronoun in terms of gender and number.

Phrase	Meaning	Category	الاسم الموصول	صلة
مَا جَزَاءُ مَنْ يَفْعَلُ ذَلِكَ	What is the recompense for the person who does this			
وَارْزُقْ أَهْلَهُ مِنَ الثَّمَرَاتِ مَنْ آمَنَ مِنْهُمْ بِاللهِ	And provide fruits for its those residents that bring faith on Allah			
إِنَّ الَّذِيْنَ آمَنُوْا	Verily those people that brought faith	جمع مذكر	الذين	آمنوا
مُخْرِجٌ مَا كُنْتُمْ تَكْتُمُوْنَ	Take out that which you concealed			
وَإِذَا لَقُوْا الَّذِيْنَ آمَنُوْا	When they meet those people who brought faith			

ACTIVITY: 29

Fill in the gaps in the following sentences with suitable relative pronouns, and write the category of the relative pronoun.

Phrase	Meaning	الاسم الموصول	Category
نَصَرَتْ عَمَّاتُكُمْ .... جِئْنَ أَمْسِ	Your aunts helped who came yesterday.		
ذَهَبَتْ فَاطِمَةُ .... زَارَتْ أَهْلَنَا	That Fatimah went who visited our family.		
أَكْرِمْ .... عَلَّمُوْكَ	Respect those who have taught you.	الَّذِيْنَ	جمع مذكر
جَاءَنِي الطُّلَّابُ .... نَجَحُوْا	Those students came that were successful.		
ذَهَبَ الرَّجُلَانِ .... أَرَادَا الْحَجَّ	The two men went who intended to do Hajj		

LESSON 18: GRAMMATICAL STATES FOR NOUNS

Earlier it was mentioned that **nouns** have **three** grammatical states. These are:

	State	Meaning
1	حَالَة الرَّفْعِ	This is when the word is in the *rafa'* state (حالة الرفع). In **basic Arabic words**, this will be seen by the *dhammah* (ـُ) added onto the last letter.
		Example: The word اَلْحَمْدُ in the sentence اَلْحَمْدُ لِلّٰهِ is in the ***rafa'* state,** therefore the ***dhammah*** can be seen on the last letter.
2	حَالَة النَّصْب	This is when the word is in the *nasab* state (حالة النصب). In **basic Arabic words**, this will be seen by the *fathah* (ـَ) added onto the last letter.
		Example: The word الصِّرَاطَ in the sentence اِهْدِنَا الصِّرَاطَ is in the ***nasab* state,** therefore the ***fathah*** can be seen on the last letter.
3	حَالَة الجَرّ	This is when the word is in the *jarr* state (حالة الجر). In **basic Arabic words**, this will be seen by the *kasrah* (ـِ) added onto the last letter.
		Example: The word الْمَغْضُوْبِ in the phrase غَيْرِ الْمَغْضُوْبِ is in the ***jarr* state,** therefore the ***kasrah*** can be seen on the last letter.

Depending on the state of the noun, it is referred to as the following:

	State		Name of the noun (singular)	Name of the noun (plural)
1	حَالَة الرَّفْعِ	=	مَرْفُوْع	مَرْفُوْعَات
2	حَالَة النَّصْب	=	مَنْصُوْب	مَنْصُوْبَات
3	حَالَة الجَرّ	=	مَجْرُوْر	مَجْرُوْرَات

Now, the question is when will a noun be in the *rafa'* state, when will it be in the *nasab* state and when will it be in the *jarr* state?

The following table lists the scenarios.
Further detail for each scenario will appear in the following chapters.[11]

[11] The students of grammar should learn these lists well before proceeding onto the detail – understanding the scenarios will come later in the book.

مَرْفُوعَات (8 in total)
فَاعِل (doer)
نَائِب فَاعِل (substitute doer)
مُبْتَدَأ (subject)
خَبْر (news/information)
خَبْرُ "إِنَّ" (news/information of إِنَّ)
خَبْرُ "لَا" لِنَفْي الْجِنْس (news/information of لَا which comes to negate the full genus)
إِسْمُ "كَانَ" (Subject of كَانَ)
إِسْمُ "مَا" و"لَا" الْمُشَبَّهَتَانِ بِ(لَيْس) (subject of "ما" and "لا" similar to "لَيْسَ")

مَنْصُوْبَات (12 in total)
مَفْعُوْل بِهِ (object)
مَفْعُوْل مُطْلَق (root noun)
مَفْعُوْل لَهُ (reason)
مَفْعُوْل مَعَهُ (object mentioned after *waaw* in the meaning of 'with')
مَفْعُوْل فِيْهِ (place/time)
حَال (state)
تَمْيِيْز (clarification)
إِسْمُ "إِنَّ" (subject of إِنَّ)
إِسْمُ "لَا" لِنَفْي الْجِنْس (subject of لَا which comes to negate the full genus)
خَبْرُ "كَانَ" (news/information of كَانَ)
خَبْرُ "مَا" و"لَا" الْمُشَبَّهَتَانِ بِ(لَيْس) (news/information of "ما" and "لا" similar to "لَيْسَ")

مَجْرُوْرَات (2 in total)
مُضَافُ إِلَيْهِ (possessor)
مَجْرُوْر بِحَرْفِ الْجَرِّ (occurs after the particle of *jarr)*

Further information regarding each scenario is coming in the following chapters.

LESSON 19: MARFU'AAT

One of the states of nouns is the *rafa'* state. A noun in this state is referred to as from amongst the مَرْفُوْعَات.

There are **eight** مَرْفُوْعَات; they are mentioned with a brief explanation and an example in the following table.

	Type	Meaning
1	فَاعِل (doer)	This is the **doer** of the action that is mentioned.
		Example: The word يُوْسُفُ in the sentence قَامَ يُوْسُفُ (Yusuf stood up) is the **doer** of the action 'standing' – hence, it is the فاعل .
2	نَائِب فَاعِل (Substitute doer)	This is the person/thing **upon which** the action was done **and the doer is unknown.**
		Example: The word يَحْيَى in the sentence نُصِرَ يَحْيَى (Yahya was helped) is referring to the person upon whom the action (of 'helping') was done, he never did the action himself. Further, the doer of the actual action is not mentioned or is unknown. Hence, the word يَحْيَى is a نائب فاعل .
3	مُبْتَدَأ (subject)	This is when news is given regarding someone/something (the **subject**).
		Example: The word يُوْسُفُ in the sentence يُوْسُفُ طَوِيْلٌ (Yusuf is tall) is the مبتدأ as news has been given regarding him.
4	خَبْر (news/information)	This is the **news** (information) itself that has been given regarding someone/something.
		Example: The word طَوِيْلٌ in the sentence يُوْسُفُ طَوِيْلٌ (Yusuf is tall) is the خبر as it is **giving news** regarding the subject – يوسف .
5	خَبْرُ "إِنَّ" (news/information of إِنَّ)	This is when the particle إِنَّ (or some other particles – detail coming later) enters upon a 'subject' and 'news' sentence – these particles will cause the **'news'** to be in *rafa'* state.
		Example: The word مُجْتَهِدٌ (hardworking) in the sentence إِنَّ مُحَمَّدًا مُجْتَهِدٌ (Verily, Muhammad is hardworking) is in the *rafa'* state as it is the 'news' of إِنَّ .
6	خَبْرُ "لَا" لِنَفْيِ الْجِنْس (news/information of لَا which comes to negate the full genus)	This is when the particle لَا which comes to **negate the full genus** enters upon a 'subject' and 'news' sentence – this particle will cause the 'news' to be in *rafa'* state.
		Example: The word قَائِمٌ (standing) in the sentence لَا رَجُلَ قَائِمٌ (there is not a single man standing) is in the *rafa'* state as it is the 'news' of such a لَا which is negating the full genus.

7	**اِسْمُ "كَانَ"** (Subject of كَانَ)	This is when the particle كَانَ (or some other verbs – detail coming later) enters upon a 'subject' and 'news' sentence – these verbs will cause the **'subject'** to be in *rafa'* state. Example: The word مُحَمَّدٌ in the sentence كَانَ مُحَمَّدٌ مُجْتَهِدًا (Muhammad was hardworking) is in the *rafa'* state as it is the 'subject' of كَانَ.
8	**اِسْمُ "مَا" و"لَا" الْمُشَبَّهَتَانِ بِ(لَيْسَ)** (Subject of "ما" and "لا" similar to "لَيْسَ")	This is when the particle مَا (in the meaning of 'no') or the particle لَا (in the meaning of 'no') enter upon a 'subject' and 'news' sentence – these particles will casue the **'subject'** to be in *rafa'* state. Example: The word يُوْسُفُ in the sentence مَا يُوْسُفُ قَائِمًا (Yusuf is not standing) is in the *rafa'* state as it is the 'subject' of مَا.

Above, the **eight** مَرْفُوْعَات are mentioned with a brief explanation and an example. An activity will follow to consolidate the basic ideas and then in the following chapters, each type of the **eight** مَرْفُوْعَات will be explained in some more detail.

ACTIVITY: 30

Place a ***harakah* on the last letter** of the underlined words, then write the state of the word with reason. Write the state and reason in Arabic.

Sentence	Grammatical state	Reason
فُتِحَ الْبَاب The door was opened.		
قَرَأَ مُحَمّد الْكِتَابَ Muhammad read the book.		
كَانَ الْكِتَاب كَبِيْرًا The book was big.		
إِنَّ السَّاعَةَ رَخِيْصَة Verily, the watch is cheap.		
لَا دُكَّانَ مَفْتُوْحٌ No shop is open.	حالة الرفع	خبر "لا" لنفي الجنس
الدَّرْس سَهْل The lesson is easy.		
أَكَلَ يُوْسف الطَّعَامَ Yusuf ate the food.		
لا رَجُل جَالِسًا A man is not sitting.		
نُصِرَ حَامد Hamid was helped.		
كَانَ مُحَمّد نَائِمًا Muhammad was sleeping.		
إِنَّ الطَّالِبَ غَائِب Verily, the student is absent.		
لَا طَالِبَ غَائِب No student is absent.		
مَا يُوْسُف جَالِسًا Yusuf is not sitting.		
المَسْجِدُ قَرِيْب The Masjid is close.	حالة الرفع	المبتدأ

LESSON 20: THE فاعل & نائب فاعل

From amongst the مَرْفُوْعَات is the فَاعِل.

The فَاعِل is the **doer** of the action that has been mentioned.
Example: The word يُوْسُفُ in the sentence قَامَ يُوْسُفُ (Yusuf stood up) is the **doer** of the action 'standing' – hence, he is the فاعل.

Some rules regarding the فَاعِل:

1) The normal sentence **sequence** is to bring the verb (فعل) first, then the doer (فاعل) and then the done-upon (مفعول به).[12]

Example:

مُحَمَّدًا	يُوْسُفُ	نَصَرَ
مفعول به	فاعل	فعل

Although, sometimes, this sequence can change. This may have some further rules and conditions which are studied in more advanced grammar books.

2) The فَاعِل can sometimes be mentioned in words (ظاهر) and it can sometimes be a pronoun (ضمير).

Example:

	فاعل	Meaning
1	ظَاهِر (apparent)	This is when the **doer** is apparent (mentioned in words).
		Example: The word يُوْسُفُ in the sentence قَامَ يُوْسُفُ (Yusuf stood up) is clearly mentioned in the words (after the verb), it is a ظاهر doer.
2	ضَمِيْر (hidden)	This is when the **doer** is hidden (not mentioned in words) – it is a pronoun.
		Example: The doer in the sentence دَخَلُوْا (they entered) is not clearly mentioned in words (after the verb), rather it is hidden within the verb (and translated as 'they'), it is a ضمير doer.

[12] More detail regarding the done-upon (مفعول به) will come later in the منصوبات chapter.

3) If the فَاعِل is mentioned in words (ظاهر), then the verb (prior to it) will always be brough as a **singular** verb irrespective of the فَاعِل being dual or plural; however, the gender of the verb will change from masculine to feminine if the doer is feminine.

Example:

Sentence	Meaning	فعل	فاعل
لَعِبَتْ الطَّالِبَاتُ فِيْ الْمَلْعَبِ	The female students played in the playground.	لعبتْ	الطالبات
نَصَرَتْ فَاطِمَةُ الطَّالِبَةَ	Fatimah helped the student.	نصرتْ	فاطمة
فَتَحَ زَيْدٌ وَمُحَمَّدٌ الْبَابَ	Zaid and Muhammad opened the door.	فتح	زيد ومحمد
نَصَرَ الرِّجَالُ الْمُدِيْرَ	The men helped the principal.	نصر	الرجال

In all the above examples, the verb has remained **singular** (whether masculine or feminine), as the verb was mentioned in words (ظاهر).

4) If the فَاعِل is a pronoun (ضمير), then the verb will correspond to the فاعل in terms of number and gender. For example, if the فاعل is **dual and feminine,** then the verb will also be **dual and feminine.**

Sentence	Meaning	فعل	فاعل
لَعِبْنَ	They (many women) played.	لعب	هُنَّ
نَصَرَتَا	Them two (women) helped.	نصر	هُمَا
فَتَحَا	Them two (men) opened.	فتح	هُمَا
سَمِعْتُمْ	You (many) men heard.	سمع	أَنْتُمْ

In all the above examples, the verb changed in appearance based on the number and gender of the doer; the doer was a pronoun within the verb.

<u>From amongst the مَرْفُوْعَات is the نَائِب فَاعِل</u>

The نَائِب فَاعِل is the **substitute doer** of the action that has been mentioned.

In other words, it is **not** the doer, rather it is the person/thing **upon which** the action was done; however, as the **doer is unknown** (therefore missing from the sentence)**,** the substitute doer takes its grammatical place and accepts the *rafa'* case.

<u>Example</u>: The word يُوْسُفُ in the sentence نُصِرَ يُوْسُفُ (Yusuf was helped) is the نَائِب فَاعِل (substitute doer) of the action 'helping'. Yusuf never did the action of helping, rather he was helped. However, as we do not know who the doer (helper) was, there is no فَاعِل in the sentence. Instead, the person who was helped (Yusuf) has taken the grammatical place of the فَاعِل and is in the *rafa'* case. Hence, يُوْسُفُ is the نَائِب فَاعِل (substitute doer).

<u>Some rules regarding the نَائِب فَاعِل</u>:

1) The نائب فاعل is regarded as the فاعل in regards to grammar rules, not in terms of meaning. Hence, all the grammar rules mentioned for the فاعل will also normally apply to the نائب فاعل.

2) The نائب فاعل is also called مَفْعُوْل مَا لَمْ يُسَمَّ فَاعِلُهُ (the object (done-upon) whose doer is not mentioned) – as in literal terms, that is what a نائب فاعل is.

3) The نائب فاعل will have a فعل مجهول (passive verb) prior to it. Further detail regarding فعل مجهول (passive verb) is discussed in Sarf (Arabic morphology) books and briefly later within this book.

ACTIVITY: 31

Place a *harakah* on the last letters of the underlined words. Also, mention which grammatical state these words are in and mention the type.

Sentence	Grammatical state	Reason
كَسَرَ الطِّفْل الْقَلَمَ The student broke the pen.		
غُسِلَتْ السَّيَّارَة The car was washed.		
غَسَلَتْ آمِنَة الْمِنْدِيلَ Aminah washed the handkerchief.		
حُفِظَتِ السُّوْرَة The surah is memorised.	حالة الرفع/مرفوعات	نائب فاعل
كَتَبَتْ الْمُدَرِّسَة الدَّرْسَ The teacher wrote the lesson.	حالة الرفع/مرفوعات	فاعل
سَمِعَ بِلَال الْأَذَانَ Bilal heard the adhaan.		
يَذْهَبُ الطَّالِب إِلَى الْمَدْرَسَةِ The student is going to the madrasah.		
يَلْعَبُ الطِّفْل مَعَ أُخْتِهِ The child is playing with his sister.		
أُكِلَ التَّمْر The dates were eaten.		
كُسِرَ الْكُرْسِيّ The chair was broken.		
أَكَلَ أُسَامَة الْعِنَبَ Usamah ate the grape.		
قُتِلَ الْحَيَوَان The animal was killed.		
حَفِظَ حَمْزَة الْقُرْآنَ Hamzah memorised the Qur'an.		
سُئِلَ الْمُدِيْر The principal was asked.		

LESSON 21: THE مبتدأ & خبر

From amongst the مَرْفُوْعَات are the مُبْتَدَأ and the خَبَرْ

	Type	Meaning
3	مُبْتَدَأ (subject)	This is when news is given regarding someone/something (the **subject**).
		Example: The word يُوْسُفُ in the sentence يُوْسُفُ طَوِيْلٌ (Yusuf is tall) is the مبتدأ as news has been given **regarding him**.
4	خَبَرْ (news/information)	This is the **news** (information) that has been given regarding someone/something.
		Example: The word طَوِيْلٌ in the sentence يُوْسُفُ طَوِيْلٌ (Yusuf is tall) is the خبر as it is **giving news** regarding the subject – يوسف .

Some rules regarding the مُبْتَدَأ and the خَبَرَ:

1) The مُبْتَدَأ and خَبَرَ usually occur together – as the news (خبر) is given regarding the subject (مبتدأ).

2) In terms of the sentence order, the subject (مبتدأ) usually comes **first** and the news (خبر) usually comes **second.**[13]

3) The subject (مبتدأ) is usually **specific** (معرفة) and the news (خبر) is usually **common** (خبر).[14]

4) The subject (مبتدأ) and the news (خبر) form together to make a **nominal informative sentence** – this is called **جُمْلَة اِسْمِيَّة خَبْرِيَّة** in Arabic.

[13] Sometimes the order does change; this can be studied in more advanced books.

[14] Sometimes the subject can be common, or the news can be specific; however, these changes are only allowed in unique scenarios which are studied in more advanced books.

5) The subject (مبتدأ) and the news (خبر) usually correspond in gender – so, both will be masculine, or both will be feminine.

6) The subject (مبتدأ) and the news (خبر) usually correspond in number – so, both will be singular, or both will be dual, or both will be plural.

7) One subject (مبتدأ) can have **more than one** news (خبر).

Example: مُحَمَّدٌ عَاقِلٌ عَالِمٌ مُجْتَهِدٌ (Muhammad is intelligent, a scholar and hardworking).

In this example, **three** sets of news were given regarding Muhammad.

Overall example (with explanation):

طَوِيْلٌ	يُوْسُفُ
خبر	مبتدأ
جملة اسميّة خبريّة	

Notice in this example:

- the subject (مبتدأ) which was يوسف appeared first,
- the subject (مبتدأ) is specific (معرفة) and the news (خبر) is common (نكرة),
- the subject (مبتدأ) and the news (خبر) both are masculine (مذكّر),
- the subject (مبتدأ) and the news (خبر) both are singular (واحد),
- the subject (مبتدأ) and the news (خبر) together form a جملة اسميّة خبريّة .

ACTIVITY: 32

Analyse the following example by filling in the gaps and then writing an explanation. Use the above example for the method of analysis.

كَبِيْرَانِ	اَلْكِتَابَانِ

Analysis:

....

....

....

....

ACTIVITY: 33

Place a *harakah* on the last letters of the underlined words. Also, mention which grammatical state these words are in and mention the type.

Sentence	Grammatical state	Reason
الْذَّهَب رَخِيْص The gold is cheap.		
الْمَاءُ بَارِد The water is cold.		
يُوْسُف عَالِمٌ Yusuf is a scholar.	حالة الرفع/مرفوعات	مبتدأ
حُفِظَتِ السُّوْرَة The surah was memorised.	حالة الرفع/مرفوعات	نائب فاعل
كَتَبَتْ الْمُدَرِّسَة الدَّرْس The teacher wrote the lesson.	حالة الرفع/مرفوعات	فاعل
النَّافِذَة مَكْسُوْرَة The window is broken.		
الْبَابَانِ مَفْتُوْحَان The two doors are open.		
الْطَّالِبَة غَائِبَةٌ The student is absent.		
كَسَرَ الرَّجُل الْمِلْعَقَةَ The man broke the spoon.		
يَحْيَى أُسْتَاذٌ Yahya is a teacher.		
النُّجُوْم كَثِيْرَةٌ The stars are many.		
الْإِمْتِحَان قَرِيْبٌ The examination is close.		

LESSON 22: The "إن" خبر & خبر "لا" لنفي الجنس

From amongst the مَرْفُوْعَات are the "إِنَّ" خَبَرُ and the خَبَرُ "لَا" لِنَفْيِ الْجِنْس

	Type	Meaning
5	خَبَرُ "إِنَّ" (news/information of إِنَّ)	This is when the particle إِنَّ (or some other particles – detail coming later) enter upon a 'subject' and 'news' sentence – these particles will give the **'news'** a *rafa'* state. Example: The word مُجْتَهِدٌ (hardworking) in the sentence إِنَّ مُحَمَّدًا مُجْتَهِدٌ (Verily, Muhammad is hardworking.) is in the *rafa'* state as it is the 'news' of إِنَّ .
6	خَبَرُ "لَا" لِنَفْيِ الْجِنْس (news/information of لَا which comes to negate the full genus)	This is when the particle لَا which comes to **negate the full genus** enters upon a 'subject' and 'news' sentence – this particle will give the **'news'** a *rafa'* state. Example: The word قَائِمٌ (standing) in the sentence لَا رَجُلَ قَائِمٌ (there is not a single man standing) is in the *rafa'* state as it is the 'news' of such a لَا which is negating the full genus.

Further detail regarding خَبَرُ "إِنَّ":

There are **six** particles which are referred to as إِنَّ وَأَخَوَاتُهَا (إنّ and its sisters). They are given this name of 'sisters' as the remaining five particles have the same grammatical rule as إنّ.

These particles are also called الْحُرُوْفُ الْمُشَبَّهَةُ بِالْفِعْلِ (particles that are similar to a verb).[15]

[15] Each particle is referred to as الْحَرْف الْمُشَبَّه بِالْفِعْل (in singular format, when referring to only one of the six particles).
Also, the reason for similarity with verbs is studied in intermediate level Nahw books.

These **six particles** are:

	Type	Meaning
1	إِنَّ Verily	The particle إِنَّ means **'verily'**. It comes at the beginning of the sentence and creates the meaning of **emphasis**. Example: إِنَّ مُحَمَّدًا مُجْتَهِدٌ (Verily, Muhammad is hardworking.) Notice the particle إِنَّ has come at the beginning and is creating the meaning of emphasis.
2	أَنَّ That	The particle أَنَّ means **'that'**. It comes within a sentence (not at the beginning) and it creates a meaning of **emphasis**. Example: بَلَغَنِيْ أَنَّ يُوْسُفَ نَاجِحٌ (It has reached me that Yusuf is successful.) Notice the particle أَنَّ has come in-between (not at the beginning). Also, it is translated as 'that', although it does create a (hidden) emphasised meaning of its following sentence. This meaning of emphasis is not normally translated.
3	كَأَنَّ As though	The particle كَأَنَّ means **'as though'**. Example: كَأَنَّ مُعَاوِيَةَ قَائِمٌ (It is as though Muawiyah is standing).
4	لَكِنَّ However	The particle لَكِنَّ means **'however'**. Example: غَابَ يَحْيَى لَكِنَّ يُوْسُفَ حَاضِرٌ (Yahya was absent, however, Yusuf was present).
5	لَيْتَ I wish	The particle لَيْتَ means **'I wish'**. It comes to express a 'wish' of something which is **impossible**. Example: لَيْتَ الشَّبَابَ يَعُوْدُ (I wish youth would return!).
6	لَعَلَّ Hope	The particle لَعَلَّ means **'(I have) hope'**. It comes to express a 'hope' of something which is **possible**. Example: لَعَلَّ الْمُسَافِرَ قَادِمٌ (I have hope the traveller will return).

The **overall grammatical rule** for all these six particles is that:

- they will enter upon a مبتدأ (subject) and a خبر (news) – hence, overall, they will follow similar grammatical rules to the مبتدأ and the خبر ;
- they will give the مبتدأ (subject) a *nasab* case (that will mean a *fathah* for simple words);
- they will give the خبر (news) a *rafa'* case (that will mean a *dhammah* for simple words);
- the مبتدأ (subject) will now be called "إِسْمُ إنّ" (or whichever particle is used instead of إِنّ);

- the خبر (news) will now be called "خَبَرُ "إن (or whichever particle is used instead of إن).

Example one:

طَوِيْلٌ	يُوْسُفَ	إنَّ
خبر "إنّ"	اسم "إنّ"	الحرف المشبّه بالفعل
جملة اسميّة خبريّة		

Notice in this example:

- the "اسم "إن which was يوسف appeared first and is in the *nasab* case (which is shown by the *fathah);*
- the "خبر "إن which was طويل appeared second and is in the *rafa'* case (which is shown by the *dhammah);*
- the "اسم "إن is specific (معرفة) (as is the مبتدأ normally) and the "خبر "إن is common (نكرة) (as is the خبر normally),
- the اسم "إنّ" and the خبر "إنّ" both are masculine (مذكّر),
- the اسم "إنّ" and the خبر "إنّ" both are singular (واحد),
- the "اسم "إن and the خبر "إنّ" together form a جملة اسميّة خبريّة .

Example two:

قَادِمٌ	الْمُسَافِرَ	لَعَلَّ
خبر "لعلّ"	اسم "لعلّ"	الحرف المشبّه بالفعل
جملة اسميّة خبريّة		

ACTIVITY: 34

Fill in the gaps in the following table.

قَائِمٌ	مُعَاوِيَةَ	كَأَنَّ

Further detail regarding خَبَرُ "لَا" لِنَفْيِ الْجِنْسِ

From amongst the nouns which are in the *rafa'* state is the خبر (news/information) of that particle لَا which gives the meaning of **negating the full genus.**

Example: The word قَائِمٌ (standing) in the sentence لَا رَجُلَ قَائِمٌ (there is **not a single man** standing) is in the *rafa'* state as it is the 'news' of such a لَا which is negating the full genus.

Some rules regarding "لَا" لِنَفْيِ الْجِنْسِ:

1) The "لَا" لِنَفْيِ الْجِنْسِ comes to negate the **full genus**, not just one or two individuals.

2) The subject (اسم) of the "لَا" لِنَفْيِ الْجِنْسِ will be in the *nasab* case, and the news (خبر) of the "لَا" لِنَفْيِ الْجِنْسِ will be in the *rafa'* case.

3) The subject (اسم) of the "لَا" لِنَفْيِ الْجِنْسِ will be a common noun (نكرة) generally. This is contrary to the normal subject (مبتدأ) which is usually specific (معرفة).

4) It is common for the subject (اسم) of the "لَا" لِنَفْيِ الْجِنْسِ to be a possessive structure (مضاف ومضاف إليه).[16]

Example:

قَائِمٌ	رَجُلَ	لَا
خبر "لا" لنفي الجنس	اسم "لا" لنفي الجنس	"لا" لنفي الجنس
جملة اسميّة خبريّة		

[16] More detail of the possessive structure is covered in the chapter of *majrooraat* (مجرورات) later.

LESSON 23: The "كان" اسم & "لا" و"ما" اسم

From amongst the مَرْفُوْعَات are the "كَانَ" اِسْمُ and the "مَا" و"لَا" اِسْمُ which is similar to لَيْسَ

	Type	Meaning
7	اِسْمُ "كَانَ" (Subject of كَانَ)	This is when the particle كَانَ (or some other verbs – detail coming later) enter upon a 'subject' and 'news' sentence – these verbs will give the 'subject' a *rafa'* state.
		Example: The word مُحَمَّدٌ in the sentence كَانَ مُحَمَّدٌ مُجْتَهِدًا (Muhammad was hardworking) is in the *rafa'* state as it is the 'subject' of كَانَ .
8	اِسْمُ "مَا" و"لَا" الْمُشَبَّهَتَانِ بِ(لَيْسَ) (Subject of "ما" and "لا" similar to "لَيْس")	This is when the particle مَا (in the meaning of 'no') or the particle لَا (in the meaning of 'no') enter upon a 'subject' and 'news' sentence – these particles will give the 'subject' a *rafa'* state.
		Example: The word يُوْسُفُ in the sentence مَا يُوْسُفُ قَائِمًا (Yusuf is not standing) is in the *rafa'* state as it is the 'subject' of مَا .

Further detail regarding "كَانَ" اِسْمُ :

There are **thirteen**[17] verbs which are referred to as كَانَ and its sisters (as these remaining twelve verbs have the same grammatical rule as كَانَ).

These verbs are also called الْأَفْعَالُ النَّاقِصَةُ (incomplete verbs – i.e. verbs which don't follow all the normal rules of a verb).[18]

[17] In more detailed books, **seventeen** verbs are mentioned.
[18] Each verb is referred to as الْفِعْلُ النَّاقِصُ (in singular format).

These **thirteen verbs** are:

	Type	Example
1	كَانَ Was	Example: كَانَ مُحَمَّدٌ غَائِبًا (Muhammad **was** absent.)
2	صَارَ Became	Example: صَارَ إِبْرَاهِيْمُ غَنِيًّا (Ibrahim **became** rich.)
3	أَصْبَحَ To do in the morning	Example: أَصْبَحَ إِسْمَاعِيْلُ ذَاكِرًا (Ismaeel was doing *dhikr* in the **morning.**)
4	أَمْسَى To do in the evening	Example: أَمْسَى إِسْمَاعِيْلُ ذَاكِرًا (Ismaeel was doing *dhikr* in the **evening.**)
5	أَضْحَى To do in the late-morning	Example: أَضْحَى إِسْمَاعِيْلُ ذَاكِرًا (Ismaeel was doing *dhikr* in the **late morning.**)
6	ظَلَّ To spend the day	Example: ظَلَّ مُعَاوِيَةُ كَاتِبًا (Muawiyah **spent the day** writing.)
7	بَاتَ To spend the night	Example: بَاتَ مُعَاوِيَةُ كَاتِبًا (Muawiyah **spent the night** writing.)
8	مَا زَالَ To be continuously	Example: مَا زَالَ فَهِيْمٌ أَمِيْرًا (Faheem **continuously** remained a leader.)
9	مَا فَتِئَ To be continuously	Example: مَا فَتِئَ فَهِيْمٌ أَمِيْرًا (Faheem **continuously** remained a leader.)
10	مَا بَرِحَ To be continuously	Example: مَا بَرِحَ فَهِيْمٌ أَمِيْرًا (Faheem **continuously** remained a leader.)
11	مَا انْفَكَّ To be continuously	Example: مَا انْفَكَّ فَهِيْمٌ أَمِيْرًا (Faheem **continuously** remained a leader).
12	مَا دَامَ To do continuously **until**	Example: أَقُوْمُ مَا دَامَ الْأَمِيْرُ جَالِسًا (I will stand **until** the leader is sitting).
13	لَيْسَ Not	Example: لَيْسَ يُوْسُفُ غَائِبًا (Yusuf was **not** absent).

The **overall grammatical rule** for all these thirteen verbs is that:

- they will enter upon a مبتدأ (subject) and a خبر (news) – hence, overall, they will follow similar grammatical rules to the مبتدأ and the خبر ;
- they will give the مبتدأ (subject) a *rafa'* case (that will mean a *dhammah* for *simple words);*
- they will give the خبر (news) a *nasab* case (that will mean a *fathah* for simple words);
- the مبتدأ (subject) will now be called "إِسْمُ كَان" (or whichever verb is used instead of كَان);

- the خبر (news) will now be called "كَانَ" خَبَرُ (or whichever verb is used instead of كَانَ).
- As these words are verbs, the overall sentence will be considered as a 'verbal informative sentence' (جُمْلَة فِعْلِيَّة خَبْرِيَّة).

Example one:

حَاضِرًا	يُوْسُفُ	كَانَ
خبر "كَانَ"	اسم "كَانَ"	الفعل الناقص
جملة فعليّة خبريّة		

Notice in this example:

- the "اسم" "كان" which was يوسف appeared first and is in the *rafa'* case (which is shown by the *dhammah);*
- the "خبر" "كان" which was حاضر appeared second and is in the *nasab* case (which is shown by the *fathah);*
- the "اسم" "كان" is specific (معرفة) (as is the مبتدأ normally) and the "خبر" "كان" is common (نكرة) (as is the خبر normally);
- the "اسم" "كان" and the "خبر" "كان" are both masculine (مذكّر)
- the "اسم" "كان" and the "خبر" "كان" are both singular (واحد);
- the "كَانَ" اسم and the "كَانَ" خبر together form a جملة فعليّة خبريّة .

Example two:

ذَاكِرًا	إِسْمَاعِيْلُ	أَصْبَحَ
خبر "أصبح"	اسم "أصبح"	الفعل الناقص
جملة فعليّة خبريّة		

ACTIVITY: 34

Fill in the gaps in the following table.

غَائِبًا	يُوْسُفُ	لَيْسَ

Further detail regarding "لَا" و"مَا" اِسْمُ which is similar to لَيْسَ

	Type	Meaning
8	اِسْمُ "مَا" و"لَا" الْمُشَبَّهَتَانِ بِ(لَيْسَ) (subject of "ما" and "لا" similar to "لَيْسَ")	This is when the particle مَا (in the meaning of 'no') or the particle لَا (in the meaning of 'no') enter upon a 'subject' and 'news' sentence – these particles will give the 'subject' a *rafa'* state.
		Example: The word يُوْسُفُ in the sentence مَا يُوْسُفُ قَائِمًا (Yusuf is not standing) is in the *rafa'* state as it is the 'subject' of مَا .

Further rules:

1) The "مَا" or "لَا" which comes to give a basic negative meaning of 'no' is similar to لَيْسَ as it gives the same meaning and follows similar grammatical rules.
2) The subject (اسم) of this "مَا" and "لَا" will be in the *rafa'* case, and the news (خبر) of this "مَا" and "لَا" will be in the *nasab* case.

3) This "مَا" and "لَا" will enter upon a 'nominal informative sentence' (جُمْلَة اسْمِيَّة خَبْرِيَّة).

4) The particle "مَا" enters upon specific (معرفة) and common (نكرة) nouns.

Example: مَا يُوْسُفُ قَائِمًا (Yusuf is not standing)	In this example, the particle "مَا" has entered upon the word يُوْسُف which is a proper noun; hence, specific (معرفة).
Example: مَا رَجُلٌ قَائِمًا (A man is not standing)	In this example, the particle "مَا" has entered upon the word رَجُل which is a common noun; hence, common (نكرة).

5) The particle "لَا" can only enter upon a common (نكرة) noun.

Example: لَا رَجُلٌ قَائِمًا (A man is not standing)	In this example, the particle "لَا" has entered upon the word رَجُل which is a common noun; hence, common (نكرة).

LESSON 24: RECAP OF مرفوعات

The **eight** مَرْفُوْعَات have been discussed over the previous few chapters. The following activities aims to embed the knowledge of the مَرْفُوْعَات .

ACTIVITY: 35

Mention all the types of مَرْفُوْعَات with examples (and explanation), also mention the English term for each type in the following table.

	Type	English Term	Example (with brief explanation)
1			
2			
3			
4			
5			
6			
7			
8			

ACTIVITY: 36

Place a *harakah* on the last letters of the underlined words. Also, mention which grammatical state these words are in and the type.

Sentence	Grammatical state	Reason
كَانَ الْذَّهَب رَخِيْصًا The gold was cheap		
مَا الْمَاء بَارِدًا The water is not cold		
يُوْسُف عَالِمٌ Yusuf is a scholar	حالة الرفع/مرفوعات	مبتدأ
حُفِظَتِ السُّوْرَة The surah is memorised		
كَتَبَتْ الْمُدَرِّسَة الكِتَابَ The teacher wrote the book		
إِنَّ النَّافِذَةَ مَكْسُوْرَة Verily, the window is broken		
الْبَابَانِ مَفْتُوْحَان The two doors are open		
صَارَتِ الْطَّالِبَة نَاجِحَةً The female student became successful		
كَسَرَ الرَّجُل الْمِلْعَقَةَ The man broke the spoon		
لَيْسَ إِسْمَاعِيْل أُسْتَاذًا Ismaeel is not a teacher		
كَأَنَّ النُّجُوْمَ كَثِيْرَة It is as though the stars are many		
لَعَلَّ الْإِمْتِحَانَ قَرِيْب Hopefully the examination is close		
لَا طَالِبَةَ غَائِبَة No female student is absent		
مَا زَالَ الرَّجُل جَالِسًا The man continuously is sitting		
إِنَّ اللهَ غَفُوْر Verily, Allah is all-forgiving		

ACTIVITY: 37

Analyse the following text/sentences. The words underlined are in the *rafa'* case, explain why. Then, give three more examples, with reason, of words in the *rafa'* case from the following text.

وكَانَ اسْمُ هَذَا الرَّجُلِ آزرَ ، قَالَ إِبْرَاهِيْمُ: أَنَا أَكْسِرُ الْأَصْنَامَ إِذَا ذَهَبَ النَّاسُ
وَخَرَجَ النَّاسُ لِلْعِيْدِ وَخَرَجَ الْأَطْفَالُ ، قَالَ إِبْرَاهِيْمُ: أَنَا سَقِيْمٌ
وَسَكَتَتِ الْأَصْنَامُ لِأَنَّهَا حِجَارَةٌ لَا تَنْطِقُ ، وَسَكَتَتِ الْأَصْنَامُ وَمَا نَطَقَتْ
وَكَانُوْا يَعْرِفُوْنَ أَنَّ الصَّنَمَ الْأَكْبَرَ أَيْضًا حَجَرٌ ، كَانَتِ النَّارُ بَرْدًا وَسَلَامًا عَلَى إِبْرَاهِيْمَ
أَنَّ إِبْرَاهِيْمَ مَسْرُوْرٌ وَأَنَّ إِبْرَاهِيْمَ سَالِمٌ وَدُهِشَ النَّاسُ ، إِنَّ اللهَ حَيٌّ لَا يَمُوْتُ

	Word	Reason for *rafa'* case
1	اسم	
2	إبراهيم	
3	الأطفال	
4	سقيم	
5	الأصنام	
6	حجارة	
7	حجر	
8	النار	
9	مسرور	
10	الناس	
11		
12		
13		

ACTIVITY: 38

Fill in the gaps in the following tables.

مَسْرُوْرٌ	إِبْرَاهِيْمَ	أَنَّ
	اسم "أَنَّ"	

بَرْدًا	النَّارُ	كَانَتِ

النَّاسُ	خَرَجَ

النَّاسُ	دُهِشَ

سَقِيْمٌ	أَنَا

حَيٌّ	اللّٰهَ	إِنَّ

LESSON 25: THE MANSOOBAAT

One of the states of nouns is the *nasab* state – the noun in such a state is referred to as from amongst the مَنْصُوْبَات .

There are **twelve** مَنْصُوْبَات, they are mentioned with a brief explanation and example in the following table.

	Type	Meaning
1	مَفْعُوْل بِهِ (object)	This is **who/what** the action was done upon. Example: The word مُحَمَّدًا in the sentence نَصَرَ يُوْسُفُ مُحَمَّدًا (Yusuf helped Muhammad) is the مفعول به – as the action of helping was done to/upon him.
2	مَفْعُوْل مُطْلَق (root noun)	This is when the **root noun** *(masdar)* of the verb mentioned previously is mentioned. The purpose of bringing this root noun could differ, further detail will be mentioned in the following chapters. Example: The word نَصْرًا in the sentence نَصَرَ يُوْسُفُ مُحَمَّدًا نَصْرًا (Yusuf definitely helped Muhammad.) is the مفعول مطلق – as it is a root noun which has come after the same meaning verb.
3	مَفْعُوْل لَهُ (reason)	This is **why** the action took place, i.e. it gives a **reason** for the action. Example: The word إِكْرَامًا in the sentence قُمْتُ لِأُمِّيْ إِكْرَامًا (I stood up for my mother out of respect for her).
4	مَفْعُوْل مَعَهُ (with)	This is when a noun comes after the particle *waaw* that has the meaning of 'with' in the sentence. The noun after the particle *waaw* is **attached together with** the doer/object which was mentioned before the it. Example: The word الْكِتَاب in the sentence جَاءَنِيْ يُوْسُفُ وَالْكِتَاب (Yusuf came to me **with** the book) is a مفعول معه – as it comes after a *waaw* in the meaning of 'with'; thereby attaching the book with Yusuf.
5	مَفْعُوْل فِيْهِ (time/place)	This indicates **when** or **where** the action took place. In other words, it tells you the **time** or the **place** where and action took place. Example: The word أَمَامَ in the sentence صَلَّيْتُ أَمَامَكَ (I prayed in front of you) is a مفعول فيه as it shows the place of the action.
6	حَال (state)	This is when the word is describing the **state** of the doer (فاعل) and/or the object (مفعول به). Example: The word مَاشِيًا in the sentence جَاءَنِيْ عَبْدُ الرَّحْمَنِ مَاشِيًا ('Abdurrahman came to me **walking**) is the حال (state) as it shows the **state** of the doer, 'Abdurrahman.

7	**تَمْيِيْز** (specification)	This is when the noun comes to **remove** some **ambiguity** that was created by the early part of the sentence. <u>Example</u>: The word كَوْكَبًا (stars) in the sentence رَأَيْتُ أَحَدَ عَشَرَ كَوْكَبًا (I saw eleven stars) is the تمييز (specification) as it **specifies** (and clarifies) the ambiguity created by 'eleven' since it raises the question, what was it? Eleven cars? Eleven books? This ambiguity was removed by the word 'stars'.
8	**مُسْتَثْنَى** (excluded)	This is the noun that is **excluded** from an earlier part of the sentence and it occurs after the 'particles of excluding'. The 'particles of excluding' will be discussed in a later lesson. <u>Example</u>: The word إِسْمَاعِيْل in the sentence جَاءَنِيْ الْقَوْمُ إِلَّا إِسْمَاعِيْل (The people came to me except Ismaeel.) is مستثنى as it is **excluding** إسماعيل from the 'people' that were mentioned earlier in the sentence.
9	**اِسْمُ "إِنَّ"** (Subject of إِنَّ)	This is when the particle **إِنَّ** (and the other sister particles) enter upon a 'subject' and 'news' sentence – these particles will give the **'subject'** a *nasab* state. <u>Example</u>: The word مُحَمَّدًا in the sentence إِنَّ مُحَمَّدًا مُجْتَهِدٌ (Verily, Muhammad is hardworking.) is in the *nasab* state as it is the 'subject' of إِنَّ.
10	**اِسْمُ "لَا" لِنَفْيِ الْجِنْس** (Subject of لَا which comes to negate the full genus)	This is when the particle **لَا** which comes to **negate the full genus** enters upon a 'subject' and 'news' sentence – this particle will give the **'subject'** a *nasab* state. <u>Example</u>: The word رَجُلَ (man) in the sentence لَا رَجُلَ قَائِمٌ (there is not a single man standing) is in the *nasab* state as it is the 'subject' of such a لَا which is negating the full genus.
11	**خَبَرُ "كَانَ"** (news/information of كَانَ)	This is when the particle **كَانَ** (or its other sister verbs) enters upon a 'subject' and 'news' sentence – these verbs will give the **'news'** a *nasab* state. <u>Example</u>: The word مُجْتَهِدًا in the sentence كَانَ مُحَمَّدٌ مُجْتَهِدًا (Muhammad was hardworking.) is in the *nasab* state as it is the 'news' of كَانَ.
12	**خَبَرُ "مَا" و"لَا" الْمُشَبَّهَتَانِ بِ(لَيْسَ)** (news/information of "ما" and "لا" similar to "لَيْسَ")	This is when the particle **مَا (in the meaning of 'no') or the particle لَا (in the meaning of 'no')** enter upon a 'subject' and 'news' sentence – these particles will give the **'news'** a *nasab* state. <u>Example</u>: The word قَائِمًا in the sentence مَا يُوْسُفُ قَائِمًا (Yusuf is not standing.) is in the *nasab* state as it is the 'news' of مَا .

Above, the **twelve** مَنْصُوْبَات are mentioned with a brief explanation and an example. An activity will follow to consolidate the basic ideas and then in the following chapters, each type of the **twelve** مَنْصُوْبَات will be explained in some more detail.

ACTIVITY: 39

Place a ***harakah*** **on the last letter** of the underlined words, then write the state of the word with reason in Arabic.

Sentence	Grammatical state	Reason
فَتَحَ مُحَمَّدٌ الْبَابَ إِكْرَاما لِيُوْسُفَ Muhammad opened the door, out of honour for Yusuf.		
قَرَأَ مُحَمّدٌ الْكِتَاب Muhammad read the book.		
كَانَ الْكِتَابُ كَبِيْرا The book was big.		
إِنَّ السَّاعَة رَخِيْصَةٌ Verily, the watch is cheap.		
لَا دُكَّانَ مَفْتُوْحٌ No shop is open.	حالة النصب/منصوبات	اسم "لا" لنفي الجنس
سَجَدَ الْمَلَائِكَةُ إِلَّا إِبْلِيْس The angels prostrated except Iblees.		
جَلَسَ يُوْسفُ خَلْفكَ Yusuf sat behind you.		
لا رَجُلٌ جَالِسا A man is not sitting.		
عِنْدِيْ ثَلَاثَةَ عَشَرَ دِرْهَما I have thirteen dirhams.		
سَكَنْتُ مَكَّةَ شَهْرا I lived in Makkah for a month.		
كَفَاكَ وَإِبْرَاهِيْم دِرْهَمٌ One dirham is enough for you along with Ibrahim (collectively).		
لَا طَالِب غَائِبٌ No student is absent.		
مَا يُوْسُفٌ جَالِسا Yusuf is not sitting.		
قَرَأَ مُحَمّدٌ الْكِتَابَ قِرَاءَة Muhammad definitely read the book.		

LESSON 26: THE FIVE MAFA'EEL

From amongst the **twelve** مَنْصُوْبَات , there were **five مَفْعُوْل** – in plural form, they are referred to as **مَفَاعِيْل .**

The **five مَفَاعِيْل** are:

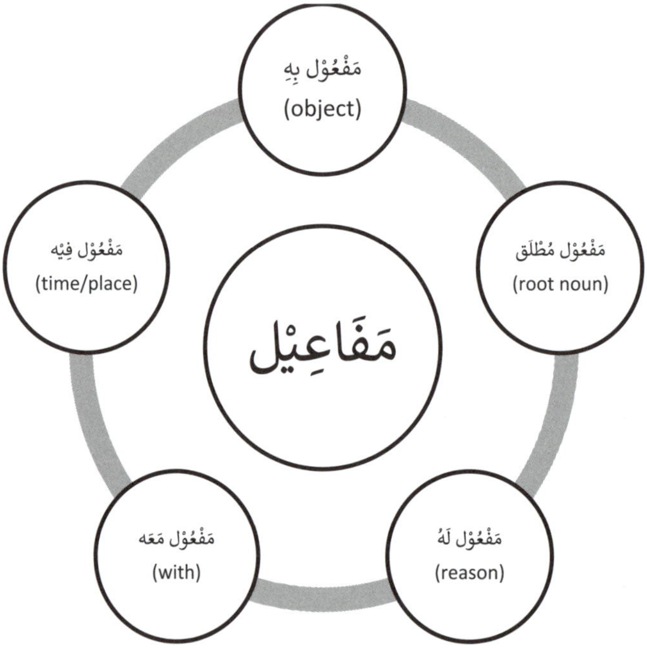

These **five مَفَاعِيْل** are briefly defined below with an example for each.

	Type	Meaning
1	**مَفْعُوْل بِهِ** (object)	This is **who/what** the action was done upon.
		Example: The word مُحَمَّدًا in the sentence نَصَرَ يُوْسُفُ مُحَمَّدًا (Yusuf helped Muhammad) is the مفعول به – as the action of helping was done to/upon him.
2	**مَفْعُوْل مُطْلَق** (Root noun)	This is when the **root noun** *(masdar)* of a previous verb in the sentence is mentioned. The purpose for bringing this root noun could differ, further detail will be mentioned in the following chapters.

		Example: The word نَصْرًا in the sentence نَصَرَ يُوْسُفُ مُحَمَّدًا نَصْرًا (Yusuf definitely helped Muhammad.) is the مفعول مطلق – as it is a root noun which has come after the same meaning verb.
3	مَفْعُوْل لَه (reason)	This is **why** the action took place. So, it gives the **reason** for why a certain action took place.
		Example: The word إِكْرَامًا in the sentence قُمْتُ لِأُمِّيْ إِكْرَامًا (I stood up for my mother, **out of respect** for her).
4	مَفْعُوْل مَعَهُ (with)	This is when a noun comes after the particle *waaw* in a sentence, such a *waaw* which is in the meaning of 'with'. The noun after the letter *waaw* is **attached together with** the doer/object which was mentioned before the particle *waaw*.
		Example: The word الْكِتَابَ in the sentence جَاءَنِيْ يُوْسُفُ وَالْكِتَابَ (Yusuf came to me **with** the book.) is a مفعول معه – as it comes after a *waaw* in the meaning of 'with'; attaching the book with Yusuf.
5	مَفْعُوْل فِيْهِ (time/place)	This tells you the **time** or the **place** where an action took place.
		Example: The word أَمَامَ in the sentence صَلَّيْتُ أَمَامَكَ (I prayed in front of you) is a مفعول فيه – as it shows the **place** of the action.

Some rules regarding the مَفْعُوْل بِهِ

1) Normally, when the word مَفْعُوْل is used, it is predominantly used in the meaning of مَفْعُوْل بِهِ. This is the **most common** type of مفعول.

2) The **normal sentence sequence** is to bring the verb (فعل) first, then the doer (فاعل) and then the object (مفعول به).

Example: نَصَرَ يُوْسُفُ مَحَمَّدًا (Yusuf helped Muhammad.)

مُحَمَّدًا	يُوْسُفُ	نَصَرَ
مفعول به	فاعل	فعل

However, it is also permissible to bring the مفعول به before the فاعل (doer) or even before the فعل (verb).

Example: نَصَرَ مُحَمَّدًا يُوْسُفُ (Yusuf definitely helped Muhammad.)

يُوْسُفُ	مُحَمَّدًا	نَصَرَ
فاعل	مفعول به	فعل

In this example, the مفعول به has occurred before the فاعل .

Example: مُحَمَّدًا نَصَرَ يُوْسُفُ (Yusuf definitely helped Muhammad.)

يُوْسُفُ	نَصَرَ	مُحَمَّدًا
فاعل	فعل	مفعول به

In this example, the مفعول به has occurred before the فعل as well.

As mentioned, the normal sequence is to bring the مفعول به after the فعل and the فاعل ; however, it is permissible to bring it before (as the examples above indicate). The purpose of bringing it earlier is to create extra emphasis in the sentence. Other reasons for bringing مفعول به earlier can be studied in the subject of rhetoric styles *(balagah)*.

3) Sometimes the verb (فعل) and the doer (فاعل) of the مفعول به is dropped in words; however, it can be assumed or worked out by the context.

Example: When someone comes as a guest, from amongst the greetings that Arabs give is the word أَهْلًا (family). This word is in the *nasab* state because the complete sentence is أَتَيْتَ أَهْلًا (You have come to your family (i.e. a warm welcome)). So, the sentence structure is as follows:

أَهْلًا	أَتَيْتَ
مفعول به	فعل + فاعل

In this example, the فاعل (doer) is the pronoun inside أَتَيْتَ .

Some rules regarding the مَفْعُوْل مُطْلَق

1) The مَفْعُوْل مُطْلَق is simply a **root noun** word which is in the **same meaning** as the verb prior to it.
Example: قَعَدْتُ جُلُوْسًا (A literal translation would be 'I sat, sitting.'.)
It is not necessary for the **root noun** to be the exact **same word** as the verb before it, rather simply being the same meaning (as in the example above) will suffice.

2) Grammarians have mentioned a few purposes of مَفْعُوْل مُطْلَق ; some of them include:

	Purpose	Meaning
1	تَأْكِيْد Emphasis	This is when the مفعول مطلق is used to **emphasise** the meaning of the verb. Example: The word نَصْرًا in the sentence نَصَرَ يُوْسُفُ مُحَمَّدًا نَصْرًا (Yusuf definitely helped Muhammad.) is the مفعول مطلق which is simply giving the meaning of emphasis (hence, translated as definitely).
2	عَدَد Number	This is when the مفعول مطلق is used to **show the number** of times the action (verb) occurred. Example: The word نَصْرَتَيْنِ in the sentence نَصَرَ يُوْسُفُ مُحَمَّدًا نَصْرَتَيْنِ (Yusuf helped Muhammad twice (helped two times).) is the مفعول مطلق which indicates how many times the action took place.
3	نَوْع State	This is when the مفعول مطلق is used to **show the state** of the action (verb). Example: The word جِلْسَةَ in the sentence جَلَسَ يُوسُفُ جِلْسَةَ الطَّالِبِ (Yusuf sat how a student sits (i.e. in the same manner).) is the مفعول مطلق which is indicating to the state of the action.

Some rules regarding the مَفْعُوْل فِيْه

1) The مَفْعُوْل فِيْه is when the noun indicates the **time** when or the **place** where the action took place.

2) Another name for مَفْعُوْل فِيْه is ظَرْف . This is divided into two types:

	Type	Meaning
1	ظَرْف زَمَان Time	This is when the noun is indicating the **time** of the occurrence of the action.
		Example: The word يَوْمَ الْجُمُعَة in the sentence صَلَّيْتُ يَوْمَ الْجُمُعَةِ (I prayed in front of you) is a ظرف زمان – as it shows the **place** of the action.
2	ظَرْف مَكَان Place	This is when the noun is indicating the **place** of the occurrence of the action.
		Example: The word أَمَامَ in the sentence صَلَّيْتُ أَمَامَكَ (I prayed in front of you) is a ظرف مكان – as it shows the **place** of the action.

Example which includes all the types of the مفاعيل :

The following is an example of all the five مفاعيل combined in one sentence:

حَمِدْتُ فَاطِمَةَ وَعَبْدَ الرَّحْمَنِ حَمْدًا رِعَايَةَ شُكْرِهَا الْيَوْمَ I praised Fatimah **with** 'Abdurrahman, praising a lot **because of** the gratitude she showed **today.**					
الْيَوْمَ	رِعَايَةَ شُكْرِهَا	حَمْدًا	وَعَبْدَ الرَّحْمَنِ	فَاطِمَةَ	حَمِدْتُ
مفعول فيه (زمان)	مفعول له	مفعول مطلق	مفعول معه	مفعول به	فعل + فاعل
جملة الفعليّة خبريّة					

Further examples of sentences with the different مفاعيل :

The following examples are further examples of sentences with the different types of مفاعيل . A grammatical sentence breakdown *(tarkeeb)* has been presented for each example.

Example one:

الْيَوْمَ	إِبْرَاهِيْمُ	ذَهَبَ
مفعول فيه (ظرف زمان)	فاعل	فعل
جملة فعليّة خبريّة		

Example two:

مَكَّةَ	يُوْسُفُ	دَخَلَ
مفعول فيه (ظرف مكان)	فاعل	فعل
جملة فعليّة خبريّة		

Example three:

وَالْكِتَابَ	يَحْيَى	جَاءَنِيْ
مفعول معه	فاعل	فعل + مفعول به
جملة فعليّة خبريّة		

Example four:

ذَهَابًا	عَبْدُ الرَّحْمَنِ	ذَهَبَ
مفعول مطلق	فاعل	فعل
جملة فعليّة خبريّة		

ACTIVITY: 40

Place a ***harakah* on the last letter** of the underlined words, then write the state of the word with reason. Write the state and reason in Arabic.

Sentence	Grammatical state	Reason
فَتَحَ مُحَمَّدٌ الْبَابَ إِكْرَاما لِيُوْسُفَ Muhammad opened the door out of honour for Yusuf.		
قَرَأَ مُحَمَّدٌ الْكِتَاب Muhammad read the book.		
جَلَسَ يُوْسفُ خَلْفك Yusuf sat behind you.		
سَكَنْتُ مَكَّة شَهْرًا I lived in Makkah for a month.		
كَفَاكَ وَإِبْرَاهِيْم دِرْهَمٌ One dirham is enough for you along with (i.e. and) Ibrahim.	حالة النصب (منصوبات)	مفعول معه
هَدَى اللهُ الطَّالِب Allah guided the student.		
قَعَدْتُ عَنِ الْحَرْبِ جُبْنا I stayed away from the war out of cowardice.		
جَاءَنِيْ عَبْدُ الرَّحْمَنِ وَأُخْته 'Abdurrahman came to me with his sister.		
لَقِيْتُ يُوْسُفَ يَوْم الْجُمُعَةِ I met Yusuf on the day of Jumu'ah.		
جَلَسْتُ مَعَ مُحَمَّدٍ جَلْسَتَيْن I sat with Muhammad twice.		
أَنَا أَكْسِرُ الْقَلَم I will break the pen.		
رَأَى إِبْرَاهِيْمُ الْقَمَر Ibrahim saw the moon.		
قَرَأَ مُحَمَّدٌ الْكِتَابَ قِرَاءَة Muhammad definitely read the book.		
قَامَ الْمُعَلِّمُ أَمَام الطُّلَّابِ The teacher stood in front of the students.		

ACTIVITY: 41

Complete the gaps in the following grammatical sentence breakdowns *(tarkeebs).*

Sentence one:

اللهَ	يُوْسُفُ	حَمِدَ

Sentence two:

ذِكْرًا	فَاطِمَةُ	ذَكَرَتْ

Sentence three:

شَهْرًا	يَحْيَى	صَامَ

Sentence four:

الرَّجُلَ	الْمَوْتُ	جَاءَ

Sentence five:

الْيَوْمَ	الْقُرْآنَ	سَمِعْتُ

LESSON 27: STATE, SPECIFICATION & EXCLUSION

From amongst the **twelve** مَنْصُوْبَات are the following **three:**

	Type	Meaning
6	حَال (state)	This is when the word is describing the **state** of the doer (فاعل) and/or the object (مفعول به). Example: The word مَاشِيًا in the sentence جَاءَنِيْ عَبْدُ الرَّحْمَنِ مَاشِيًا ('Abdurrahman came to me **walking**) is the حال (state) as it shows the **state** of the doer, 'Abdurrahman.
7	تَمْيِيْز (specification)	This is when the noun comes to **remove** some **ambiguity** that was created by the early part of the sentence. Example: The word كَوْكَبًا (stars) in the sentence رَأَيْتُ أَحَدَ عَشَرَ كَوْكَبًا (I saw eleven stars) is the تمييز (specification) as it **specifies** (and clarifies) the ambiguity created by 'eleven' since it raises the question, what was it? Eleven cars? Eleven books? This ambiguity was removed by the word 'stars'.
8	مُسْتَثْنَى (excluded)	This is the noun that is excluded from an earlier part of the sentence and it occurs after a 'particle of excluding'. Example: The word إِسْمَاعِيْل in the sentence جَاءَنِيْ الْقَوْمُ إِلَّا إِسْمَاعِيْلَ (the people came to me except Ismaeel.) is مستثنى as it is **excluding** إسماعيل from the 'people' that were mentioned earlier in the sentence.

Some rules regarding the حَال

1) The حَال gives information of the **state** of the doer (فاعل) or the object (مفعول به) or the state of **both**.

Examples:

State (حال) for?	Example
فَاعِل (doer)	Example: The word مَاشِيًا (walking) in the sentence جَاءَنِيْ مُحَمَّدٌ مَاشِيًا (Muhammad came to me in a state that he was walking) is the حال for the doer (فاعل).
مَفْعُوْل بِهِ (object)	Example: The word تَبَسُّمًا (smiling) in the sentence لَقِيْتُ يُوْسُفَ تَبَسُّمًا (I met Yusuf in a state that he was smiling.) is the حال for the object (مفعول به).
فَاعِل + مَفْعُوْل بِهِ (doer + object (i.e. both))	Example: The word مَاشِيَيْنِ (walking) in the sentence لَقِيْتُ الطَّالِبَ مَاشِيَيْنِ (I met the student whilst both of us were (in the state of) walking.) is the حال for the doer (فاعل) and the object (مفعول به).

2) The حال always indicates to the **state** of something – this person/thing whose state it is mentioning is called the ذُوْ الْحَالِ (literally translated as the person/thing of the 'state').

Example:

تَبَسُّمًا	يُوْسُفَ	لَقِيْتُ
حال	مفعول به (+ ذو الحال)	فعل + فاعل
جملة فعليّة خبريّة		

In this example, the 'state' of Yusuf is explained, hence, Yusuf is the ذو الحال . Yusuf is also the مفعول به in the sentence, as he was the object of the action (verb).

3) The حال is generally نَكِرَة (common) and the ذُوْ الْحَالِ is generally مَعْرِفَة (specific).

Example: In the above example, لَقِيْتُ يُوْسُفَ تَبَسُّمًا , the ذو الحال which was يُوْسُف was مَعْرِفَة (specific) and the حال which was تَبَسُّمًا was نَكِرَة (common).

4) If the ذُوْ الْحَالِ is نَكِرَة (common), then it **must** come **after** the حال in the sentence.

Example:

رَجُلًا	تَبَسُّمًا	لَقِيْتُ
مفعول به (+ ذو الحال)	حال	فعل + فاعل
جملة فعليّة خبريّة		

In this example, the person regarding whom the 'state' is mentioned (ذو الحال) is نكرة (common) – that is رَجُلًا (a man), therefore it **must** come after the 'state' (حال) – that is تَبَسُّمًا.

5) The حال is generally مُفْرَد (singular), however, it can also be a sentence, i.e. a nominal sentence (جملة اسميّة) or a verbal sentence (جملة فعليّة).

Examples:

Type	Example
مُفْرَد (singular)	Example: The word مَاشِيًا (walking) in the sentence جَاءَنِي مُحَمَّدٌ مَاشِيًا (Muhammad came to me in a state that he was walking.) is the حال. The حال is a singular word here.
جُمْلَة اِسْمِيَّة (nominal sentence)	Example: The phrase وَهُوَ جَالِسٌ (whilst he was sitting) in the sentence لَقِيْتُ يُوْسُفَ وَهُوَ جَالِسٌ (I met Yusuf in a state that he was sitting.) is the حال . The حال is a nominal sentence.
جُمْلَة فِعْلِيَّة (verbal sentence)	Example: The phrase يَسْعَى (in a state of running) in the sentence لَقِيْتُ يُوْسُفَ يَسْعَى (I met Yusuf in a state that he was running.) is the حال. The حال is a verbal sentence.

ACTIVITY: 42

Complete the gaps in the following grammatical sentence breakdowns *(tarkeebs)* regarding حال and also analyse the examples based on the rules mentioned above.

Sentence one:

مَاشِيًا	عَبْدُ الرَّحْمَنِ	جَاءَنِي

Analysis: ....

....

....

Sentence two:

مَفْتُوْحًا	الْمَسْجِدَ	رَأَيْتُ

Analysis: ....

....

....

Some rules regarding the تَمْيِيْز (specification)

1) The تَمْيِيْز removes ambiguity. The word (or phrase) that it removes the ambiguity from is called the مُمَيَّز (clarified).

<u>Examples</u>: رَأَيْتُ أَحَدَ عَشَرَ كَوْكَبًا (I saw eleven stars).

<table>
<tr><th>كَوْكَبًا</th><th>أَحَدَ عَشَرَ</th><th>رَأَيْتُ</th></tr>
<tr><td>تمييز</td><td>مميّز</td><td rowspan="2">فعل + فاعل</td></tr>
<tr><td colspan="2">مفعول به</td></tr>
<tr><td colspan="3">جملة فعليّة خبريّة</td></tr>
</table>

2) The تَمْيِيْز is always نَكِرَة (common). In the example above, the word كَوْكَبًا(stars) was نكرة .

3) The تَمْيِيْز commonly comes to remove the ambiguity for the following:

Type	Example
عَدَد (number)	<u>Example</u>: The word كَوْكَبًا(stars) in the sentence رَأَيْتُ أَحَدَ عَشَرَ كَوْكَبًا (I saw eleven stars.) has come to clarify the **number** أَحَدَ عَشَرَ – the question was 'eleven what?' The word كَوْكَبًا clarified this.
وَزْن (weight)	<u>Example</u>: The word تَمْرًا (dates) in the sentence اِشْتَرَيْتُ كِيْلُوْ تَمْرًا (I purchased a kilo of dates.) has come to clarify the **weight** كِيْلُوْ – the question was 'a kilo of what?' The word تَمْرًا clarified.
مَسَاحَة (distance/length)	<u>Example</u>: The word ثَوْبًا (cloth) in the sentence اِشْتَرَيْتُ مِتْرًا ثَوْبًا (I purchased a meter of cloth) has come to clarify the **length** مِتْر – the question was 'a meter of what?' The word ثَوْبًا clarified.

Some rules regarding the مُسْتَثْنَى (excluded):

1) The مُسْتَثْنَى comes to **exclude** someone/thing from an earlier group/items.

   Example: The word إِسْمَاعِيْل in the sentence جَاءَنِيْ الْقَوْمُ إِلَّا إِسْمَاعِيْلَ (The people came to me except Ismaeel.) is مستثنى as إسماعيل is **excluded** from the 'people' that were mentioned earlier in the sentence.

2) The sentence which includes a مُسْتَثْنَى would normally have **three** main components for the مُسْتَثْنَى related part. These are:

Part	Example Example: In the sentence جَاءَنِيْ الْقَوْمُ إِلَّا إِسْمَاعِيْلَ (the people came to me except Ismaeel) ...
مُسْتَثْنَى مِنْهُ (Excluded from)	The word الْقَوْمُ is the مُسْتَثْنَى مِنْه as that is what the مُسْتَثْنَى has been **excluded from.**
حَرْفُ الْإِسْتِثْنَاء (particle for excluding)	The particle إِلَّا is the حَرْفُ الْإِسْتِثْنَاء – it is the **particle** used to exclude.
مُسْتَثْنَى (excluded)	The word إِسْمَاعِيْل is the مُسْتَثْنَى as he is **excluded** from the overall group.

3) The grammatical sentence breakdown of the basic مُسْتَثْنَى examples would as follows:

إِسْمَاعِيْلَ	إِلَّا	الْقَوْمُ	جَاءَنِيْ
مستثنى	حرف الاستثناء	مستثنى منه	فعل + مفعول به
فاعل			
جملة فعليّة خبريّة			

4) The حُرُوْف الْإِسْتِثْنَاء (particles for excluding) are:

8	7	6	5	4	3	2	1
مَا عَدَا	مَا خَلَا	عَدَا	خَلَا	حَاشَا	سِوَى	غَيْرَ	إِلَّا
All of these words have the meaning of 'except' (when used in the context of 'exclusion')							

The first **three** of these particles are the most commonly used.

5) The مُسْتَثْنَى can be divided into **two types** based on its connection to the مُسْتَثْنَى مِنْهُ .

	Type	Meaning
1	**مُسْتَثْنَى مُتَّصِل** (exclusion from a category it was part of)	This is when the مُسْتَثْنَى was **originally part** of the مُسْتَثْنَى مِنْهُ – however, after the exclusion, it was separated.
		Example: The word إِسْمَاعِيْل in the sentence جَاءَنِيْ الْقَوْمُ إِلَّا إِسْمَاعِيْلَ (The people came to me except Ismaeel.) is مستثنى متّصل as إِسْمَاعِيْل was originally part of the مستثنى منه – it is only after the exclusion he was separated from them.
2	**مُسْتَثْنَى مُنْفَصِل/مُنْقَطِع** (exclusion from a category it was not part of)	This is when the مُسْتَثْنَى was **never** originally a part of the مُسْتَثْنَى مِنْهُ, rather only in the sentence it has been excluded .[19]
		Example: The word حِمَارًا in the sentence جَاءَنِيْ الْقَوْمُ إِلَّا حِمَارًا (The people came to me except the donkey.) is مستثنى منقطع as the donkey was **never** originally a part of the مستثنى منه i.e. the 'people'!

6) In most cases the مُسْتَثْنَى is in the *nasab* state (حالة النصب); however, this does change based on the حَرْف الإِسْتِثْنَاء used.

The particle used	Grammatical state of the مُسْتَثْنَى	Example
إِلَّا	Mostly[20] حَالَة النصب	جَاءَنِيْ الْقَوْمُ إِلَّا مُحَمَّدًا
خَلَا	Always حَالَة النصب	جَاءَنِيْ الْقَوْمُ خَلَا مُحَمَّدًا
عَدَا	Always حَالَة النصب	جَاءَنِيْ الْقَوْمُ عَدَا مُحَمَّدًا
مَا خَلَا	Always حَالَة النصب	جَاءَنِيْ الْقَوْمُ مَا خَلَا مُحَمَّدًا
مَا عَدَا	Always حَالَة النصب	جَاءَنِيْ الْقَوْمُ مَا عَدَا مُحَمَّدًا
غَيْرَ	Always حَالَة الْجَرّ	جَاءَنِيْ الْقَوْمُ غَيْرَ مُحَمَّدٍ
سِوَى	Always حَالَة الْجَرّ	جَاءَنِيْ الْقَوْمُ سِوَى مُحَمَّدٍ
حَاشَا	Always حَالَة الْجَرّ	جَاءَنِيْ الْقَوْمُ حَاشَا مُحَمَّدٍ

[19] This could be done for some rhetorical features studied in books of *balagah*.

[20] Detail of the different scenarios of إِلَّا are discussed in more advanced books.

ACTIVITY: 43

Complete the gaps in the following grammatical sentence breakdowns *(tarkeebs)* regarding مستثنى or تمييز .

Sentence one: أَخَذْتُ ثَلَاثَةَ عَشَرَ جُنَيْهًا (I took thirteen pounds.)

<table>
<tr><th>جُنَيْهًا</th><th>ثَلَاثَةَ عَشَرَ</th><th>اِشْتَرَيْتُ</th></tr>
<tr><td></td><td></td><td rowspan="2"></td></tr>
<tr><td colspan="2"></td></tr>
<tr><td colspan="3"></td></tr>
</table>

Sentence two: جَاءَنِيْ الطُّلَّابُ مَا خَلَا عَبْدَ الرَّحْمَنِ (The students came to me, except 'Abdurrahman.)

<table>
<tr><th>عَبْدَ الرَّحْمَنِ</th><th>مَا خَلَا</th><th>الطُّلَّابُ</th><th>جَاءَنِيْ</th></tr>
<tr><td></td><td></td><td></td><td rowspan="2"></td></tr>
<tr><td colspan="3"></td></tr>
<tr><td colspan="4"></td></tr>
</table>

Sentence three: سَجَدَ الْمَلَائِكَةُ إِلَّا إِبْلِيْسَ (The angels prostrated except *Iblees.)*

<table>
<tr><th>إِبْلِيْسَ</th><th>إِلَّا</th><th>الْمَلَائِكَةُ</th><th>سَجَدَ</th></tr>
<tr><td></td><td></td><td></td><td rowspan="2"></td></tr>
<tr><td colspan="3"></td></tr>
<tr><td colspan="4"></td></tr>
</table>

Sentence four: ذَهَبَ الْقَوْمُ عَدَا زَيْدًا (The people went except Zaid.)

<table>
<tr><th>زَيْدًا</th><th>عَدَا</th><th>الْقَوْمُ</th><th>ذَهَبَ</th></tr>
<tr><td></td><td></td><td></td><td rowspan="2"></td></tr>
<tr><td colspan="3"></td></tr>
<tr><td colspan="4"></td></tr>
</table>

LESSON 28: REMAINING MANSOOBAAT

So far, **eight of** the **twelve** مَنْصُوْبَات have been covered. The remaining **four** are ones that have been discussed in the مَرْفُوْعَات chapter. Overall, they are:

9	اِسْمُ "إِنَّ" (Subject of إِنَّ)	This is when the particle إِنَّ (and the other sister particles) enter upon a 'subject' and 'news' sentence – these particles will give the 'subject' a *nasab* state.
		Example: The word مُحَمَّدًا in the sentence إِنَّ مُحَمَّدًا مُجْتَهِدٌ (Verily, Muhammad is hardworking.) is in the *nasab* state as it is the 'subject' of إِنَّ .
10	اِسْمُ "لَا" لِنَفْيِ الْجِنْس (Subject of لَا which comes to negate the full genus)	This is when the particle لَا which comes to negate the **full genus** enters upon a 'subject' and 'news' sentence – this particle will give the 'subject' a *nasab* state.
		Example: The word رَجُلَ (man) in the sentence لَا رَجُلَ قَائِمٌ (There is not a single man standing.) is in the *nasab* state as it is the 'subject' of such a لَا which is negating the full genus.
11	خَبَرُ "كَانَ" (news/information of كَانَ)	This is when the particle كَانَ (or some other sister verbs) enter upon a 'subject' and 'news' sentence – these verbs will give the 'news' a *nasab* state.
		Example: The word مُجْتَهِدًا in the sentence كَانَ مُحَمَّدٌ مُجْتَهِدًا (Muhammad was hardworking.) is in the *nasab* state as it is the 'news' of كَانَ .
12	خَبَرُ "مَا" و"لَا" الْمُشَبَّهَتَانِ بِ(لَيْسَ) (news/information of "ما" and "لا" similar to "لَيْسَ")	This is when the particle مَا (in the meaning of 'no') or the particle لَا (in the meaning of 'no') enter upon a 'subject' and 'news' sentence – these particles will give the 'news' a *nasab* state.
		Example: The word قَائِمًا in the sentence مَا يُوْسُفُ قَائِمًا (Yusuf is not standing.) is in the *nasab* state as it is the 'news' of مَا .

These very same types were discussed in the مَرْفُوْعَات chapter with additional rules. The only difference is that, for example, in the مَرْفُوْعَات chapter, if it was discussing the "إِنَّ" خبر ; then in the منصوبات chapter, the discussion will be about the "إنّ" اسم.

Example:

طَوِيْلٌ	يُوْسُفَ	إِنَّ
خبر "إنّ"	اسم "إنّ"	الحرف المشبّه بالفعل
جملة اسميّة خبريّة		

Notice, the "إِنَّ" اسم is in the *nasab* state and the "إِنَّ" خبر is in the *rafa'* state.

ACTIVITY: 44

Mention all the types of مَنْصُوْبَات with examples (and explanation), also mention the English term for each type in the following table.

	Type	English Term	Example (with brief explanation)
1			
2			
3			
4			
5			
6			
7			
8			
9			
10			
11			
12			

ACTIVITY: 45

Place a *harakah* on the last letters of the underlined words. Also, mention which grammatical state these words are in and the reason for this state.

Sentence	Grammatical state	Reason
كَانَ الْذَّهَبُ رَخِيْصا The gold was cheap.		
مَا الْمَاءُ بَارِدا The water is not cold.		
أَعْطَى الرَّجُلُ الْقَلَمَ The man gave the pen.	حالة النصب/منصوبات	مفعول به
حَفِظَ يُوْسُفُ السُّوْرَة Yusuf memorised the surah.		
كَتَبَتْ الْمُدَرِّسَةُ الكِتَاب The teacher wrote the book.		
إِنَّ النَّافِذَة مَكْسُوْرَةٌ Verily, the window is broken.		
ذَهَبَ الطُّلَّابُ إِلَّا يُوْسُف The students went except Yusuf.		
صَارَتِ الْطَّالِبَةُ نَاجِحَة The female student became successful.		
كَسَرَ الرَّجُلُ الْمِلْعَقَة The man broke the spoon.		
لَيْسَ إِسْمَاعِيْلُ أُسْتَاذا Ismaeel is not a teacher.		
كَأَنَّ النُّجُوْم كَثِيْرَةٌ It is as though the stars are many.		
لَعَلَّ الِامْتِحَان قَرِيْبٌ Hopefully the examination is close.		
لَا طَالِبَة غَائِبَةٌ No female student is absent.		
مَا زَالَ الرَّجُلُ جَالِسا The man is continuously sitting.		
إِنَّ اللهِ غَفُوْرٌ Verily, Allah is all-forgiving.		

ACTIVITY: 46

Analyse the following text/sentences. The words underlined are in the *nasab* case - explain why. Then, give three more examples, with reason, of words in the *nasab* case from this text.

وكَانَ اسْمُ هَذَا الرَّجُلِ آزَرَ ، قَالَ إِبْرَاهِيْمُ: أَنَا أَكْسِرُ الْأَصْنَامَ إِذَا ذَهَبَ النَّاسُ ، حِيْنَئِذٍ غَضِبَ إِبْرَاهِيْمُ وَأَخَذَ الْفَأْسَ
وَكَانُوْا يَعْرِفُوْنَ أَنَّ الصَّنَمَ الْأَكْبَرَ أَيْضًا حَجَرٌ ، كَانَتِ النَّارُ بَرْدًا وَسَلَامًا عَلَى إِبْرَاهِيْمَ ، قَتَلْتُ رَجُلًا وَتَرَكْتُ رَجُلًا
وَكَانَ إِبْرَاهِيْمُ حَلِيْمًا فَقَالَ لِوَالِدِهِ ، وَيَدْعُوَ النَّاسَ إِلَى اللهِ ، وَتَرَكَ إِبْرَاهِيْمُ زَوْجَهُ هَاجَرَ وَوَلَدَهُ إِسْمَاعِيْلَ
وَأَرَادَتْ أُمُّهُ أَنْ تَسْقِيَهُ مَاءً ، وَنَصَرَ اللهُ هَاجَرَ وَنَصَرَ إِسْمَاعِيْلَ ، وَكَانَ إِبْرَاهِيْمُ نَبِيًّا صَادِقًا وَكَانَ مَنَامُهُ مَنَامًا صَادِقًا

	Word	Reason for nasab' case
1	آزر	
2	الأصنام	
3	الفأس	
4	الصنم	
5	بردا	
6	رجلا	
7	حليما	
8	الناس	
9	زوج	
10	ماء	
11		
12		
13		

LESSON 29: MAJROORAAT

One of the states of a noun is the *jarr* state – the noun in such state is referred to as from amongst the مَجْرُوْرَات .

There are **two** مَجْرُوْرَات, they are mentioned with a brief explanation and an example in the following table.

	Type	Meaning
1	مُضَافٌ إِلَيْهِ (possessor)	This is the **possessor** in a possessive structure. Example: The word مُحَمَّد in the phrase قَلَمُ مُحَمَّدٍ (Muhammad's pen) is the **possessor**, hence in the *jarr* state. The sentence is a possessive structure where it is showing an item (the pen) being the possession of a person (Muhammad).
2	مَجْرُوْرٌ بِحَرْفِ الْجَرِّ (after *harf jarr*)	This is a noun that comes **after** the particle of *jarr.*[21] Example: The word مُحَمَّد in the phrase بِمُحَمَّدٍ (with Muhammad) is occurring after a particle of *jarr* (which is the particle *baa* in this example), hence, the word مُحَمَّد is in the *jarr* state.

Detailed rules for the 'possessive structure':

1) The possessive structure is called إِضَافَة in the Arabic language. The إِضَافَة is made of two main parts:

1	مُضَاف	This is the **possession.**
2	مُضَافٌ إِلَيْهِ	This is the **possessor** of a thing/item.

2) The مُضَاف (possession) has the following rules:

- The مُضَاف will come **first** in the sentence structure,
- *Alif-laam* (ال) will **never** enter at the beginning of it. For example, it will not be الْقَلَمُ مُحَمَّدٍ .
- It will **never** have a *tanween.* Example, it will not be قَلَمٌ مُحَمَّدٍ, so the word قلم will not have a *tanween.*
- There is no fixed grammatical state for the مُضَاف, rather it is dependent on what is before it in the sentence which will impact its grammatical state.

[21] The particles of *jarr* will be mentioned soon.

3) The مُضَاف إِلَيْهِ (possessor) has the following rules:
- The مُضَاف إِلَيْه will come **second** in the sentence structure,
- The مُضَاف إِلَيْهِ (possessor) will **always** be fixed in the *jarr* state (حَالَة الْجَرّ).

4) The translation of a possessive structure is normally shown with 'of' or 's.

   Example: قَلَمُ مُحَمَّدٍ (Muhammad's pen). This has 's in the translation.

Example: كِتَابُ مُحَمَّدٍ (Muhammad's book)

مُحَمَّدٍ	كِتَابُ
مضاف إليه	مضاف

Notice the following in this example:
1) The English translation has an ('s) in it.
2) The مُضَاف does not have an (ال) before it.
3) The مُضَاف does not have a *tanween.*
4) The مُضَاف comes **first** in the sentence, the مُضَاف إِلَيْه comes **second**.
5) The مُضَاف إِلَيْه is in the *jarr* state.

Examples of the state of the مُضَاف:

As mentioned, the مُضَاف does not have a **fixed** state – rather its grammatical state is impacted by the words before it.

State	Example	Explanation
حالة الرفع	جَاءَنِي وَلَدُ مُحَمَّدٍ Muhammad's child came to me.	The مُضَاف , which is وَلَد , is in the *rafa'* state as it is the **doer (فاعل).**
حالة النصب	فَتَحْتُ بَابَ الْمَسْجِدِ I opened the door of the *masjid.*	The مُضَاف , which is بَاب ,is in the *nasab* state as it is the object **(مفعول به).**
حالة الجرّ	كَتَبْتُ عَلَى دَفْتَرِ مُحَمَّدٍ I wrote on Muhammad's notebook.	The مُضَاف ,which is دَفْتَر ,is in the *jarr* state, as it is occurring after a particle of *jarr.*

ACTIVITY: 47

Complete the gaps in the following grammatical sentence breakdowns *(tarkeebs)* regarding إضافة and its rules.

Sentence one: بَابُ الْمَسْجِدِ (The door of the *masjid).*

الْمَسْجِدِ	بَابُ

Analysis: ....

....

....

....

....

....

....

....

....

Sentence two: قَلَنْسُوَةُ مُحَمَّدٍ (Muhammad's hat)

مُحَمَّدٍ	قَلَنْسُوَةُ

Analysis: ....

....

....

....

....

....

....

....

....

Detailed rules for the 'nouns that come after the particles of *jarr*':

1) Only **nouns** can appear **after** the particles of *jarr.*

2) There are **seventeen** particles of *jarr.* They are:

9	8	7	6	5	4	3	2	1
حَتَّى	كَ	عَنْ	فِيْ	عَلَى	إِلَى	مِنْ	لِ	بِ
Until	Like	regarding	In	upon	To	From	For	With
	17	16	15	14	13	12	11	10
	مُذْ	مُنْذُ	عَدَا	خَلَا	حَاشَا	تَ	وَ	رُبَّ
	Since	Since	Except	Except	Except	By (oath)	By (oath)	Some

3) All the particles are listed below with examples for each.

	Particle	Example
1	بِ	كَتَبْتُ بِالْقَلَمِ (I wrote **with** the pen.)
2	لِ	كَتَبْتُ لِمُحَمَّدٍ (I wrote **for** Muhammad.)
3	مِنْ	سَافَرْتُ مِنْ مِكَّةَ إِلَى الْمَدِيْنَةِ (I travelled **from** Makkah to Madinah)
4	إِلَى	سَافَرْتُ مِنْ مِكَّةَ إِلَى الْمَدِيْنَةِ (I travelled from Makkah **to** Madinah.)
5	عَلَى	صَعَدْتُ عَلَى الْبَيْتِ (I climbed **upon** the house.)
6	فِيْ	دَخَلْتُ فِيْ الْمَسْجِدِ (I enter **in** the Masjid.)
7	عَنْ	سَأَلْتُ الْأُسْتَاذَ عَنِ الدَّرْسِ (I asked the teacher **regarding** the lesson.)
8	كَ	يُوْسُفُ كَالْأَسَدِ (Yusuf is **like** a lion.)
9	حَتَّى	سِرْتُ حَتَّى السُّوْقِ (I travelled **until** the market.)
10	رُبَّ	رُبَّ رَجُلٍ كَرِيْمٍ لَقِيْتُهُ (I have only met with **some** generous people.)
11	وَ	وَاللهِ إِنَّ يُوْسُفَ لَقَائِمٌ (**By** Allah, verily Yusuf is most certainly standing.)
12	تَ	تَاللهِ إِنَّ يُوْسُفَ لَقَائِمٌ (**By** Allah, verily Yusuf is most certainly standing.)
13	حَاشَا	جَاءَ الْقَوْمُ حَاشَا مُحَمَّدٍ (The people came **except** Muhammad.)
14	خَلَا	جَاءَ الْقَوْمُ خَلَا مُحَمَّدٍ (The people came **except** Muhammad.)
15	عَدَا	جَاءَ الْقَوْمُ عَدَا مُحَمَّدٍ (The people came **except** Muhammad.)
16	مُنْذُ	مَا رَأَيْتُهُ مُنْذُ يَوْمِ الْجُمُعَةِ (I have not seen him **since** Friday.)
17	مُذْ	مَا رَأَيْتُهُ مُذْ يَوْمِ الْجُمُعَةِ (I have not seen him **since** Friday.)

4) Some of the particles for *jarr* are also particles in other chapters – usually the context determines which type of particle it is.

Example: The particle *waaw* (و) is a particle of *jarr* (in the meaning of 'by' (as an oath)); however, it is also a particle of joining[22] (in the meaning of 'and).

1	وَاللهِ هَذَا يُوْسُفُ By Allah, this is Yusuf	In this example, the particle *waaw* is a particle of *jarr,* hence the following word is in *jarr* state.
2	قَامَ يُوْسُفُ وَمُحَمَّدٌ Yusuf and Muhammad stood up	In this example, the particle *waaw* is a particle of joining, hence the following word is just copying the grammatical state of the earlier word.[23]

5) In some cases, some particles of *jarr* may also be particles of other chapters and there is no reason to give preference to one meaning over the other; in those cases, either option is possible.

Example: The particle حَاشَا can be a particle of *jarr* or a particle of exclusion. It is up to the speaker/reader whichever particle they intend, the meaning of حَاشَا will be based on that.

If it is regarded as a particle of exclusion, then the following word will be in the *nasab* state.

If it is regarded as a particle of *jarr*, then the following word will be in the *jarr* state.

6) The particle of *jarr* **links** the word after it with the verb prior to it. Hence, the linked word with the particle of *jarr* is called مُتَعَلِّق (attached). See the following sentence breakdown.

الْقَلَمِ	بِ	كَتَبْتُ
مجرور بحرف الجرّ	حرف الجرّ	فعل + فاعل
متعلّق بـ(كَتَبْتُ)		
جملة فعليّة خبريّة		

Note: Sometimes, the verb it is attached to may be hidden.

[22] The particles of 'joining' will be studied later.

[23] The rulings of this will be studied in more detail later.

ACTIVITY: 48

Complete the gaps in the following grammatical sentence breakdowns *(tarkeebs)* regarding حرف الجرّ formations.

Sentence one: كَتَبْتُ لِمُحَمَّدٍ (I wrote **for** Muhammad.)

<table>
<tr><th>مُحَمَّدٍ</th><th>لِ</th><th>كَتَبْتُ</th></tr>
<tr><td></td><td></td><td rowspan="2"></td></tr>
<tr><td colspan="2"></td></tr>
<tr><td colspan="3"></td></tr>
</table>

Sentence two: دَخَلْتُ فِيْ الْمَسْجِدِ (I entered the Masjid.)

<table>
<tr><th>الْمَسْجِدِ</th><th>فِيْ</th><th>دَخَلْتُ</th></tr>
<tr><td></td><td></td><td rowspan="2"></td></tr>
<tr><td colspan="2"></td></tr>
<tr><td colspan="3"></td></tr>
</table>

Sentence three: سَأَلْتُ الْأُسْتَاذَ عَنِ الدَّرْسِ (I asked the teacher **regarding** the lesson.)

<table>
<tr><th>الدَّرْسِ</th><th>عَنِ</th><th>الْأُسْتَاذَ</th><th>سَأَلْتُ</th></tr>
<tr><td></td><td></td><td rowspan="2"></td><td rowspan="2"></td></tr>
<tr><td colspan="2"></td></tr>
<tr><td colspan="4"></td></tr>
</table>

Sentence four: يُوْسُفُ كَالْأَسَدِ (Yusuf is (established) **like** a lion.)

<table>
<tr><th>الْأَسَدِ</th><th>كَ</th><th>[ثَبَتَ]</th><th>يُوْسُفُ</th></tr>
<tr><td></td><td></td><td rowspan="2">فعل + فاعل</td><td rowspan="3"></td></tr>
<tr><td colspan="2"></td></tr>
<tr><td colspan="3"></td></tr>
<tr><td colspan="4"></td></tr>
</table>

LESSON 30: REVISION OF مرفوعات , منصوبات & مجرورات

This lesson is focused on revising the key concepts of the three very important chapters for **nouns** in the Arabic language; the مَرْفُوْعَات, مَنْصُوْبَات and مَجْرُوْرَات .

Please complete the following activities of this lesson – this will help consolidate the knowledge of these chapters.

ACTIVITY: 49

List all of the مَرْفُوْعَات , مَنْصُوْبَات and مَجْرُوْرَات .

	مرفوعات	منصوبات	مجرورات
1			
2			
3			
4			
5			
6			
7			
8			
9			
10			
11			
12			

ACTIVITY: 50

Place a *harakah* on the last letters of the underlined words. Also, mention which grammatical state these words are in and mention the type.

Sentence	Grammatical state	Reason
يَرْفَعُ إِبْرَاهِيمْ الْقَوَاعِدَ Ibrahim raised the walls (foundation).		
اِسْتَوْقَدَ نَارًا He ignited the fire.		
أَعْطَى الرَّجُلُ الْقَلَمَ The man gave the pen.	حالة النصب/منصوبات	مفعول به
حَفِظَ يُوْسُفُ السُّوْرَة Yusuf memorised the surah.		
فَسَجَدُوْا إِلَّا إِبْلِيْسَ Thus, they prostrated except *Iblees*.		
إِنَّ النَّافِذَة مَكْسُوْرَةٌ Verily, the window is broken.		
اِنْفَجَرَتْ مِنْهُ اثْنَتَا عَشْرَةَ عَيْنًا Twelve streams gushed from it.		
كَانَ عَدُوًّا لِلّٰهِ He was an enemy of Allah.		
أَعِذْنَا مِنْ عَذَابِ النَّارِ Protect us from the fire of hell (punishment).		
لَا تَلْبِسُوْا الْحَقَّ بِالْبَاطِلِ Don't confuse the truth with falsehood.		
لَا يُخَفَّفُ عَنْهُمُ الْعَذَابُ The punishment will not be lightened for them.		
أَنَّهُ الْحَقُّ مِنْ رَبِّهِمْ That it is the truth from their lord.		
يُؤْمِنُوْنَ بِالْغَيْبِ They bring faith in the unseen.		
اَنْتُمْ تَتْلُوْنَ الْكِتَابَ You read the book.		
يَرْفَعُ إِبْرَاهِيمْ الْقَوَاعِدَ Ibrahim raised the walls (foundation).		

ACTIVITY: 51

Analyse the following text/sentences. Write down the grammatical state of the underlined words with a reason. (The translation of the passage is given in the footnotes.[24])

سَكَنَ <u>إِبْرَاهِيْمُ</u> فِيْ <u>الشَّامِ</u> ، وَبَنَى إِسْحَاقُ <u>بَيْتًا</u> للهِ فِيْ الشَّامِ وَهُوَ الْمَسْجِدُ الْأَقْصَى الَّذِيْ بَارَكَ <u>اللهُ</u> <u>حَوْلَهُ</u>

وَبَارَكَ اللهُ فِيْ <u>أَوْلَادِ</u> إِسْحَاقَ ، <u>اسْمُهُ</u> يَعْقُوْبُ وَكَانَ <u>نَبِيًّا</u> ، كَانَ <u>يَعْقُوْبُ</u> لَهُ اثْنَا عَشَرَ <u>وَلَدًا</u>

نَحْنُ نَتَوَجَّهُ إِلَى الْكَعْبَةِ فِيْ كُلِّ <u>صَلَاةٍ</u> ، وَكَانَ <u>إِبْرَاهِيْمُ</u> يَذْكُرُ <u>اللهَ</u> وَيَدْعُوْ

	Word	Grammatical state	Reason for the grammatical state
1	إِبْرَاهِيْمُ		
2	الشَّامِ		
3	إِسْحَاقُ		
4	بَيْتًا		
5	اللهُ		
6	حَوْلَ		
7	أَوْلَادِ		
8	اِسْمُ		
9	نَبِيًّا		
10	يَعْقُوْبُ		
11	وَلَدًا		
12	صَلَاةٍ		
13	إِبْرَاهِيْمُ		
14	اللهَ		

[24] Ibrahim stayed in *Shaam.* And Ishaaq made a house for Allah in *Shaam,* which is al-Masjid al-Aqsa, that (masjid) Allah has blessed around it. And Allah blessed the children of Ishaaq. His name is Ya'qub and he was a prophet. For Ya'qub, there were twelve children. We face towards the *Ka'bah* in every *salaah.* And Ibrahim used to remember Allah and make dua.

ACTIVITY: 52

Fill in the gaps in the following grammatical breakdowns *(tarkeeb).*

نَاجِحٌ Successful	يُوْسُفَ Yusuf	إِنَّ Verily
	اسم "إنّ"	

الْبَيْتِ The house	فِيْ In	دَخَلْتُ I entered

إِبْلِيْسَ *Iblees*	إِلَّا Except	الْمَلَائِكَةُ The Angels	سَجَدَ Prostrated

جُنَيْهًا Pounds	خَمْسَةَ عَشَرَ Fifteen	إِشْتَرَيْتُ I purchased

مَفْتُوْحًا Open	الْمَسْجِدَ The Masjid	رَأَيْتُ I saw

LESSON 31: THE FOLLOWERS

After studying the three core grammatical concepts for nouns, that is the حالة الرفع , حالة النصب and the حالة الجرّ , A new concept will be studied – that is when a word is simply **following** the grammatical state of an earlier word.

There are two key terms to understand before moving on:

	Term	Meaning
1	تَابِع Follower	This is when a noun is **following** the grammatical state of an earlier noun. Example: The word نُوْحًا in the sentence نَصَرَ يُوْسُفُ مُحَمَّدًا ونُوْحًا (Yusuf helped Muhammad and Nuh) is **following** the grammatical state of the word مُحَمَّدًا – hence, both are in the *nasab* state. Therefore, the word نُوْحًا is the تَابِع.
2	مَتْبُوْع Followed	This is when the grammatical state of this noun is **followed** by a later appearing noun. Example: The word مُحَمَّدًا in the sentence نَصَرَ يُوْسُفُ مُحَمَّدًا ونُوْحًا (Yusuf helped Muhammad and Nuh) is **followed** in grammatical state by the word نُوْحًا – hence, both are in the *nasab* state. Therefore, the word مُحَمَّدًا is the مَتْبُوْع .

Overall rules:

1) The follower (تَابِع) and the followed (مَتْبُوْع) will have the **same** grammatical state.
2) The follower (تَابِع) and the followed (مَتْبُوْع) **together** form a grammatical phrase.

Grammatical analysis: جَاءَنِي رَجُلٌ طَوِيْلٌ (a tall man came to me).

طَوِيْلٌ	رَجُلٌ	جَاءَنِي
تابع	متبوع	فعل + مفعول به
فاعل		
جملة فعليّة خبريّة		

Note: Notice the متبوع and the تابع together formed the overall فاعل .

Types of 'followers' (تَوَابِع):

The plural for the word follower (تَابِع) is followers (تَوَابِع).

There are **five** تَوَابِع (followers) in total. They are:

	Type	Meaning
1	صِفَة (description/adjective)	This is the word/phrase which **describes** an earlier word. Example: The word طَوِيْل in the sentence جَاءَنِيْ رَجُلٌ طَوِيْلٌ (a tall man came to me) is describing the earlier word رَجُل – hence, the word طَوِيْل is a صفة (adjective).
2	تَأْكِيْد (emphasis)	This is the word which **emphasises** an earlier word/phrase. Example: The second word يُوْسُفُ in the sentence جَاءَنِيْ يُوْسُفُ يُوْسُفُ (Yusuf came to me, definitely Yusuf) creates the meaning of emphasis (indicating it was definitely Yusuf who came) – hence, the second يُوْسُف is a تَأْكِيْد (emphasis).
3	بَدَل (substitute)	This is the word/phrase which is a **substitution (replacement)** for an earlier word/phrase. Example: The word قَلَم in the sentence سُلِبَ مُحَمَّدٌ قَلَمُهُ (Muhammad, his pen, was robbed) is a بَدَل (substitute) as the original sentence was 'Muhammad was robbed', but then the addition of 'rather his pen' substituted the item robbed from 'Muhammad' to the 'pen'.
4	عَطْف بِالْحَرْفِ (Conjunction with a particle)	This is the word/phrase which is **connected** to an earlier word/phrase using a conjunction. Example: The word يُوْسُفُ in the sentence جَاءَنِيْ مُحَمَّدٌ وَيُوْسُفُ (Muhammad and Yusuf came to me) is **connected** to the word مُحَمَّد with the conjunction (و) – hence, the word يُوْسُف is regarded as عَطْف بِالْحَرْفِ .
5	عَطْفُ الْبَيَانِ (explanation)	This is when the word/phrase **explains/clarifies** an earlier word/phrase. Example: The word عُمَرُ in the sentence جَاءَنِيْ أَبُوْ حَفْصٍ عُمَرُ (Abu Hafs, Umar came to me.) is **clarifying** the word أَبُوْ حَفْص . When the speaker mentioned 'Abu Hafs came to me,' it was unclear. Who is 'Abu Hafs'? So, when the word, 'Umar' was added as **clarification,** it made it clear that the 'Abu Hafs (father of Hafsah)' referred to here is actually Umar – hence, the word عُمَر is regarded as عَطْف الْبَيَانِ .

The names of the corresponding مَتْبُوْع to each تَابِع are mentioned below with an example for each.

	تَابِع	مَتْبُوْع	Example
1	صِفَة طَوِيْل	مَوْصُوْف رَجُل	جَاءَنِيْ رَجُلٌ طَوِيْلٌ
2	تَأْكِيْد يُوْسُف	مُؤَكَّد يُوْسُف	جَاءَنِيْ يُوْسُفُ يُوْسُفُ
3	بَدَل قَلَم	مُبْدَل مِنْه مُحَمَّد	سُلِبَ مُحَمَّدٌ قَلَمُهُ
4	عَطْف بِالْحَرْفِ /مَعْطُوْف يُوْسُف	مَعْطُوْف عَلَيْه مُحَمَّد	جَاءَنِيْ مُحَمَّدٌ وَيُوْسُفُ
5	عَطْفُ الْبَيَانِ عُمَر	مَعْطُوْف عَلَيْه أَبُوْ حَفْص	جَاءَنِيْ أَبُوْ حَفْصٍ عُمَرُ

Before moving onto the detail of each of the five تَوَابِع in the following lessons, all the names of the different مَتْبُوْع and their تَابِعshould be learnt (with an example).

ACTIVITY: 53

Fill in the gaps in the following diagram with the **five** تَوَابِع (followers). Also, write the relevant مَتْبُوْع names.

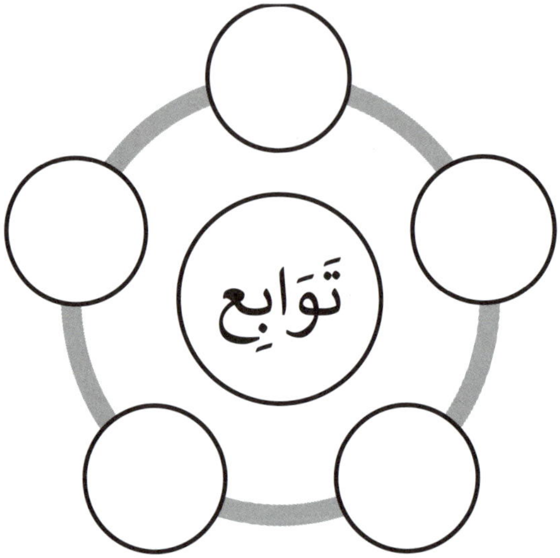

ACTIVITY: 54

Mention, with reason, which type of تَوَابِع the following are:

Sentence	Type	Reason
سَافَرَ يُوْسُفُ يُوْسُفُ Yusuf, definitely Yusuf, travelled.		
حَضَرَ عَبْدُ الرَّحْمَنِ وَيُوْسُفُ Abdurrahman and Yusuf were present.		
ذَهَبَ طَالِبٌ مُجْتَهِدٌ The hardworking student went	صفة	The word مُجْتَهِد is describing the word طَالِب
قَالَ أَبُوْ الْقَاسِمِ مُحَمَّدٌ Abul Qasim, Muhammad said ...		
جَاءَنِيْ مُحَمَّدٌ أَخُوْكَ Muhammad came to me, your brother.		
نَجَحَ رَجُلٌ عَالِمٌ A knowledgeable man was successful.		

LESSON 32: THE DESCRIPTION/ADJECTIVES

One of the types of تَوَابِع (followers) is the صِفَة (description/adjective).

There are two key terms to understand before moving on:

	Term	Meaning
1	صِفَة Description/adjective	This is the word/phrase which **describes** an earlier word.
2	مَوْصُوْف Described	This is the earlier word/phrase that is **described** by an adjective.
	Example: In the sentence جَاءَنِيْ رَجُلٌ طَوِيْلٌ (a tall man came to me): - the word رَجُل is the مَوْصُوْف as it is the **described** word, - the word طَوِيْل is the صِفَة as it is the **adjective/describing** word.	

Overall rules:

1) The adjective (صِفَة) is also called نَعْت in Arabic grammar.
2) The described word/phrase (مَوْصُوْف) is also called مَنْعُوْت in Arabic grammar.
3) The adjective (صِفَة) and the described (مَوْصُوْف) will correspond in the following **four** features:

	Feature	Meaning
1	إِعْرَاب Grammatical state	In terms of the **three** grammatical states for nouns; *rafa', nasab* and *jarr,* whichever state the مَوْصُوْف has, the صِفَة will follow the **same state**.
2	عَدَد Number	In terms of number (singular, dual or plural), the صِفَة will correspond to the مَوْصُوْف.
3	جِنْس Gender	In terms of gender (masculine & feminine), the صِفَة will correspond to the مَوْصُوْف.
4	تَخْصِيْص Definiteness	In terms of definiteness (specific or common), the صِفَة will correspond to the مَوْصُوْف.

Grammatical analysis: جَاءَنِيْ رَجُلٌ طَوِيْلٌ (a tall man came to me).

<table>
<tr><th>طَوِيْلٌ</th><th>رَجُلٌ</th><th>جَاءَنِيْ</th></tr>
<tr><td>صفة/نعت</td><td>موصوف/منعوت</td><td rowspan="2">فعل + مفعول به</td></tr>
<tr><td colspan="2">فاعل</td></tr>
<tr><td colspan="3">جملة فعليّة خبريّة</td></tr>
</table>

Further analysis: In the above example, the word طَوِيْل is the صِفَة (adjective). It corresponds to the word رَجُل which is the مَوْصُوْف in all **four** features. Both are:

- **in the *rafa'* case** – hence, correspond in إِعْرَاب (grammatical state),
- **singular (وَاحِد)** – hence, correspond in عَدَد (number),
- **masculine (مُذَكَّر)** – hence, correspond in جِنْس (gender),
- **common (نَكِرَة)** – hence, correspond in تَخْصِيْص (definiteness).

ACTIVITY: 55

Complete the grammatical analysis, with further analysis/explanation, for the following sentence.

<table>
<tr><th>الْمُجْتَهِدَةُ</th><th>فَاطِمَةُ</th><th>ذَهَبَتْ</th></tr>
<tr><td></td><td></td><td rowspan="2"></td></tr>
<tr><td colspan="2"></td></tr>
<tr><td colspan="3"></td></tr>
</table>

Further analysis: ....

....

....

....

....

....

LESSON 33: THE EMPHASIS

One of the types of the تَوَابِع (followers) is تَأْكِيْد (emphasis).

There are two key terms to understand before moving on:

	Term	Meaning
1	تَأْكِيْد Emphasis	This is a word which **emphasises** an earlier word/phrase.
2	مُؤَكَّد Emphasised	This is the earlier word which is **emphasised.**
	Example: In the sentence جَاءَنِيْ يُوْسُفُ يُوْسُفُ (Yusuf came to me, **definitely Yusuf.**): - the first word يُوْسُفُ is the مُؤَكَّد as it is the **emphasised** word, - the second word يُوْسُفُ is the تَأْكِيْد as it is **emphasising** the earlier word.	

Further rules:

There are **two** types of تَأْكِيْد (emphasis):

	Type	Meaning
1	تَأْكِيْد لَفْظِيّ (word-based emphasis)	This is when the word being emphasised is **repeated.** Example: The second word يُوْسُفُ in the sentence جَاءَنِيْ يُوْسُفُ يُوْسُفُ (Yusuf came to me, **definitely Yusuf.**) creates the meaning of emphasis by **repeating** the word 'Yusuf'. So, if there was any doubt whether it was 'Yusuf' or someone else that came, the repetition of the word removed any doubt.
2	تَأْكِيْد مَعْنَوِيّ (Meaning-based emphasis)	This is when the word being emphasised is emphasised by different word to create the meaning of **emphasis**. Example: The word كُلُّهُمْ in the sentence سَجَدَ الْمَلَائِكَةُ كُلُّهُمْ (The angels did *sajdah*, **all of** them.) creates the meaning of emphasis – although it is not a repeated word. There may have been doubt whether all of the angels did *sajdah* or only some, the word كُلُّهُمْ (all of them) removed any such doubt.

Further detail for تَأْكِيْد مَعْنَوِيّ (meaning-based emphasis):

The تَأْكِيْد مَعْنَوِيّ is commonly done using the following words:

	Word	Example with explanation
1	نَفْس Self	Example: جَاءَنِيْ يُوْسُفُ نَفْسُهُ (Yusuf came to me, **himself**). The word نَفْس (self) is emphasising that it was Yusuf **himself** that came – not some representative of his.
2	عَيْن Self	Example: جَاءَنِيْ يُوْسُفُ عَيْنُهُ (Yusuf came to me, **himself**). The word عَيْن (self) is emphasising that it was Yusuf **himself** that came – not some representative of his.
3	كِلَا Both (male)	Example: قَامَ الرَّجُلَانِ كِلَاهُمَا (The two men stood up, **both** of them). The word كِلَا (both) is creating the meaning of emphasis by emphasising that it was definitely **both** that stood up.
4	كِلْتَا Both (female)	Example: قَامَتِ الْمَرْأَتَانِ كِلْتَاهُمَا (The two women stood up, **both** of them). The word كِلْتَا (both) is creating the meaning of emphasis showing that it was definitely **both** that stood up.
5	كُلّ All	Example: سَجَدَ الْمَلَائِكَةُ كُلُّهُمْ (The angels did *sajdah,* **all** of them). The word كُلّ (all) is creating the meaning of emphasis by removing any doubt that only 'some' may have done *sajdah.*
6	أَجْمَعُ All/together	Example: جَاءَنِيْ الْقَوْمُ أَجْمَعُوْنَ (The people came to me, **all** of them). The word أَجْمَعُوْنَ (all) (plural for أَجْمَعُ) is creating the meaning of emphasis by removing any doubt that only 'some' came.

__Grammatical analysis__: جَاءَنِيْ يُوْسُفُ يُوْسُفُ (Yusuf came to me, **definitely Yusuf**).

<table>
<tr><th>يُوْسُفُ</th><th>يُوْسُفُ</th><th>جَاءَنِيْ</th></tr>
<tr><td>تأكيد</td><td>مؤكّد</td><td rowspan="2">فعل + مفعول به</td></tr>
<tr><td colspan="2">فاعل</td></tr>
<tr><td colspan="3">جملة فعليّة خبريّة</td></tr>
</table>

__Grammatical analysis__: سَجَدَ الْمَلَائِكَةُ كُلُّهُمْ (The angels did *sajdah,* **all of** them).

<table>
<tr><th>هُمْ</th><th>كُلُّ</th><th>الْمَلَائِكَةُ</th><th>سَجَدَ</th></tr>
<tr><td>مضاف إليه</td><td>مضاف</td><td rowspan="2">مؤكّد</td><td rowspan="3">فعل</td></tr>
<tr><td colspan="2">تأكيد</td></tr>
<tr><td colspan="3">فاعل</td></tr>
<tr><td colspan="4">جملة فعليّة خبريّة</td></tr>
</table>

ACTIVITY: 56

Identify the مُؤَكَّد and تَأْكِيْد in the following examples and mention the type of تَأْكِيْد .

Sentence	مُؤَكَّد	تَأْكِيْد	Type
نَصَرَ الْمُسْلِمُوْنَ كُلُّهُمْ النَّاسَ The Muslims, **all of them,** helped the people.			
حَضَرَ عَبْدُ الرَّحْمَنِ عَيْنُهُ Abdurrahman, **himself**, was present.			
اِشْتَرَيْتُ الْكِتَابَ الْكِتَابَ I purchased the book, **definitely the book.**	First الْكِتَابَ	Second الْكِتَابَ	تأكيد لفظي
أَكَلَ يُوْسُفُ نَفْسُهُ اللَّحْمَ Yusuf, **himself,** ate the meat.			
نَصَرَ يَحْيَى يَحْيَى عَبْدَ الرَّحْمَنِ Yahya, **definitely Yahya**, helped ‘Abdurrahman.			
نَجَحَتِ الطَّالِبَتَانِ كِلْتَاهُمَا The two female students, **both**, were successful.			

ACTIVITY: 57

Complete the grammatical analysis for the following sentences.

<table>
<tr><th>عَبْدَ الرَّحْمَنِ</th><th>يَحْيَى</th><th>يَحْيَى</th><th>نَصَرَ</th></tr>
<tr><td></td><td></td><td></td><td rowspan="2"></td></tr>
<tr><td></td><td colspan="2">فاعل</td></tr>
<tr><td colspan="4"></td></tr>
</table>

<table>
<tr><th>النَّاسَ</th><th>هُمْ</th><th>كُلُّ</th><th>الْمُسْلِمُوْنَ</th><th>نَصَرَ</th></tr>
<tr><td rowspan="3">مفعول به</td><td></td><td>مضاف</td><td rowspan="2"></td><td rowspan="3"></td></tr>
<tr><td colspan="2">تأكيد</td></tr>
<tr><td colspan="3"></td></tr>
<tr><td colspan="5"></td></tr>
</table>

LESSON 34: THE SUBSTITUTE

One of the types of تَوَابِع (followers) is بَدَل (substitute).

There are two key terms to understand before moving on:

	Term	Meaning
1	بَدَل Substitute	This is the word which **replaces/substitutes** an earlier word/phrase. It is this substitute that is really intended in the speech; not what it has replaced.
2	مُبْدَل مِنْه Substituted from (replaced)	This is the earlier word which is **replaced/substituted.**
	Example: In the sentence سُلِبَ مُحَمَّدٌ قَلَمُهُ (Muhammad, **his pen,** was robbed): - the word مُحَمَّد is the مُبْدَل مِنْه as it is **substituted/replaced** (originally, it seemed as though Muhammad was robbed!), - the second word قَلَم is the بَدَل as it is **replacing/substituting** the earlier word (now we know it was the pen that was robbed, and not Muhammad).	

Further rules:

There are **four** types of بَدَل (substitute):

	Type	Meaning
1	بَدْل الْكُلّ (Substitute of the **full**)	This is when the بَدَل (substitute) and the مُبْدَل مِنْه are referring to **exactly the same full/complete** concept.
		Example: The word أَخُوْكَ in the sentence جَاءَنِيْ يُوْسُفُ أَخُوْكَ (Yusuf, your brother, came to me) is **replacing/substituting** the word يُوْسُف. The word أَخُوْكَ is referring to exactly the **same person** i.e. يُوْسُف; it is بَدْلُ الْكلّ
2	بَدْل الْبَعْضِ (Substitute of the **part**)	This is when the بَدَل (substitute) is referring to the same **concept/genus** as that of the مُبْدَل مِنْه – but, to only **part** of the concept/genus.
		Example: The word رَأْسُهُ in the sentence ضُرِبَ زَيْدٌ رَأْسُهُ (Zaid, his head, was hit) is **replacing/substituting** the word زَيْد. The word رَأْسُهُ is talking about **part** of the **same person;** it is بَدْلُ الْبَعْض.
3	بَدْل الْإِشْتِمَال (Substitute of something **connected**)	This is when the بَدَل (substitute) is referring to something **connected** to the مُبْدَل مِنْه, not to the actual مُبْدَل مِنْه itself.
		Example: The word قَلَمُهُ in the sentence سُلِبَ مُحَمَّدٌ قَلَمُهُ (Muhammad, his pen, was robbed) is **replacing/substituting** the word مُحَمَّد. The word قَلَمُهُ is talking about something **connected** to the مُبْدَل مِنْه; it is بَدْلُ الْإِشْتِمَال.

<table>
<tr><td rowspan="2">4</td><td rowspan="2">بَدْل الْغَلَط
(Substitute due to a mistake)</td><td>This is when the بَدَل (substitute) comes to correct the مُبْدَل منه as the مُبْدَل مِنْه was a mistake.</td></tr>
<tr><td><u>Example</u>: The word حِمَارًا in the sentence رَأَيْتُ فَرَسًا حِمَارًا (I saw a horse, actually a donkey) is replacing/substituting the word فَرَسا . The مُبْدَل مِنْه which was فَرَسًا was actually said mistakenly, it was soon corrected using the بَدَل which was حِمَارًا .</td></tr>
</table>

<u>Grammatical analysis</u>: جَاءَنِيْ يُوْسُفُ أَخُوْكَ (Yusuf, your brother, came to me.)

<table>
<tr><th>كَ</th><th>أَخُوْ</th><th>يُوْسُفُ</th><th>جَاءَنِيْ</th></tr>
<tr><td>مضاف إليه</td><td>مضاف</td><td rowspan="2">مبدل منه</td><td rowspan="3">فعل + مفعول به</td></tr>
<tr><td colspan="2">بدل (بدل الكلّ)</td></tr>
<tr><td colspan="3">فاعل</td></tr>
<tr><td colspan="4">جملة فعليّة خبريّة</td></tr>
</table>

<u>Grammatical analysis</u>: ضُرِبَ زَيْدٌ رَأْسُهُ (Zaid, his head, was hit.)

<table>
<tr><th>هُ</th><th>رَأْس</th><th>زَيْدٌ</th><th>ضُرِبَ</th></tr>
<tr><td>مضاف إليه</td><td>مضاف</td><td rowspan="2">مبدل منه</td><td rowspan="3">فعل</td></tr>
<tr><td colspan="2">بدل (بدل البعض)</td></tr>
<tr><td colspan="3">مفعول ما لم يسمّ فاعله (نائب فاعل)</td></tr>
<tr><td colspan="4">جملة فعليّة خبريّة</td></tr>
</table>

<u>Grammatical analysis</u>: سُلِبَ مُحَمَّدٌ قَلَمُهُ (Muhammad, his pen, was robbed.)

<table>
<tr><th>هُ</th><th>قَلَمُ</th><th>مُحَمَّدٌ</th><th>سُلِبَ</th></tr>
<tr><td>مضاف إليه</td><td>مضاف</td><td rowspan="2">مبدل منه</td><td rowspan="3">فعل</td></tr>
<tr><td colspan="2">بدل (بدل الاشتمال)</td></tr>
<tr><td colspan="3">مفعول ما لم يسمّ فاعله (نائب فاعل)</td></tr>
<tr><td colspan="4">جملة فعليّة خبريّة</td></tr>
</table>

<u>Grammatical analysis</u>: رَأَيْتُ فَرَسًا حِمَارًا (I saw a horse, **actually a donkey**.)

<table>
<tr><th>حِمَارًا</th><th>فَرَسًا</th><th>رَأَيْتُ</th></tr>
<tr><td>بدل (بدل الغلط)</td><td>مبدل منه</td><td rowspan="2">فعل + فاعل</td></tr>
<tr><td colspan="2">مفعول به</td></tr>
<tr><td colspan="3">جملة فعليّة خبريّة</td></tr>
</table>

ACTIVITY: 58

Fill in the gaps in the following diagram with the **four** types of بَدَل (substitute). Also, write a brief description and example for each type around each circle.

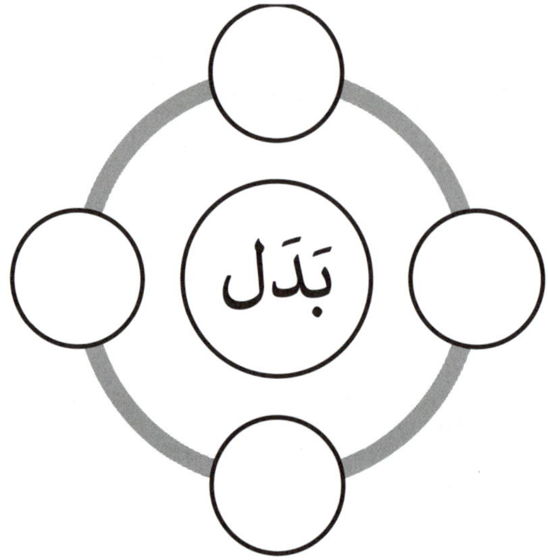

ACTIVITY: 59

Identify the مُبْدَل مِنْه and the بَدَل in the following examples along with the type of بَدَل .

Sentence	مُبْدَل مِنْه	بَدَل	Type
أَعْجَبَنِي يُوسُفُ أَخْلَاقُهُ I was pleased at Yusuf, **his manners.**			
حَفِظْتُ الْقُرْآنَ نِصْفَهُ I memorised the Qur'an, **half of it.**			
عَدَلَ الْخَلِيْفَةُ عُمَرُ The Calip, **Umar,** was just.	الْخَلِيْفَةُ	عُمَرُ	بدل الكلّ
قَبَّلْتُ الْوَالِدَ يَدَهُ I kissed the father, **his hand.**			
نَظَرْتُ إِلَى سَيَّارَةٍ ، طَائِرَةٍ I saw a car, **actually a plane.**			
قَرَأْتُ الْكِتَابَ الْقُرْآنَ I read the book, **the Qur'an.**			

ACTIVITY: 60

Complete the grammatical analysis for the following sentences.

<table dir="rtl">
<tr><th>حَفِظْتُ</th><th>الْقُرْآنَ</th><th>نِصْفَ</th><th>هُ</th></tr>
<tr><td rowspan="3"></td><td rowspan="2"></td><td></td><td></td></tr>
<tr><td colspan="2"></td></tr>
<tr><td colspan="3">مفعول به</td></tr>
<tr><td colspan="4"></td></tr>
</table>

<table dir="rtl">
<tr><th>عَدَلَ</th><th>الْخَلِيْفَةُ</th><th>عُمَرُ</th></tr>
<tr><td rowspan="2">فعل</td><td></td><td></td></tr>
<tr><td colspan="2"></td></tr>
<tr><td colspan="3"></td></tr>
</table>

<table dir="rtl">
<tr><th>نَظَرْتُ</th><th>إِلَى</th><th>سَيَّارَةٍ</th><th>طَائِرَةٍ</th></tr>
<tr><td rowspan="3"></td><td rowspan="2"></td><td></td><td></td></tr>
<tr><td colspan="2">مجرور بحرف الجرّ</td></tr>
<tr><td colspan="3">متعلّق بـ(نَظَرْتُ)</td></tr>
<tr><td colspan="4"></td></tr>
</table>

<table dir="rtl">
<tr><th>قَبَّلْتُ</th><th>الْوَالِدَ</th><th>يَدَ</th><th>هُ</th></tr>
<tr><td rowspan="3"></td><td rowspan="2"></td><td></td><td>مضاف إليه</td></tr>
<tr><td colspan="2">بدل (بدل البعض)</td></tr>
<tr><td colspan="3"></td></tr>
<tr><td colspan="4"></td></tr>
</table>

LESSON 35: THE CONJUNCTION ('ATF)

One of the types of تَوَابِع (followers) is the عَطْف بِالْحَرْف (conjunction with a particle).

There are three key terms to understand before moving on:

	Term	Meaning
1	**عَطْف بِالْحَرْف / مَعْطُوْف** Conjunction with a particle	This is the word/phrase which is **connected** to an earlier word/phrase using a conjunction.
2	**مَعْطُوْف عَلَيْه** Conjoined	This is the earlier word/phrase **conjoined** by a later word/phrase.
3	**حَرْف الْعَطْف** Particle of conjunction	This is the **particle** that is used to **join** two words or phrases together.
	Example: In the sentence جَاءَنِي مُحَمَّدٌ وَيُوْسُفُ (Muhammad and Yusuf came to me.): - the word مُحَمَّد is the مَعْطُوْف عَلَيْه as it is **conjoined** by a later word, - the second word يُوْسُف is the مَعْطُوْف as it is **joining/connected** to the earlier word, - the particle وَ is the حَرْف الْعَطْف – as it is the particle used to **join** the two words.	

Further rules:

The particles of conjunction are **ten**, they are:

5	4	3	2	1
أَوْ	حَتَّى	ثُمَّ	فَ	وَ
Or	Then (slight delay)	Then (with delay)	Then (without delay)	And
10	**9**	**8**	**7**	**6**
لَكِنْ	بَلْ	لَا	أَمْ	إِمَّا
However	Instead	No	Or	Or

All the particles are listed below with examples for each.

	Particle	Example
1	**وَ**	جَاءَنِي يُوْسُفُ وَعَبْدُ الرَّحْمَنِ (Yusuf **and** 'Abdurrahman came to me.)
2	**فَ**	قَامَ يُوْسُفُ فَعَبْدُ الرَّحْمَنِ (Yusuf stood up, **then** (very soon after) 'Abdurrahman stood up.)

3	ثُمَّ	قَامَ يُوْسُفُ ثُمَّ عَبْدُ الرَّحْمَنِ (Yusuf stood up, **then** (after a while) 'Abdurrahman stood up.)
4	حَتَّى	قَامَ يُوْسُفُ حَتَّى عَبْدُ الرَّحْمَنِ (Yusuf stood up, **then** (after a short while) 'Abdurrahman stood up.)
5	أَوْ	جَاءَنِيْ يُوْسُفُ أَوْ عَبْدُ الرَّحْمَنِ (Yusuf **or** 'Abdurrahman came to me.)
6	إِمَّا	الْعَدَدُ إِمَّا زَوْجٌ وَإِمَّا فَرْدٌ (The number is either odd **or** even.)
7	أَمْ	أَيُوْسُفُ عِنْدَكَ أَمْ عَبْدُ الرَّحْمَنِ (Is Yusuf by you **or** 'Abdurrahman?)
8	لَا	جَاءَنِيْ يُوْسُفُ لَا عَبْدُ الرَّحْمَنِ (Yusuf came to me, **not** 'Abdurrahman.)
9	بَلْ	جَاءَنِيْ يُوْسُفُ بَلْ عَبْدُ الرَّحْمَنِ (Yusuf came to me, **rather** 'Abdurrahman.)
10	لَكِنْ	مَا جَاءَنِيْ يُوْسُفُ لَكِنْ عَبْدُ الرَّحْمَنِ جَاءَ (Yusuf never came to me, **however,** 'Abdurrahman came to me.)

Grammatical analysis: جَاءَنِيْ يُوْسُفُ لَا عَبْدُ الرَّحْمَنِ (Yusuf came to me, **not** 'Abdurrahman.)

عَبْدُ الرَّحْمَنِ	لَا	يُوْسُفُ	جَاءَنِيْ
معطوف	حرف العطف	معطوف عليه	فعل + مفعول به
فاعل			
جملة فعليّة خبريّة			

Grammatical analysis: قَامَ يُوْسُفُ فَعَبْدُ الرَّحْمَنِ (Yusuf stood up, **then** (very soon) 'Abdurrahman stood up.)

عَبْدُ الرَّحْمَنِ	فَ	يُوْسُفُ	قَامَ
معطوف	حرف العطف	معطوف عليه	فعل + مفعول به
فاعل			
جملة فعليّة خبريّة			

Grammatical analysis: رَأَيْتُ يُوْسُفَ وَعَبْدَ الرَّحْمَنِ (I saw Yusuf and 'Abdurrahman).

عَبْدَ الرَّحْمَنِ	وَ	يُوْسُفَ	رَأَيْتُ
معطوف	حرف العطف	معطوف عليه	فعل + فاعل
مفعول به			
جملة فعليّة خبريّة			

ACTIVITY: 61

Identify the مَعْطُوْف عَلَيْه , the حَرْف الْعَطْف and the مَعْطُوْف in the following examples.

Sentence	مَعْطُوْف عَلَيْه	حَرْف الْعَطْف	مَعْطُوْف
أَمُحَمَّدٌ مُسَافِرٌ أَمْ يَحْيَى Is Muhammad travelling **or** Yahya?			
ذَكَرَ اسْمَ رَبِّهِ فَصَلَّى He mentioned the name of his lord, **then** (very soon) prayed salaah.			
اِذْهَبْ إِلَى الْأُسْتَاذِ بَلْ الْمُدِيْرِ Go to the teacher, **rather** the principal.	الْأُسْتَاذ	بَلْ	الْمُدِيْر
زُرْتُ الْقَاهِرَةَ بَلْ الْإِسْكَنْدَرِيَّةَ I visited Cairo, **actually** Alexandria.			
اِشْتَرَيْتُ كِتَابًا ثُمَّ قَلَمًا I purchased a book, **then** (after a while) a pen.			
صَدَقَ اللهُ وَرَسُوْلُهُ Allah **and** his messenger have said the truth.			

ACTIVITY: 62

Complete the grammatical analysis for the following sentences.

<table>
<tr><th>قَلَمًا</th><th>ثُمَّ</th><th>كِتَابًا</th><th>اِشْتَرَيْتُ</th></tr>
<tr><td></td><td></td><td></td><td rowspan="2"></td></tr>
<tr><td colspan="3">مفعول به</td></tr>
<tr><td colspan="4"></td></tr>
</table>

<table>
<tr><th>هُ</th><th>رَسُوْلُ</th><th>وَ</th><th>اللهُ</th><th>صَدَقَ</th></tr>
<tr><td></td><td>مضاف</td><td rowspan="2"></td><td rowspan="2"></td><td rowspan="3"></td></tr>
<tr><td colspan="2"></td></tr>
<tr><td colspan="4">فاعل</td></tr>
<tr><td colspan="5"></td></tr>
</table>

LESSON 36: THE EXPLANATION ('ATF BAYAAN)

One of the types of تَوَابِع (followers) is عَطْف الْبَيَانِ (explanation).

There are **two** key terms to understand before moving on:

	Term	Meaning
1	عَطْف الْبَيَانِ Explanation	This is the word/phrase that **explains/clarifies** an **earlier** word/phrase.
2	مَعْطُوْف عَلَيْه Explained	This is the word/phrase that is **explained/clarified** by a **later** word/phrase.
	Example: In the sentence جَاءَنِيْ أَبُوْ حَفْصٍ عُمَرُ (Abu Hafs, 'Umar came to me.): - the word أَبُوْ حَفْصٍ is the مَعْطُوْف عَلَيْه as it is **explained** by a later word, - the word عُمَرُ is the عَطْف الْبَيَانِ as it is an **explanation** to the earlier word.	

Further rules:

1) The explanation (عَطْف الْبَيَان) and the explained (مَعْطُوْف عَلَيْه) will correspond in the following **four** features (same as the صِفَة and the مَوْصُوْف):

	Feature	Meaning
1	إِعْرَاب Grammatical state	In terms of the **three** grammatical states for nouns; *rafa'*, *nasab* and *jarr*, whichever state the مَعْطُوْف عَلَيْه has, the عَطْف الْبَيَان will follow the **same state**.
2	عَدَد Number	In terms of number (singular, dual or plural), the عَطْف الْبَيَان will correspond to the مَعْطُوْف عَلَيْه .
3	جِنْس Gender	In terms of gender (masculine & feminine), the عَطْف الْبَيَان will correspond to the مَعْطُوْف عَلَيْه .
4	تَخْصِيْص Definiteness	In terms of definiteness (specific or common), the عَطْف الْبَيَان will correspond to the مَعْطُوْف عَلَيْه .

2) عَطْف الْبَيَان and بَدَل can be very similar; hence, in a sentence, it can be assumed as either one of the two. Although in advanced books, there are methods mentioned to sometimes distinguish between the two.

Grammatical analysis: جَاءَنِيْ أَبُوْ حَفْصٍ عُمَرُ (Abu Hafs, 'Umar came to me):

<table>
<tr><th>عُمَرُ</th><th>حَفْصٍ</th><th>أَبُوْ</th><th>جَاءَنِيْ</th></tr>
<tr><td rowspan="2">عطف البيان</td><td>مضاف إليه</td><td>مضاف</td><td rowspan="3">فعل + مفعول به</td></tr>
<tr><td colspan="2">معطوف عليه</td></tr>
<tr><td colspan="3">فاعل</td></tr>
<tr><td colspan="4">جملة فعليّة خبريّة</td></tr>
</table>

Grammatical analysis: قَالَ أَبُوْ الْقَاسِمِ مُحَمَّدٌ (Abu al-Qasim, Muhammad said ...):

<table>
<tr><th>مُحَمَّدٌ</th><th>الْقَاسِمِ</th><th>أَبُوْ</th><th>قَالَ</th></tr>
<tr><td rowspan="2">عطف البيان</td><td>مضاف إليه</td><td>مضاف</td><td rowspan="3">فعل</td></tr>
<tr><td colspan="2">معطوف عليه</td></tr>
<tr><td colspan="3">فاعل</td></tr>
<tr><td colspan="4">جملة فعليّة خبريّة</td></tr>
</table>

ACTIVITY: 63

Mention the **five** types of تَوَابِع , give an example for each and explain the example.

	Type	Example	Explanation
1			
2			
3			
4			
5			

LESSON 37: MISCELLANEOUS NOUNS

The اسم (noun) has **three** grammatical states. The state of each noun will dictate its **end-case** depending on the **form** of the noun.

We have now studied enough Nahw where we have covered the majority of the different types of nouns that need to be discussed in the **three** grammatical states.

However, a few types of nouns have not been mentioned yet. So, for completion purposes, it would be good for students to familiarise themselves with these nouns as well.

The **three** main nouns that will be discussed briefly in this chapter are:

1) The 'six nouns' (الْأَسْمَاء السِّتَّة),
2) The *ism maqsoor* (الْإِسْم الْمَقْصُوْر),
3) The *ism manqoos* (الْإِسْم الْمَنْقُوْص).

The 'six nouns' (الْأَسْمَاء السِّتَّة):

There are **six unique nouns** in the Arabic language, that have their own unique method for the end-case depending on their grammatical state. These six nouns are:

6	5	4	3	2	1
ذُوْ	فُوْ	هَن	حَم	أَخ	أَب
Possessor	Mouth	Swear word (in Arabic)	Father-in-law	Brother	Father

Notes and rules:

1) The word هَن is no longer used in the Arabic language.
2) The word فُوْ is actually from the word فَمٌ, the letter *meem* has dropped off. Now in the *rafa'* case, it will become فُوْ, in the *nasab* case, it will become فَا and in the *jarr* case, it will become فِيْ .
3) These 'six nouns' will only follow the unique end-case (which will be mentioned in the 'magic chart' chapter) when it is singular and in a possessive (مضاف) structure.

The *ism maqsoor* (الْإِسْم الْمَقْصُوْر):

This is a noun which has an *alif* (sometimes written as a *yaa)* as the last letter, and the second-to-last letter has a *fathah* upon it.

Example one: The word مُوْسَى is an *ism maqsoor* as it has an *alif* (written as a *yaa)* as the last letter and it has a *fathah* on the second-to-last letter.

Example two: The word عَصَا (stick) is an *ism maqsoor* as it has an alif as the last letter and it has a *fathah* on the second-to-last letter.

The *ism manqoos* (الْإِسْم الْمَنْقُوْص):

This is a noun which has a *yaa* as the last letter, and the second-to-last letter has a *kasrah* upon it.

Example: The word قَاضِي is an *ism manqoos* as it has a *yaa* as the last letter and it has a *kasrah* on the second-to-last letter.

LESSON 38: THE 'MAGIC CHART' FOR NOUNS

The اسم (noun) has **three** grammatical states. The state of each noun will dictate the **end-case** of the noun depending on the **form** of the noun.

If a student of grammar can do the following (in order), then they will find adding diacritical marks to the endings of nouns simple, with the permission of Almighty Allah.

1) For each noun, identify which **grammatical state** (حَالَة) it is in,
2) Then, identify which **form** of noun it is.
3) Then, choose the end-case using the 'magic chart (for nouns)' below.

MAGIC CHART (FOR NOUNS)

	Forms	Examples	Grammatical states: حالة الرفع	حالة النصب	حالة الجرّ
1	الْإِسْمِ الْمُفْرَد Singular noun (also called 'basic noun')	الرَّجُل or رَجُل	ends with a ـٌ or ـُ	ends with a ـً or ـَ	ends with a ـٍ or ـِ
			الرَّجُلُ or رَجُلٌ	الرَّجُلَ or رَجُلًا	الرَّجُلِ or رَجُلٍ
2	الْجَمْع الْمُكَسَّر Broken plural	الرِّجَال or رِجَال	ends with a ـٌ or ـُ	ends with a ـً or ـَ	ends with a ـٍ or ـِ
			الرِّجَالُ or رِجَالٌ	الرِّجَالَ or رِجَالًا	الرِّجَالِ or رِجَالٍ
3	غَيْر الْمُنْصَرِف Diptote	عُمَرُ	ends with a ـُ	ends with a ـَ	
			عُمَرُ	عُمَرَ	عُمَرَ
4	جَمْع مُؤَنَّث سَالِم Sound feminine plural	مُسْلِمَات or الْمُسْلِمَات	ends with ـاتٌ or ـاتُ	ends with ـاتٍ or ـاتِ	
			مُسْلِمَاتٌ or الْمُسْلِمَاتُ	مُسْلِمَاتٍ or الْمُسْلِمَاتِ	مُسْلِمَاتٍ or الْمُسْلِمَاتِ
5	الْأَسْمَاء السِّتَّة The **six** nouns	أب ، أَخ ، حَم ، هَن ، فُو ، ذُوْ	ends with a ـُوْ	ends with a ـَا	ends with a ـِيْ
			أَبُوْ ، أَخُوْ ، حَمُوْ ، هَنُوْ ، فُو ، ذُوْ	أَبَا ، أَخَا ، حَمَا ، هَنَا ، فَا ، ذَا	أَبِيْ ، أَخِيْ ، حَمِيْ ، هَنِيْ ، فِيْ ، ذِيْ

6	**تَثْنِيَة** Dual	رَجُلَان/رَجُلَيْن	ends with ـَانِ	ends with ـَيْنِ	
			رَجُلَانِ	رَجُلَيْنِ	رَجُلَيْنِ
7	**اِثْنَانِ/اِثْنَتَانِ** These are two specific words which mean 'two'. These are singular words but have a dual meaning.	اِثْنَانِ/اِثْنَيْنِ	ends with ـَانِ	ends with ـَيْنِ	
			اِثْنَانِ	اِثْنَيْنِ	اِثْنَيْنِ
8	**كِلَا/كِلْتَا** These two specific words. They mean 'two'. They will only follow the end-case rule mentioned here if they are in a possessive (مضاف) structure – they are possessed by a **pronoun**.	كِلَا/كِلَيْ	ends with ـَانِ	ends with ـَيْنِ	
			كِلَاهُمَا	كِلَيْهِمَا	كِلَيْهِمَا
9	**جَمْع مُذَكَّر سَالِم** Sound masculine plural	مُسْلِمُوْنَ/مُسْلِمِيْنَ	ends with ـُوْنَ	ends with ـِيْنَ	
			مُسْلِمُوْنَ	مُسْلِمِيْنَ	مُسْلِمِيْنَ
10	**عِشْرُوْنَ ...** Twenty ... This rule includes all the tens from twenty to ninety	عِشْرُوْنَ/عِشْرِيْنَ	ends with ـُوْنَ	ends with ـِيْنَ	
			عِشْرُوْنَ	عِشْرِيْنَ	عِشْرِيْنَ
11	**أُوْلُوْ** Possessor They will only follow the end-case rule mentioned here if they are in a possessive (مضاف) structure – they are possessed.	أُوْلُوْ/أُوْلِيْ	ends with ـُوْ	ends with ـِيْ	
			أُوْلُوْ مَالٍ	أُوْلِيْ مَالٍ	أُوْلِيْ مَالٍ
12	**الْإِسْم الْمَقْصُوْر** *Ism maqsoor*	مُوْسَى	Hidden end case (on last letter)		
			مُوْسَى	مُوْسَى	مُوْسَى
13	**الْإِسْم الْمُضَاف إِلَى "يْ"** A noun that is in a possessive (مضاف) structure as a possession for the first person pronoun (يْ).	كِتَابِيْ	Hidden end case (on last letter)		
			كِتَابِيْ	كِتَابِيْ	كِتَابِيْ
14	**الْإِسْم الْمَنْقُوْص** *Ism manqoos*	الْقَاضِي	Hidden end case (on last letter)	ends with a ـَ	Hidden end case (on last letter)
			الْقَاضِيْ	الْقَاضِيَ	الْقَاضِيْ

In the above table:

1) The change in the end-case was based on the ***harakah*** in forms **one-four**. This is called الْإِعْرَاب بِالْحَرَكَات .
2) The change in the end-case was based on **letters** in forms **five-eleven**. This is called الْإِعْرَاب بِالْحُرُوْف .
3) The change in the end-case was based on **hidden** changes in forms **twelve-fourteen**. This is called الْإِعْرَاب التَّقْدِيْرِيّ .

ACTIVITY: 64

Write, with examples, the **forms** of nouns for each of the following categories.

	الْإِعْرَاب بِالْحَرَكَات	الْإِعْرَاب بِالْحُرُوْف	الْإِعْرَاب التَّقْدِيْرِيّ
1			
2	الجمع المكسّر (رِجَال)		الاسم المضاف إلى "ي" (قَلَمِيْ)
3			
4			
5		جمع مذكّر سالم (مُسْلِمُوْنَ)	
6			
7			

ACTIVITY: 65

Analyse the following sentences. Write the grammatical state, with reason, for each noun underlined; thereafter, write the form of the noun and then finally from the magic chart write the end-case for a noun in such a case.[25]

وَكَانَ اسْمُ هَذَا الرَّجُلِ آزَرَ ، أَنَا أَكْسِرُ الْأَصْنَامَ إِذَا ذَهَبَ النَّاسُ ، كَانَتِ النَّارُ بَرْدًا وَسَلَامًا عَلَى إِبْرَاهِيْمَ ، وَكَانَ إِبْرَاهِيْمُ نَبِيًّا صَادِقًا ، الْحَمْدُ لِلّٰهِ رَبِّ الْعَالَمِيْنَ ، لَا رَيْبَ فِيْهِ ، هُدًى لِلْمُتَّقِيْنَ ، خَتَمَ اللهُ عَلَى قُلُوْبِهِمْ ، تَرَكَهُمْ فِيْ ظُلُمَاتٍ ، قَالَ مُوْسَى لِقَوْمِهِ ، تَذْبَحُوْا بَقَرَةً ، أَصْحَاب الْجَنَّةِ ،

	Word	Grammatical state	Reason for grammatical state	Noun form	End-case
1	اسْمُ				
2	الْأَصْنَامَ				
3	النَّاسُ				
4	إِبْرَاهِيْمَ				
5	نَبِيًّا				
6	الْعَالَمِيْنَ				
7	رَيْبَ				
8	مُتَّقِيْنَ	حالة الجرّ	مجرور بحرف الجرّ	جمع مذكّر سالم	ـِيْنَ
9	قُلُوْب				
10	ظُلُمَاتٍ				
11	مُوْسَى				
12	بَقَرَةً				
13	الْجَنَّةِ				

[25] The translations for the Arabic sentences are: [1] And this man's name was Aazar, [2] I will break the idols when the people go, [3] The fire was cold and peaceful upon Ibrahim A.S., [4] And Ibrahim A.S. was a truthful prophet, [5] All (the) praise is for Allah, lord of the worlds, [6] There is no doubt in it (at all), [7] Guidance for the god-conscious people,[8] Allah has sealed (covered) their hearts. [9] He left them in abundant darkness, [10] Musa A.S. said to his people, [11] Sacrifice a cow, [12] People of Jannah.

LESSON 39: GOVERNING NOUNS

In the Arabic language, the grammatical state of a word is impacted by **governors**. These governors will 'act-upon' the following word(s).

There are **two** key terms to understand before moving on:

	Term	Meaning
1	عَامِل Governor	This is the word which is **governing** (impacting) its following words grammatically.
2	مَعْمُوْل Governed	This is the word(s) which are being **governed** (impacting) grammatically by an earlier governor.
	Example: In the sentence نَصَرَ يُوْسُفُ عَبْدَ الرَّحْمَنِ (Yusuf helped 'Abdurrahman.) - the verb نَصَرَ is the governor (عامل), - the words يُوْسُفُ and عَبْدَ الرَّحْمَنِ are being governed (معمول).	

<u>Grammatical analysis</u>: نَصَرَ يُوْسُفُ عَبْدَ الرَّحْمَنِ (Yusuf helped 'Abdurrahman).

عَبْدَ الرَّحْمَنَ	يُوْسُفُ	نَصَرَ
مفعول به (معمول)	فاعل (معمول)	فعل (عامل)
جملة فعليّة خبريّة		

<u>What are the governors (عَامِل) in the Arabic language</u>?

The following are the governors (عَامِل) in the Arabic language:

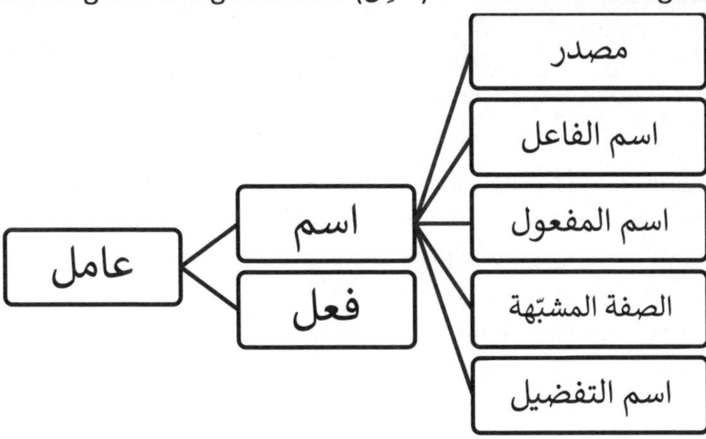

	Governors	Meaning
1	فِعْل (verb)	All **verbs** are governors. Further detail regarding verbs will come in the verb chapters. Example: The verb نَصَرَ in the sentence نَصَرَ يُوْسُفُ عَبْدَ الرَّحْمَنِ (Yusuf helped Abdurrahman.) is an عَامِل – it is governing the following words يُوْسُفُ and عَبْدَ الرَّحْمَن .
2	مَصْدَر (Root noun)	The **root** noun can be a governor (with some conditions). Example: The root noun نَصْر in the sentence أَعْجَبَنِيْ نَصْرُ مُحَمَّدٍ زَيْدًا (I was very pleased with Muhammad's help for Zayd.) is an عَامِل – it is governing its following words مُحَمَّدٍ and زَيْدًا .
3	اِسْمُ الْفَاعِل (Doer noun)	The **doer** noun can be a governor (with some conditions). Example: The doer noun نَاصِرٍ in the sentence مَرَرْتُ بِرَجُلٍ نَاصِرٍ مُحَمَّدًا (I passed by a person who was helping Muhammad.) is an عَامِل – it is governing the following word مُحَمَّدًا.
4	اِسْمُ الْمَفْعُوْل (Done-upon noun)	The **done-upon** noun can be a governor (with some conditions). Example: The done-upon noun مَنْصُوْر in the sentence مَرَرْتُ بِرَجُلٍ مَنْصُوْرٍ وَلَدُهُ (I passed by a person whose child was helped) is an عَامِل – it is governing the following word وَلَدُ .
5	الصِّفَةُ الْمُشَبَّهَة (Quality similar (to the doer) noun)	The special noun used to denote a **quality** (it gives a similar meaning to the doer noun) can be a governor (with some conditions). Example: The quality similar (to the doer) noun حَسَن in the sentence مَرَرْتُ بِرَجُلٍ حَسَنِ الْخُلُقِ (I passed by a person who had good manners). is an عَامِل – it is governing the following word الْخُلُق .
6	اِسْمُ التَّفْضِيْل (Comparative superlative noun)	The **comparative superlative** noun can be a governor (with some conditions). Example: The comparative superlative noun أَنْصَر in the sentence مَرَرْتُ بِرَجُلٍ هُوَ أَنْصَرُ النَّاسِ (I passed by a person who is the most helpful from the people.) is an عَامِل – it is governing the following word النَّاس .

<u>Note</u>:

1) In brief, **all verbs** will **govern**; however, only **selected** types of **nouns** will **govern**.
2) As for the governing **nouns**, many of them only act as grammatical governors with some conditions – these conditions are studied in more detail books of Arabic grammar (nahw).
3) Further detail regarding all the above nouns, their complete definitions and their scales are studied in more detail in the books of Arabic morphology (sarf).

Grammatical analysis: نَصَرَ يُوْسُفُ عَبْدَ الرَّحْمَنِ (Yusuf helped Abdurrahman.)

عَبْدَ الرَّحْمَنِ	يُوْسُفُ	نَصَرَ
مفعول به	فاعل	فعل
جملة فعليّة خبريّة		

Grammatical analysis: أَعْجَبَنِيْ نَصْرُ مُحَمَّدٍ زَيْدًا (I was very pleased with Muhammad's help for Zayd.)

<table>
<tr><th>زَيْدًا</th><th>مُحَمَّدٍ</th><th>نَصْرُ</th><th>أَعْجَبَنِيْ</th></tr>
<tr><td>مفعول به لـ(نصر)</td><td>مضاف إليه (لفظا)
فاعل لـ(نصر) (معنى)</td><td>مضاف
+ مصدر (عامل)</td><td rowspan="2">فعل + مفعول به</td></tr>
<tr><td colspan="3">فاعل لـ(أعجبني)</td></tr>
<tr><td colspan="4">جملة فعليّة خبريّة</td></tr>
</table>

<u>Note</u>: In this example, the word مُحَمَّد is in the *jarr* state (hence ends with a *kasrah)* as it is the مضاف إليه in terms of the word نَصْر . However, as the word نَصْر is a مصدر which is an عامل in this example, the word مُحَمَّدٍ will also be the فاعل of the (نصر) مصدر – although, the end-case of it being a فاعل does not show (as the state for the مضاف إليه will be given preference in wording). The word زَيْدًا is also governed by the (نصر) مصدر – it is the مفعول به ; hence, in the *nasab* state.

Grammatical analysis: مَرَرْتُ بِرَجُلٍ نَاصِرٍ مُحَمَّدًا (I passed by a person who was helping Muhammad.)

<table>
<tr><th>مُحَمَّدًا</th><th>نَاصِرٍ</th><th>رَجُلٍ</th><th>بِـ</th><th>مَرَرْتُ</th></tr>
<tr><td>مفعول به لـ(ناصر)</td><td>اسم الفاعل (عامل)
+ فاعل لـ(ناصر)</td><td rowspan="2">موصوف</td><td rowspan="3">حرف الجرّ</td><td rowspan="4">فعل + فاعل</td></tr>
<tr><td colspan="2">صفة</td></tr>
<tr><td colspan="3">مجرور بحرف الجرّ</td></tr>
<tr><td colspan="4">متعلّق بـ(مَرَرْتُ)</td></tr>
<tr><td colspan="5">جملة فعليّة خبريّة</td></tr>
</table>

<u>Note</u>: In this example, the word نَاصِر (helper) is an اسم الفاعل which is an عامل. It has a فاعل which is a pronoun within the اسم الفاعل in this example (which refers to the word رجل). It also has a مفعول به which is the word مُحَمَّدًا.

Grammatical analysis: مَرَرْتُ بِرَجُلٍ مَنْصُوْرٍ وَلَدُهُ (I passed by a person whose child was helped.)

<table>
<tr><th>ه</th><th>وَلَدُ</th><th>مَنْصُوْرٍ</th><th>رَجُلٍ</th><th>بِ</th><th>مَرَرْتُ</th></tr>
<tr><td>مضاف إليه</td><td>مضاف</td><td rowspan="2">اسم المفعول (عامل)</td><td rowspan="3">موصوف</td><td rowspan="4">حرف الجرّ</td><td rowspan="5">فعل + فاعل</td></tr>
<tr><td colspan="2">نائب الفاعل لـ(مَنْصُوْر)</td></tr>
<tr><td colspan="3">صفة</td></tr>
<tr><td colspan="4">مجرور بحرف الجرّ</td></tr>
<tr><td colspan="5">متلّق بـ(مَرَرْتُ)</td></tr>
<tr><td colspan="6">جملة فعليّة خبريّة</td></tr>
</table>

Grammatical analysis: مَرَرْتُ بِرَجُلٍ حَسَنِ الْخُلُقِ (I passed by a person who had good manners.)

<table>
<tr><th>الْخُلُقِ</th><th>حَسَنِ</th><th>رَجُلٍ</th><th>بِ</th><th>مَرَرْتُ</th></tr>
<tr><td>مضاف إليه (لفظا)
مفعول به لـ(حَسَن) (معنى)</td><td>المضاف +
الصفة المشبّهة (عامل)
+ فاعل لـ(حَسَن)</td><td rowspan="2">موصوف</td><td rowspan="3">حرف الجرّ</td><td rowspan="4">فعل + فاعل</td></tr>
<tr><td colspan="2">صفة</td></tr>
<tr><td colspan="3">مجرور بحرف الجرّ</td></tr>
<tr><td colspan="4">متعلّق بـ(مَرَرْتُ)</td></tr>
<tr><td colspan="5">جملة فعليّة خبريّة</td></tr>
</table>

Note: In this example, the word حَسَن (good) is an عامل . It has a فاعل which is a pronoun within the الصفة المشبّهة in this example (which refers to the word رجل). It also has a مفعول به (in meaning) which is the word الْخُلُقِ . However, in terms of wording the phrase حَسَن الْخُلُقِ will be considered as a possessive (so a مضاف + مضاف إليه) structure.

Grammatical analysis: مَرَرْتُ بِرَجُلٍ هُوَ أَنْصَرُ النَّاسِ (I passed by a person who is the most helpful from the people.)

<table>
<tr><th>النَّاسِ</th><th>أَنْصَرُ</th><th>هُوَ</th><th>رَجُلٍ</th><th>بِ</th><th>مَرَرْتُ</th></tr>
<tr><td>مضاف إليه (لفظا)
مفعول به لـ(أَنْصَر) (معنى)</td><td>مضاف + اسم
التفضيل (عامل) +
فاعل لـ(أَنْصَر)</td><td rowspan="2">مبتدأ</td><td rowspan="4">موصوف</td><td rowspan="5">حرف الجرّ</td><td rowspan="6">فعل + فاعل</td></tr>
<tr><td colspan="2">خبر</td></tr>
<tr><td colspan="3">جملة اسميّة خبريّة</td></tr>
<tr><td colspan="3">صفة</td></tr>
<tr><td colspan="4">مجرور بحرف الجرّ</td></tr>
<tr><td colspan="5">متعلّق بـ(مَرَرْتُ)</td></tr>
<tr><td colspan="6">جملة فعليّة خبريّة</td></tr>
</table>

Note: The word أَنْصَر (most helpful) is an عامل . It has a فاعل which is a pronoun within the اسم التفضيل in this example (which refers to the word رجل). It also has a مفعول به (in meaning) which is the word النَّاس . However, in terms of wording the phrase أَنْصَرُ النَّاسِ will be considered as a possessive structure (so a مضاف + مضاف إليه).

LESSON 40: VERBS

In the Arabic language, there are **three** types of words (as mentioned earlier).

	Term	Meaning
1	اِسْم	This is a **noun** – a name or an object, etc. Nouns are not limited to a time. Example: The word 'pen' (قَلَم), this is the name of an object, hence a **noun.**
2	فِعْل	This is a **verb** – an action. Verbs are limited to a time; either past, present or future tense. Example: The word 'he wrote' (كَتَبَ), this is an 'action' word, hence a **verb.** This is an example of a past tense verb.
3	حَرْف	This is a **particle** – usually a 1 or 2 lettered word used to 'join' between two nouns or a verb and a noun. Example: The word 'in' (فِيْ), this is a 2 lettered particle. The word فِيْ would be used in sentence like: دَخَلَ مُحَمَّدٌ فِيْ الْمَسْجِدِ (Muhammad entered **in** the Masjid).

In the books of Nahw, the majority discussion is regarding **nouns** (اِسْم). As for **verbs** (فِعْل), the detailed discussion regarding them is captured in the books of Sarf (Arabic morphology). However, the different types of verbs will be mentioned briefly in the table below.

The following are different types of verbs:

	Type	Meaning
1	فِعْل مَاضِيْ (Past tense verb)	This is a verb which usually indicates upon **past** tense. Example: The verb جَاءَ (came) in the sentence جَاءَنِيْ يُوْسُفُ (Yusuf came to me) gives a past tense meaning, hence it is a فِعْل ماضي .
2	فِعْل مُضَارِع (Present/future verb)	This is a verb which usually indicates upon the **present** or the **future** tense. Example: The verb يَنْصُرُ (is helping/will help) in the sentence يَنْصُرُ يُوْسُفُ يَحْيَى (Yusuf is helping/will help Yahya) is giving a present or future tense meaning, hence it is a فِعْل مُضَارِع .
3	فِعْل أَمْر (Imperative verb)	This is verb which indicates upon an **imperative** meaning. Example: The verb اُنْصُرْ (help) in the sentence اُنْصُرْ عَبْدَ الرَّحْمَنِ (Help Abdurrahman) is giving an imperative meaning (i.e. commanding the addressee), hence it is فِعْل أَمْر .

4	**فِعْل نَهْي** (Prohibition verb)	This is a verb which indicates upon a **prohibiting** meaning. Example: The verb لَا تَنْصُرْ (Don't help) in the sentence لَا تَنْصُرْ ظَالِمًا (Don't help the oppressor) is giving a prohibiting meaning – hence فِعْل نَهْي .
5	**فِعْل مَعْرُوْف** (Active verb)	This is a verb that is in the **active** form – **we know** who did the action. Example: The verb نَصَرَ (he helped) in the sentence نَصَرَ يُوْسُفُ يَحْيَى (Yusuf helped Yahya) is a فِعْل مَعْرُوْف (active) as we know who did the action – يُوْسُف .
6	**فِعْل مَجْهُوْل** (Passive verb)	This is a verb that is in the **passive** form – we **don't** know who did the action; rather, we only know who the action was **done** upon. Example: The verb نُصِرَ (he was helped) in نُصِرَ عَبْدُ الرَّحْمَنِ (Abdurrahman was helped) is a فِعْل مَجْهُوْل (passive) as we **don't** know who did the action, rather we only know who the action was done upon – عَبْدُ الرَّحْمَن .
7	**فِعْل لَازِم** (Intransitive verb)	This is such a verb that does **not** have a مَفْعُوْل بِهِ (object) – rather, it suffices with the فَاعِل (doer). Example: The verb كَرُمَ in the sentence كَرُمَ زَيْدٌ (Zaid was generous) does **not** have a مَفْعُوْل بِهِ – hence, it is a فِعْل لَازِم (intransitive verb).
8	**فِعْل مُتَعَدِّي** (Transitive verb)	This is such a verb that **does** have a مَفْعُوْل بِهِ (object) for the completion of the sentence. Example: The نَصَرَ in the sentence نَصَرَ يُوْسُفُ عَبْدَ الرَّحْمَنِ (Yusuf helped Abdurrahman) has a مَفْعُوْل بِهِ – without it, the sentence would remain incomplete. Hence, it is a فِعلْ مُتَعَدِّي (transitive verb).
9	**أَفْعَالُ الْقُلُوْبِ** (Verb of the heart)	These are **seven** special verbs whose meanings relate to the **'heart'**. Some further detail regarding أَفْعَال الْقُلُوْب is mentioned later. Example: The verb عَلِمَ (he knew) in the sentence عَلِمْتُ مُحَمَّدًا صَادِقًا (I knew Muhammad was truthful) is from amongst the أَفْعَال الْقُلُوْب – as **knowing** is something connected to the mind/heart.
10	**الْأَفْعَالُ النَّاقِصَةُ** (Incomplete verbs)	These are some special verbs which don't follow the normal rules of verbs – hence, regarded as **incomplete** verbs. In some grammar books, **thirteen** such verbs are mentioned. They were discussed earlier, with rules, in the chapter of *marfu'aat.* Example: The verb كَانَ (was) in the sentence كَانَ التِّلْمِيذُ مُجْتَهِدًا (The student was hardworking.) is an **incomplete** verb, it is not followed by a فَاعِل (doer) (as most verbs would); rather it has a مُبْتَدَأ (subject) and a خَبَر (news) after it. Refer to the *marfu'aat* chapter for further detail.

11	**أَفْعَالُ الْمُقَارَبَةِ** (Verb of closeness)	These are **seven** special verbs which have the meaning of **'closeness'**. Some further detail regarding أَفْعَال الْمُقَارَبَة is mentioned later. Example: The verb عَسَى (hope) in the sentence عَسَى يُوْسُفُ أَنْ يَقُوْمَ (There is **hope** Yusuf is **close** to standing.) is from amongst the أَفْعَال الْمُقَارَبَة – as it gives the meaning of hope and closeness of the doer completing an action.
12	**أَفْعَالُ التَّحْوِيْل** (Verb of change)	These are **seven** special verbs which have the meaning of **'changing'** something to another. Some further detail regarding أَفْعَال التَّحْوِيْل is mentioned later. Example: The verb جَعَلَ (made) in the sentence جَعَلَ اللهُ الْأَرْضَ فِرَاشًا (Allah **made** the land into a bedding/resting place.) is from amongst the أَفْعَال التَّحْوِيْل – as it gives the meaning of changing something (land) into another (resting place).
13	**فِعْل التَّعَجُّبِ** (Verb of amazement)	This is a verb on **two special scales** which gives the meaning of **'amazement'.** The **two** scales are: مَا أَفْعَلَهُ and أَفْعِلْ بِهِ . Example one: The verb مَا أَنْصَرَ in the sentence مَا أَنْصَرَ إِبْرَاهِيْمَ! (How helpful is Ibrahim!) is a فِعْل التَّعَجُّب as it is on the scale of مَا أَفْعَلَ – hence, creating the meaning of amazement. Example two: The verb أَنْصِرْ in the sentence أَنْصِرْ بِإِبْرَاهِيْمَ! (How helpful is Ibrahim!) is a فِعْل التَّعَجُّب as it is on the scale of أَفْعِلْ – hence, creating the meaning of amazement.
14	**فِعْل الْمَدْح** (Verb of praise)	These are **two** specific verbs that are used to **praise** the doer. The **two** scales are: نِعْمَ and حَبَّ . Some further detail regarding فِعْل الْمَدْح is mentioned later. Example one: The verb نِعْمَ in the sentence نِعْمَ الرَّجُلُ زَيْدٌ (Zaid is a very **good** person) is a فِعْل الْمَدْح – hence, creating the meaning of 'praise'. Example two: The verb حَبَّ in the sentence حَبَّذَا زَيْدٌ (Zaid is a very **good** person) is a فِعْل الْمَدْح – hence, creating the meaning of 'praise'.
15	**فِعْل الذَّمِّ** (Verb of disgrace)	These are **two** specific verbs that are used to **disgrace** the doer. The **two** scales are: بِئْسَ and سَاءَ . Some further detail regarding فِعْل الذَّمّ is mentioned later. Example one: The verb بِئْسَ in the sentence بِئْسَ الرَّجُلُ زَيْدٌ (Zaid is a very **bad** person) is a فِعْل الذَّمّ – hence, creating the meaning of 'disgrace'. Example two: The verb سَاءَ in the sentence سَاءَ الرَّجُلُ زَيْدٌ (Zaid is a very **bad** person) is a فِعْل الذَّمّ – hence, creating the meaning of 'disgrace'.

Further detail regarding أَفْعَال الْقُلُوْب :

1) There are **seven** أَفْعَال الْقُلُوْب (verbs of the heart). They are:

7	6	5	4	3	2	1
وَجَدَ	زَعَمَ	رَأَى	خَالَ	حَسِبَ	ظَنَّ	عَلِمَ
He thought	He thought	He thought	He thought	He thought	He thought	He knew

As can be seen, the meanings of all the words are connected to the mind/heart.

2) The أَفْعَال الْقُلُوْبِ **always** have **two** مَفْعُوْل بِهِ (objects); although, sometimes **both** maybe dropped from the text (if they are known by the context).
Example: عَلِمْتُ مُحَمَّدًا صَادِقًا (I knew Muhammad as truthful). In this example, the verb عَلِمَ is from amongst the أَفْعَال الْقُلُوْب – hence, it has **two** مَفْعُوْل بِهِ which are مُحَمَّد and صَادِق .

3) Some of the verbs mentioned in the أَفْعَال الْقُلُوْب list above can have different meanings which are not linked to the 'mind/heart'; in such a case, they will not be treated as from amongst the أَفْعَال الْقُلُوْبِ .
Example: The verb وَجَدَ can also mean 'he found (an item)'. When it has such a meaning, it will not be considered from the أَفْعَال الْقُلُوْبِ and hence will **not** follow the rules of أَفْعَال الْقُلُوْبِ .

Further detail regarding أَفْعَال الْمُقَارَبَة :

There are **seven** أَفْعَال الْمُقَارَبَة (verbs of closeness). They are:

7	6	5	4	3	2	1
أَوْشَكَ	أَخَذَ	كَرُبَ	جَعَلَ	طَفِقَ	كَادَ	عَسَى
Start	Start	Start	Start	Start	Close	Hope

These **seven verbs** with examples are:

	Type	Example
1	عَسَى Hope	Example: عَسَى إِبْرَاهِيْمُ أَنْ يَجْلِسَ (There is **hope** Ibrahim will sit.)
2	كَادَ Close	Example: كَادَ يُوْسُفُ يَرْجِعُ (It is **close** that Yusuf will return.)
3	طَفِقَ Start	Example: طَفِقَ عَبْدُ الرَّحْمَنِ يَكْتُبُ (Abdurrahman **started** to write.)
4	جَعَلَ Start	Example: جَعَلَ عَبْدُ الرَّحْمَنِ يَكْتُبُ (Abdurrahman **started** to write.)
5	كَرُبَ Start	Example: كَرُبَ عَبْدُ الرَّحْمَنِ يَكْتُبُ (Abdurrahman **started** to write.)
6	أَخَذَ Start	Example: أَخَذَ عَبْدُ الرَّحْمَنِ يَكْتُبُ (Abdurrahman **started** to write.)
7	أَوْشَكَ Start	Example: أَوْشَكَ عَبْدُ الرَّحْمَنِ أَنْ يَكْتُبُ (Abdurrahman **started** to write.)

Further detail regarding أَفْعَال التَّحْوِيْل :

There are **seven** أَفْعَال التَّحْوِيْل (verbs of change). They are:

7	6	5	4	3	2	1
خَلَقَ	رَدَّ	تَرَكَ	اِتَّخَذَ	وَهَبَ	جَعَلَ	صَيَّرَ
Created	Returned	Left	Made	Made	Made	Made

These **seven verbs** with examples are:

	Type	Example
1	صَيَّرَ Made	Example: صَيَّرَ يُوْسُفُ الْأَوْرَاقَ كِتَابًا (Yusuf **made** the pages into a book.)
2	جَعَلَ Made	Example: جَعَلَ اللهُ الْأَرْضَ فِرَاشًا (Allah **made** the land into a bedding.)
3	وَهَبَ Made	Example: وَهَبَ اللهُ الْأَرْضَ فِرَاشًا (Allah **made** the land into a bedding.)
4	اِتَّخَذَ Made	Example: اِتَّخَذَ اللهُ إِبْرَاهِيْمَ خَلِيْلًا (Allah **made** Ibrahim A.S. into a close companion.)
5	تَرَكَ Left	Example: تَرَكْتُ الرَّجُلَ حَيْرَانَ (I **left** the man perplexed.)
6	رَدَّ Returned	Example: رَدَّ اللهُ شُعُوْرَهُ الْبِيْضَ سُوْدًا (Allah **returned** his white hair into black.)
7	خَلَقَ Created	Example: خَلَقَ اللهُ الْإِنْسَانَ هَلُوْعًا (Allah created humans as impatient/anxious.)

Further detail regarding فِعْل الْمَدْح and فِعْل الذَّمّ :

1) The thing/person who is **praised** is called the مَخْصُوْص بِالْمَدْحِ .
   Example: نِعْمَ الرَّجُلُ زَيْدٌ (Zaid is a very **good** person), in this example the word زَيْد is the مَخْصُوْص بِالْمَدْحِ .

2) The thing/person who is **disgraced** is called the مَخْصُوْص بِالذَّمِّ .
   Example: بِئْسَ الرَّجُلُ زَيْدٌ (Zaid is a very **bad** person), in this example the word زَيْد is the مَخْصُوْص بِالذَّمِّ .

LESSON 41: PARTICLES

In the Arabic language, there are **three** types of words (as mentioned earlier).

In this lesson, the 'particles' (حُرُوْف) will be studied.

حَرْف	This is a **particle** – usually a 1 or 2-lettered word used to 'join' between two nouns or a verb and a noun.
	Example: The word 'in' (فِيْ), this is a 2 lettered particle. The word فِيْ would be used in sentence like: دَخَلَ مُحَمَّدٌ فِيْ الْمَسْجِدِ (Muhammad entered **in** the Masjid).

The particles (حُرُوْف) can be split into **two** main categories:

	Type	Meaning
1	حُرُوْف عَامِلَة (Governing particles)	These are particles that grammatically **govern** (impact) their following words.
		Example: The particle بِ (with) in the sentence كَتَبْتُ بِالْقَلَمِ (I wrote with the pen) is giving a *kasrah* to the following word – hence, it is a حُرُوْف عَامِلَة (governing particle).
2	حُرُوْف غَيْر عَامِلَة (non-governing particles)	These are particles that do **not** grammatically **govern** (impact) their following words.
		Example: The particle أَ (is) in the sentence أَيُوْسُفُ حَاضِرٌ (Is Yusuf present?) is not impacting the word following it grammatically – hence, it is a حُرُوْف غَيْر عَامِلَة (non-governing particle).

Each of the above **two** types has a list of particles that fall within that category. The following tables will list these particles.

The حُرُوْف عَامِلَة (governing particles) are:

	Type	Meaning
1	حُرُوْف الْجَرِّ (particles that give the *jarr* state)	These are **seventeen** particles that give the following noun a *jarr* state.
	Detail regarding this was discussed in the *majrooraat* chapter.	

2	الْحُرُوْفُ الْمُشَبَّهَةُ بِالْفِعْلِ (The particles that are similar to verbs)	These are **six** particles that enter upon a مُبْتَدَأ (subject) and a خَبَر (news) – they give the مُبْتَدَأ a *nasab* case and the خَبَر a *rafa'* case.
	Detail regarding this was discussed in the *marfu'aat* chapter.	

3	حُرُوْف النَّفْي (مَا ، لَا) (particles for negating – i.e. مَا and لَا)	These are **two** particles (مَا) and (لَا) which give a **negative** meaning. These particles enter upon a مُبْتَدَأ (subject) and a خَبَر (news) – they give the مُبْتَدَأ a *rafa'* case and the خَبَر a *nasab* case.
	Detail regarding this was discussed in the *marfu'aat* chapter.	

4	الْحُرُوْف النَّاصِبَة (Particles that give the *nasab* state)	These are **four** particles that enter upon a فِعْل مُضَارِع (present/future tense verb) and give the verb a *nasab* state.
	أَنْ	أُحِبُّ أَنْ تَتَعَلَّمَ (I love **that** you study.)
	لَنْ	لَنْ يَضْرِبَ يُوْسُفُ عَبْدَ الرَّحْمَنِ (Yusuf will **definitely not** hit 'Abdurrahman.)
	كَيْ	أَسْلَمْتُ كَيْ أَدْخُلَ الْجَنَّةَ (I accepted Islam **so that** I enter Jannah.)
	إِذَنْ	إِذَنْ تَدْخُلَ الْجَنَّةَ (**Then** you will enter Jannah.)

5	الْحُرُوْف الْجَازِمَة (particles that give the *jazm* state)	These are **five** particles that enter upon a فِعْل مُضَارِع (present/future tense verb) and give the verb a *jazm* state.
	إِنْ	إِنْ تَنْصُرْنِيْ أَنْصُرْكَ (**If** you help me, **then** I will help you.)
	لَمْ	لَمْ يَضْرِبْ يُوْسُفُ عَبْدَ الرَّحْمَنِ (Yusuf **never** hit 'Abdurrahman.)
	لَمَّا	لَمَّا يَضْرِبْ يُوْسُفُ عَبْدَ الرَّحْمَنِ (**Until now,** Yusuf has **not** hit 'Abdurrahman.)
	لِ (الأمر)	لِيَنْصُرْ يُوْسُفُ عَبْدَ الرَّحْمَنِ (Yusuf **should** help 'Abdurrahman.)
	لَا (النهي)	لَا تَضْرِبْ عَبْدَ الرَّحْمَنِ (**Don't** hit 'Abdurrahman.)

6	حُرُوْف النِّدَاء (Particles for calling)	These are **five** particles that give the meaning of 'calling' and they enter upon nouns and give them specific grammatical states.
	يَا	يَا مُحَمَّدُ (**Oh** Muhammad)!
	أَيَا	أَيَا مُحَمَّدُ (**Oh** Muhammad)!
	هَيَا	هَيَا مُحَمَّدُ (**Oh** Muhammad)!
	أَيْ	أَيْ مُحَمَّدُ (**Oh** Muhammad)!
	أَ	أَ مُحَمَّدُ (**Oh** Muhammad)!

Note: The *harakah* on the last letter of the word after the 'particle of calling' (the word مُحَمَّد in the above example), will change depending on the type of word. Further detail regarding this can be studied in more advanced books of grammar.

7	حُرُوْف الشَّرْطِ (Particles for conditions)	These are **twelve** particles that give the meaning of 'condition'. In many scenarios, when they enter upon a فِعْل مُضَارِع (present/future tense verb), they will give it a *jazm* state.
	إِنْ	إِنْ تَزُرْنِيْ أُكْرِمْكَ (**If** you visit me, **then** I will honour you.)
	لَوْ	لَوْ تَزُرْنِيْ أُكْرِمْكَ (**If** you visit me, **then** I will honour you.)
	مَنْ	مَنْ يَزُرْنِيْ أُكْرِمْهُ (**Whomsoever** visits me, **then** I will honour him.)
	مَا	مَا تَفْعَلْ أَفْعَلْ (**Whatever** you do, **then** I will (also) do.)
	أَيٌّ	أَيٌّ تَفْعَلْ أَفْعَلْ (**Whatever** you do, **then** I will (also) do.)
	مَتَى	مَتَى تَزُرْنِيْ أُكْرِمْكَ (**When** you visit me, **then** I will honour you.)
	أَنَّى	أَنَّى تَزُرْنِيْ أُكْرِمْكَ (**Wherever** you visit me, (then) I will honour you.)
	أَيْنَمَا	أَيْنَمَا تَزُرْنِيْ أُكْرِمْكَ (**Wherever** you visit me, (then) I will honour you.)
	مَهْمَا	مَهْمَا تَزُرْنِيْ أُكْرِمْكَ (**When** you visit me, **then** I will honour you.)
	إِذْمَا	إِذْمَا تَزُرْنِيْ أُكْرِمْكَ (**If** you visit me, **then** I will honour you.)
	حَيْثُمَا	حَيْثُمَا تَزُرْنِيْ أُكْرِمْكَ (**Wherever** you visit me, **then** I will honour you.)

The حُرُوْف غَيْر عَامِلَة (non-governing particles) are:

	Type	Meaning
1	حَرْف الْعَطْف Particle of conjunction	This is the particle that is used to **join** two words together. There are **ten** particles of conjunction.
	Detail regarding this was discussed in the *tawabi'* chapter.	
2	حَرْف الْإِيْجَاب (Particle of answering in the affirmative)	These are **six** particles used for answering a question.
	نَعَم	أَجَاءَكَ يُوْسُفُ؟ **نَعَمْ** (Has Yusuf come to you? **Yes**)
	بَلَى	أَلَسْتُ بِرَبِّكُمْ؟ **بَلَى** (Am I not your Lord? **Why not.**)
	إِيْ	أَحَقٌّ هُوَ؟ **إِيْ** وَرَبِّيْ (Is it the truth? **Yes**, I take an oath by my Lord.)
	أَجَلْ	أَجَاءَكَ عَبْدُ الرَّحْمَنِ؟ **أَجَلْ** (Has Abdurrahman come to you? **Yes**)
	جَيْرِ	أَجَاءَكَ يَحْيَى؟ **جَيْرِ** (Has Yahya come to you? **Yes**)
	إِنَّ	أَجَاءَكَ مُحَمَّدٌ؟ **إِنَّ** (Has Muhammed come to you? **Yes**)
3	حَرْف التَّفْسِيْر (Particle of explanation)	These are **two** particles used for explaining an ambiguous word/phrase.
	أَيْ	وَاسْئَلِ الْقَرْيَةَ **أَيْ** أَهْلَ الْقَرْيَةِ (Ask the village **i.e.** the people of the village.)
	أَنْ	وَنَادَيْنَاهُ **أَنْ** يَا إِبْرَاهِيْمُ (We called him **i.e.** O Ibrahim.)
4	حَرْف الزَّائِد (Particle which is extra)	These are **seven** particles used in sentences that don't actually have any meaning – rather they are brought as **extra** particles (for beautifying the sentence).
	إِنْ	مَا **إِنْ** يُوْسُفُ حَاضِرٌ (Yusuf is not present.)
	أَنْ	وَاللهِ **أَنْ** لَوْ قُمْتَ قُمْتُ (By Allah, if you stand, then I will stand.)
	مَا	فَبِمَا رَحْمَةٍ مِنَ اللهِ (Thus, with the mercy from Allah.)
	لَا	**لَا** أُقْسِمُ بِهَذَا الْبَلَدِ (I take an oath by the name of this city.)
	مِنْ	مَا جَاءَنِيْ **مِنْ** أَحَدٍ (Nobody came to me.)
	بِ	مَا زَيْدٌ بِقَائِمٍ (Zaid was not standing.)
	لِ or لَ	رَدِفَ لَكُمْ (He sat behind you.)
5	حَرْف الرَّدْع (Particle for rebuking)	There is **one** particle which is used to **rebuke**.
	كَلَّا	**كَلَّا!** سَوْفَ تَعْلَمُوْنَ (**Definitely not!** Soon you will know).

6	**حَرْف التَّوَقُّع** (Particle for hope)	There is **one** particle which is used to give **hope**.
	قَدْ	**قَدْ** يَقْدَمُ الْمُسَافِرُ الْيَوْمَ (There is **hope** the traveller will return today).

7	**حَرْف الْمَصْدَر** (Particle to give root-noun meaning)	These are **three** particles which give the following word or the following sentence a root-noun (single word) meaning; rather than a verb-meaning or a sentence-meaning.
	مَا	ضَاقَتْ عَلَيْهِمُ الْأَرْضُ بِمَا رَحُبَتْ (The earth was narrow for them despite **it being wide**). Note: the translation was not 'despite it **was** wide (in past tense)'.
	أَنْ	مَا كَانَ جَوَابَ قَوْمِهِ إِلَّا **أَنْ** قَالُوْا (The answer of the people was not except **their statement** ...). Note: the translation was not 'except **they said** (in past tense)'.
	أَنَّ	عَلِمْتُ أَنَّكَ حَاضِرٌ (I knew about your **presence**). Note: the translation was not 'about **you are present**' (a sentence meaning).

8	**حَرْف التَّأْكِيْد** (Particle for emphasising)	These are **three** particles which provide the meaning of **emphasis**.
	نَّ	اُنْصُرَنَّ يُوْسُفَ (**Definitely** help Yusuf.)
	نْ	اُنْصُرَنْ يُوْسُفَ (**Definitely** help Yusuf.)
	لَ	إِنَّ يَحْيَى لَحَاضِرٌ (Indeed, Yahya is **definitely** present.)

9	**حَرْف الِاسْتِفْهَام** (Particle for questioning)	These are **ten** particles which are used for **questioning**.
	أَ	أَيُوْسُفُ جَالِسٌ؟ (**Is** Yusuf sitting?)
	هَلْ	**هَلْ** يُوْسُفُ جَالِسٌ؟ (**Is** Yusuf sitting?)
	مَا	**مَا** فِيْ يَدِكَ؟ (**What** is in your hand?)
	مَنْ	**مَنْ** فِيْ الدَّارِ؟ (**Who** is in the house?)
	مَاذَا	**مَاذَا** تُرِيْدُوْنَ؟ (**What** do you wish/intend)?
	أَيٌّ	**أَيُّ** الْبِلَادِ أَحْسَنُ؟ (**Which** city is more beautiful?)
	مَتَى	**مَتَى** تَذْهَبُ؟ (**When** will you go?)
	أَيَّانَ	**أَيَّانَ** يَوْمُ الدِّيْنِ؟ (**When** is the day of resurrection?)
	أَنَّى	**أَنَّى** لَكِ هَذَا؟ (**Where** did this come to you from?)
	أَيْنَ	**أَيْنَ** بَيْتُكَ؟ (**Where** is your house?)

10	حَرْف التَّحْضِيْض (Particle for encouraging)	These are **four** particles which are used for **encouraging** someone to do an action.
	هَلَّا	هَلَّا تَنْصُرُ يُوْسُفَ؟ (**Why do you not** help Yusuf?)
	أَلَّا	أَلَّا تَنْصُرُ يُوْسُفَ؟ (**Why do you not** help Yusuf?)
	لَوْلَا	لَوْلَا تَنْصُرُ يُوْسُفَ؟ (**Why do you not** help Yusuf?)
	لَوْمَا	لَوْمَا تَنْصُرُ يُوْسُفَ؟ (**Why do you not** help Yusuf?)

11	حَرْف التَّنْبِيْه (Particle for warning)	There are **three** particle which are used to **rebuke**.
	أَلَا	أَلَا بِذِكْرِ اللهِ تَطْمَئِنُّ الْقُلُوْبُ (Listen! With the remembrance of Allah, the souls gain peace.)
	أَمَا	أَمَا إِنَّ يُوْسُفَ حَاضِرٌ (Listen! Verily Yusuf is present.)
	هَا	هَا هَذَا الْكِتَابُ سَهْلٌ جِدًّا (Listen! This book is very easy.)

LESSON 42: ARABIC NUMBERS

In the Arabic language, numbers have unique rules depending on the person or thing being 'numbered'. However, to understand these deeper rules (which are studied in intermediate to advance level syntax books), it is important to first consolidate the actual numbers themselves. Therefore, in this primer, the Arabic numbers up to 100 (and beyond) are indicated in both the cardinal and ordinal forms.

	Type	Description	Example
1	**Cardinal number**	Cardinal numbers show the **quantity** and indicate 'how many'; hence, also called 'counting numbers'.	8 cars
2	**Ordinal number**	Ordinal numbers indicate to the **order** of something; they show the position or rank. The ordinal numbers **do not** show quantity.	5th car

All the detailed rules of these numbers and formats will be avoided in this primer. Students should study more advanced books for the specific rules of Arabic numbers.

	Cardinal numbers		
	Number in Arabic	Masculine form example	Feminine form example
1	وَاحِد	عِنْدِيْ رَجُلٌ	عِنْدِيْ امْرَأَةٌ
2	اثْنَان	عِنْدِيْ رَجُلَانِ	عِنْدِيْ امْرَأَتَانِ
3	ثَلَاثَة	ثَلَاثَة رِجَالٍ	ثَلَاث نِسْوَةٍ
4	أَرْبَعَة	أَرْبَعَة رِجَالٍ	أَرْبَع نِسْوَةٍ
5	خَمْسَة	خَمْسَة رِجَالٍ	خَمْس نِسْوَةٍ
6	سِتَّة	سِتَّة رِجَالٍ	سِتّ نِسْوَةٍ
7	سَبْعَة	سَبْعَة رِجَالٍ	سَبْع نِسْوَةٍ
8	ثَمَانِيَة	ثَمَانِيَة رِجَالٍ	ثَمَانِي نِسْوَةٍ
9	تِسْعَة	تِسْعَة رِجَالٍ	تِسْع نِسْوَةٍ
10	عَشَرَة	عَشَرَة رِجَالٍ	عَشْر نِسْوَةٍ
11	أَحَدَ عَشَرَ	أَحَدَ عَشَرَ رَجُلًا	إِحْدَى عَشْرَةَ امْرَأَةً
12	اثْنَا عَشَرَ	اثْنَا عَشَرَ رَجُلًا	اثْنَتَا عَشْرَةَ امْرَأَةً
13	ثَلَاثَةَ عَشَرَ	ثَلَاثَةَ عَشَرَ رَجُلًا	ثَلَاثَ عَشْرَةَ امْرَأَةً
14	أَرْبَعَةَ عَشَرَ	أَرْبَعَةَ عَشَرَ رَجُلًا	أَرْبَعَ عَشْرَةَ امْرَأَةً
15	خَمْسَةَ عَشَرَ	خَمْسَةَ عَشَرَ رَجُلًا	خَمْسَ عَشْرَةَ امْرَأَةً
16	سِتَّةَ عَشَرَ	سِتَّةَ عَشَرَ رَجُلًا	سِتَّ عَشْرَةَ امْرَأَةً
17	سَبْعَةَ عَشَرَ	سَبْعَةَ عَشَرَ رَجُلًا	سَبْعَ عَشْرَةَ امْرَأَةً
18	ثَمَانِيَةَ عَشَرَ	ثَمَانِيَةَ عَشَرَ رَجُلًا	ثَمَانِيْ عَشْرَةَ امْرَأَةً
19	تِسْعَةَ عَشَرَ	تِسْعَةَ عَشَرَ رَجُلًا	تِسْعَ عَشْرَةَ امْرَأَةً
20	عِشْرُوْن	جَاءَنِي عِشْرُوْنَ رَجُلًا	رَأَيْتُ عِشْرِيْنَ امْرَأَةً
21	أَحَد وَعِشْرُوْن	أَحَد وَعِشْرُوْنَ رَجُلًا	إِحْدَى وَعِشْرُوْنَ امْرَأَةً
99	تِسْعَة وتِسْعُوْن	تِسْعَة وَتِسْعُوْنَ رَجُلًا	تِسْع وَتِسْعُوْنَ امْرَأَةً
100	مِائَة	مِائَة رَجُلٍ	مِائَة امْرَأَةٍ
1000	أَلْف	أَلْف رَجُلٍ	أَلْف امْرَأَةٍ
4945	أَرْبَعَة آلَافٍ وَتِسْع مِائَةٍ وَخَمْسَة وَأَرْبَعُوْن	أَرْبَعَةُ آلَافٍ وَتِسْعُ مِائَةٍ وَخَمْسَةٌ وَأَرْبَعُوْنَ رَجُلًا	أَرْبَعَةُ آلَافٍ وَتِسْعُ مِائَةٍ وَخَمْسٌ وَأَرْبَعُوْنَ امْرَأَةً

	Ordinal numbers	
	Masculine	Feminine
1st	الدَّرْسُ الْأَوَّلُ	السَّيَّارَةُ الْأُوْلَى
2nd	الدَّرْسُ الثَّانِيْ	السَّيَّارَةُ الثَّانِيَةُ
3rd	الدَّرْسُ الثَّالِثُ	السَّيَّارَةُ الثَّالِثَةُ
4th	الدَّرْسُ الرَّابِعُ	السَّيَّارَةُ الرَّابِعَةُ
5th	الدَّرْسُ الْخَامِسُ	السَّيَّارَةُ الْخَامِسَةُ
6th	الدَّرْسُ السَّادِسُ	السَّيَّارَةُ السَّادِسَةُ
7th	الدَّرْسُ السَّابِعُ	السَّيَّارَةُ السَّابِعَةُ
8th	الدَّرْسُ الثَّامِنُ	السَّيَّارَةُ الثَّامِنَةُ
9th	الدَّرْسُ التَّاسِعُ	السَّيَّارَةُ التَّاسِعَةُ
10th	الدَّرْسُ الْعَاشِرُ	السَّيَّارَةُ الْعَاشِرَةُ
11th	الدَّرْسُ الْحَادِيَ عَشَرَ	السَّيَّارَةُ الْحَادِيَةَ عَشْرَةَ
12th	الدَّرْسُ الثَّانِيَ عَشَرَ	السَّيَّارَةُ الثَّانِيَةَ عَشْرَةَ
13th	الدَّرْسُ الثَّالِثَ عَشَرَ	السَّيَّارَةُ الثَّالِثَةَ عَشْرَةَ
14th	الدَّرْسُ الرَّابِعَ عَشَرَ	السَّيَّارَةُ الرَّابِعَةُ عَشْرَةَ
15th	الدَّرْسُ الْخَامِسَ عَشَرَ	السَّيَّارَةُ الْخَامِسَةَ عَشْرَةَ
16th	الدَّرْسُ السَّادِسَ عَشَرَ	السَّيَّارَةُ السَّادِسَةَ عَشْرَةَ
17th	الدَّرْسُ السَّابِعَ عَشَرَ	السَّيَّارَةُ السَّابِعَةَ عَشْرَةَ
18th	الدَّرْسُ الثَّامِنَ عَشَرَ	السَّيَّارَةُ الثَّامِنَةَ عَشْرَةَ
19th	الدَّرْسُ التَّاسِعَ عَشَرَ	السَّيَّارَةُ التَّاسِعَةَ عَشْرَةَ
20th	الدَّرْسُ الْعِشْرُوْنَ	السَّيَّارَةُ الْعِشْرُوْنَ
21st	الدَّرْسُ الْحَادِيْ وَالْعِشْرُوْنَ	السَّيَّارَةُ الْحَادِيَةُ وَالْعِشْرُوْنَ
22nd	الدَّرْسُ الثَّانِيْ وَالْعِشْرُوْنَ	السَّيَّارَةُ الثَّانِيَةُ وَالْعِشْرُوْنَ
23rd	الدَّرْسُ الثَّالِثُ والْعِشْرُوْنَ	السَّيَّارَةُ الثَّالِثَةُ وَالْعِشْرُوْنَ
24th	الدَّرْسُ الرَّابِعُ وَالْعِشْرُوْنَ	السَّيَّارَةُ الرَّابِعَةُ وَالْعِشْرُوْنَ
25th	الدَّرْسُ الْخَامِسُ وَالْعِشْرُوْنَ	السَّيَّارَةُ الْخَامِسَةُ وَالْعِشْرُوْنَ
26th	الدَّرْسُ السَّادِسُ وَالْعِشْرُوْنَ	السَّيَّارَةُ السَّادِسَةُ وَالْعِشْرُوْنَ
27th	الدَّرْسُ السَّابِعُ وَالْعِشْرُوْنَ	السَّيَّارَةُ السَّابِعَةُ وَالْعِشْرُوْنَ

28th	الدَّرْسُ الثَّامِنُ وَالْعِشْرُوْنَ	السَّيَّارَةُ الثَّامِنَةُ وَالْعِشْرُوْنَ
29th	الدَّرْسُ التَّاسِعُ وَالْعِشْرُوْنَ	السَّيَّارَةُ التَّاسِعَةُ وَالْعِشْرُوْنَ
30th	الدَّرْسُ الثَّلَاثُوْنَ	السَّيَّارَةُ الثَّلَاثُوْنَ
40th	الدَّرْسُ الْأَرْبَعُوْنَ	السَّيَّارَةُ الْأَرْبَعُوْنَ
50th	الدَّرْسُ الْخَمْسُوْنَ	السَّيَّارَةُ الْخَمْسُوْنَ
60th	الدَّرْسُ السِّتُّوْنَ	السَّيَّارَةُ السِّتُّوْنَ
70th	الدَّرْسُ السَّبْعُوْنَ	السَّيَّارَةُ السَّبْعُوْنَ
80th	الدَّرْسُ الثَّمَانُوْنَ	السَّيَّارَةُ الثَّمَانُوْنَ
90th	الدَّرْسُ التِّسْعُوْنَ	السَّيَّارَةُ التِّسْعُوْنَ
100th	الدَّرْسُ الْمِائَةُ	السَّيَّارَةُ الْمِائَةُ
101st	الدَّرْسُ الْمِائَةُ وَالْأَوَّلُ	السَّيَّارَةُ الْمِائَةُ وَالْأُوْلَى
102nd	الدَّرْسُ الْمِائَةُ وَالثَّانِيْ	السَّيَّارَةُ الْمِائَةُ وَالثَّانِيَةُ
103rd	الدَّرْسُ الْمِائَةُ وَالثَّالِثُ	السَّيَّارَةُ الْمِائَةُ وَالثَّالِثَةُ
104th	الدَّرْسُ الْمِائَةُ وَالرَّابِعُ	السَّيَّارَةُ الْمِائَةُ وَالرَّابِعَةُ
105th	الدَّرْسُ الْمِائَةُ وَالْخَامِسُ	السَّيَّارَةُ الْمِائَةُ وَالْخَامِسَةُ
106th	الدَّرْسُ الْمِائَةُ وَالسَّادِسُ	السَّيَّارَةُ الْمِائَةُ وَالسَّادِسَةُ
107th	الدَّرْسُ الْمِائَةُ وَالسَّابِعُ	السَّيَّارَةُ الْمِائَةُ وَالسَّابِعَةُ
108th	الدَّرْسُ الْمِائَةُ وَالثَّامِنُ	السَّيَّارَةُ لْمِائَةُ وَالثَّامِنَةُ
109th	الدَّرْسُ الْمِائَةُ وَالتَّاسِعُ	السَّيَّارَةُ الْمِائَةُ وَالتَّاسِعَةُ
110th	الدَّرْسُ الْمِائَةُ وَالْعَاشِرُ	السَّيَّارَةُ الْمِائَةُ وَالْعَاشِرَةُ
200th	الدَّرْسُ الْمِائَتَانِ	السَّيَّارَةُ الْمِائَتَانِ
300th	الدَّرْسُ ثَلَاثُ مِائَةٍ	الدَّرْسُ ثَلَاثَةُ مِائَةٍ
400th	الدَّرْسُ أَرْبَعُ مِائَةٍ	الدَّرْسُ أَرْبَعَةُ مِائَةٍ
500th	الدَّرْسُ خَمْسُ مِائَةٍ	الدَّرْسُ خَمْسَةُ مِائَةٍ
600th	الدَّرْسُ سِتُّ مِائَةٍ	الدَّرْسُ سِتَّةُ مِائَةٍ
700th	الدَّرْسُ سَبْعُ مِائَةٍ	الدَّرْسُ سَبْعَةُ مِائَةٍ
800th	الدَّرْسُ ثَمَانِيْ مِائَةٍ	الدَّرْسُ ثَمَانِيَةُ مِائَةٍ
900th	الدَّرْسُ تِسْعُ مِائَةٍ	الدَّرْسُ تِسْعَةُ مِائَةٍ
1000th	الدَّرْسُ الْأَلْفُ	الدَّرْسُ الْأَلْفُ

LESSON 43: GRAMMATICAL BREAKDOWNS

Alhamdulillah, with the help from Almighty Allah, the rules needed for this primer have been covered. Before a student continues his study of the rules with more advanced books, it would be good for the student to do a complete revision of the book and concepts along with consolidating this knowledge by completing some grammatical sentence breakdowns *(tarkeeb)* with some further questions. So, until the end of this compilation, numerous sentences are given in table format, with gaps in the tables for students to fill with the correct terms. These sentences are adapted from the famous compilation of Shaykh Abul Hasan Ali an-Nadwi, namely Qisas an-Nabiyyeen. The sentences are generally taken from the earlier chapters of the book as the book commences with easier sentence structures.

Line 1: كَانَ اسْمُ هَذَا الرَّجُلِ آزَرَ (This person's name was Aazar.)

<table>
<tr><td colspan="5">كَانَ اسْمُ هَذَا الرَّجُلِ آزَرَ</td></tr>
<tr><td>آزَرَ</td><td>الرَّجُلِ</td><td>هَذَا</td><td>اسْمُ</td><td>كَانَ</td></tr>
<tr><td rowspan="3"></td><td>مشار إليه</td><td></td><td rowspan="2">مضاف</td><td rowspan="3"></td></tr>
<tr><td colspan="2"></td></tr>
<tr><td colspan="3">اسم كان</td></tr>
<tr><td colspan="5"></td></tr>
</table>

	Question	Answer
1	What will the grammatical state of the مضاف be?	
2	What is the grammatical state of the word آزَرَ and explain the reason for the single *fathah*?	

<u>Line 2</u>: كَانَ آزَرُ يَبِيْعُ الْأَصْنَامَ (Aazar used to sell idols.)

<table>
<tr><td colspan="4">كَانَ آزَرُ يَبِيْعُ الْأَصْنَامَ</td></tr>
<tr><td>الْأَصْنَامَ</td><td>يَبِيْعُ</td><td>آزَرُ</td><td>كَانَ</td></tr>
<tr><td></td><td>فعل مضارع + فاعل (هو)</td><td rowspan="2"></td><td rowspan="2"></td></tr>
<tr><td colspan="2">خبر (كان)</td></tr>
<tr><td colspan="4">جملة فعلية خبرية</td></tr>
</table>

	Question	Answer
1	What does a فعل ناقص do grammatically?	
2	What is the grammatical state of the word الْأَصْنَامَ and explain the reason for the single *fathah*?	

<u>Line 3</u>: كَانَ فِيْ هَذِهِ الْقَرْيَةِ بَيْتٌ كَبِيْرٌ (There was a big house in this village.)

<table>
<tr><td colspan="7">كَانَ فِيْ هَذِهِ الْقَرْيَةِ بَيْتٌ كَبِيْرٌ</td></tr>
<tr><td>كَبِيْرٌ</td><td>بَيْتٌ</td><td>الْقَرْيَةِ</td><td>هَذِهِ</td><td>فِيْ</td><td>[ثَابِتًا]</td><td>كَانَ</td></tr>
<tr><td></td><td>موصوف</td><td></td><td>مضاف</td><td rowspan="2">حرف الجر</td><td rowspan="3">اسم الفاعل (عامل)</td><td rowspan="4"></td></tr>
<tr><td colspan="2" rowspan="3"></td><td colspan="2">مجرور بحرف الجر</td></tr>
<tr><td colspan="3">متعلّق بـ(ثابت)</td></tr>
<tr><td colspan="4"></td></tr>
<tr><td colspan="7"></td></tr>
</table>

	Question	Answer
1	Explain the *harakah* on the letter فِيْ?	
2	Why does the word الْقَرْيَةِ have a single *kasrah?*	

Line 4: كَانَ فِيْ هَذَا الْبَيْتِ أَصْنَامٌ (There were idols in this house.)

<table>
<tr><td colspan="6">كَانَ فِيْ هَذَا الْبَيْتِ أَصْنَامٌ</td></tr>
<tr><td>أَصْنَامٌ</td><td>الْبَيْتِ</td><td>هَذَا</td><td>فِيْ</td><td>[ثَابِتًا]</td><td>كَانَ</td></tr>
<tr><td rowspan="4"></td><td></td><td>اسم الإشارة</td><td rowspan="2"></td><td rowspan="3"></td><td rowspan="4">فعل ناقص</td></tr>
<tr><td colspan="2">مجرور بحرف الجرّ</td></tr>
<tr><td colspan="3"></td></tr>
<tr><td colspan="4">خبر (كان)</td></tr>
<tr><td colspan="6"></td></tr>
</table>

	Question	Answer
1	Why can't the sentence فِيْ هَذَا الْبَيْتِ be the *ism* of كان?	
2	Explain the *harakah* on the word هَذَا?	

Line 5: كَانَ النَّاسُ يَسْجُدُوْنَ لِهَذِهِ الْأَصْنَامِ (People used to prostrate for these idols.)

<table>
<tr><td colspan="6">كَانَ النَّاسُ يَسْجُدُوْنَ لِهَذِهِ الْأَصْنَامِ</td></tr>
<tr><td>الْأَصْنَامِ</td><td>هَذِهِ</td><td>لِ</td><td>يَسْجُدُوْنَ</td><td>النَّاسُ</td><td>كَانَ</td></tr>
<tr><td>مشار إليه</td><td></td><td rowspan="2"></td><td rowspan="3">فعل + فاعل (هم)</td><td rowspan="4">اسم كان</td><td rowspan="4"></td></tr>
<tr><td colspan="2"></td></tr>
<tr><td colspan="3">متعلّق بـ(يسجدون)</td></tr>
<tr><td colspan="4"></td></tr>
<tr><td colspan="6"></td></tr>
</table>

	Question	Answer
1	What type of verb is the word يَسْجُدُوْنَ? Mention what scale it is in terms of number, gender and person.	
2	Is كَانَ a noun, verb or particle?	

Line 6: كَانَ آزَرُ يَسْجُدُ لِهَذِهِ الْأَصْنَامِ (Aazar used to prostrate for these idols.)

<table>
<tr><td colspan="6">كَانَ آزَرُ يَسْجُدُ لِهَذِهِ الْأَصْنَامِ</td></tr>
<tr><td>الْأَصْنَامِ</td><td>هَذِهِ</td><td>لِ</td><td>يَسْجُدُ</td><td>آزَرُ</td><td>كَانَ</td></tr>
<tr><td>مشار إليه</td><td></td><td rowspan="2">حرف الجرّ</td><td rowspan="3"></td><td rowspan="4"></td><td rowspan="4">فعل ناقص</td></tr>
<tr><td colspan="2"></td></tr>
<tr><td colspan="3"></td></tr>
<tr><td colspan="4">خبر كان</td></tr>
<tr><td colspan="6"></td></tr>
</table>

	Question	Answer
1	Why is there a *kasrah* on the particle لِ ?	
2	What type of noun is the word الأصْنَام ?	

Line 7: كَانَ آزَرُ يَعْبُدُ هَذِهِ الْأَصْنَامَ (Aazar used to worship these idols.)

<table>
<tr><td colspan="5">كَانَ آزَرُ يَعْبُدُ هَذِهِ الْأَصْنَامَ</td></tr>
<tr><td>الْأَصْنَامَ</td><td>هَذِهِ</td><td>يَعْبُدُ</td><td>آزَرُ</td><td>كَانَ</td></tr>
<tr><td></td><td>اسم الإشارة</td><td rowspan="2"></td><td rowspan="3"></td><td rowspan="3"></td></tr>
<tr><td colspan="2">مفعول به</td></tr>
<tr><td colspan="3">خبر كان</td></tr>
<tr><td colspan="5"></td></tr>
</table>

	Question	Answer
1	What is the grammatical state of خبر كان ?	
2	If the sentence يعبد هذه الأصنام is the *khabar* of *kana,* then why does it have a *dhammah* on the word يَعبدُ ?	

<u>Line 8</u>: كَانَ آزَرُ لَهُ وَلَدٌ رَشِيْدٌ (Aazar had an intelligent/guided child.)

<table>
<tr><td></td><td colspan="6">كَانَ آزَرُ لَهُ وَلَدٌ رَشِيْدٌ</td></tr>
<tr><td>رَشِيْدٌ</td><td>وَلَدٌ</td><td>هُ</td><td>لَ</td><td>[ثَابِتٌ]</td><td>آزَرُ</td><td>كَانَ</td></tr>
<tr><td rowspan="2">صفة</td><td rowspan="2"></td><td>مجرور بحرف الجرّ</td><td></td><td rowspan="2"></td><td rowspan="5"></td><td rowspan="5"></td></tr>
<tr><td colspan="2"></td></tr>
<tr><td colspan="2">مبتدأ</td><td colspan="3">خبر</td></tr>
<tr><td colspan="5">جملة اسمية خبريّة</td></tr>
<tr><td colspan="5">خبر كان</td></tr>
<tr><td colspan="7"></td></tr>
</table>

	Question	Answer
1	Mention the rules of صفة & موصوف briefly with an example.	
2	If the word ولدٌ is the *kabar* of *kana*, then why does it not have a *fathah?*	

<u>Line 9</u>: كَانَ فِيْ قَرْيَةٍ رَجُلٌ مَشْهُوْرٌ (There was a famous man in the village.)

<table>
<tr><td colspan="6">كَانَ فِيْ قَرْيَةٍ رَجُلٌ مَشْهُوْرٌ</td></tr>
<tr><td>مَشْهُوْرٌ</td><td>رَجُلٌ</td><td>قَرْيَةٍ</td><td>فِيْ</td><td>[ثَابِتًا]</td><td>كَانَ</td></tr>
<tr><td>صفة</td><td></td><td>مجرور بحرف الجرّ</td><td></td><td rowspan="2">اسم الفاعل (عامل)</td><td rowspan="3">الفعل الناقص</td></tr>
<tr><td colspan="2" rowspan="2">اسم كان</td><td colspan="2">متعلّق بـ(ثابت)</td></tr>
<tr><td colspan="3"></td></tr>
<tr><td colspan="6">جملة فعلية خبرية</td></tr>
</table>

	Question	Answer
1	What does جملة فعلية خبرية mean?	
2	Explain the term متعلّق and mention its usage in the *majrooraat* chapter.	

Line 10: كَانَ اسْمُ هَذَا الْوَلَدِ إِبْرَاهِيمَ (This child's name was Ibrahim.)

<table>
<tr><td colspan="5">كَانَ اسْمُ هَذَا الْوَلَدِ إِبْرَاهِيمَ</td></tr>
<tr><td>إِبْرَاهِيمَ</td><td>الْوَلَدِ</td><td>هَذَا</td><td>اسْمُ</td><td>كَانَ</td></tr>
<tr><td rowspan="3">خبر كان</td><td></td><td>اسم الإشارة</td><td rowspan="2"></td><td rowspan="3"></td></tr>
<tr><td colspan="2">مضاف إليه</td></tr>
<tr><td colspan="3"></td></tr>
<tr><td colspan="5"></td></tr>
</table>

	Question	Answer
1	Why does the word إبراهيم only have a single *fathah?*	
2	Is the word هَذَا *mu'rab* or *mabni?* Give a reason for your answer.	

Line 11: كَانَ إِبْرَاهِيمُ يَرَى النَّاسَ يَسْجُدُوْنَ لِلْأَصْنَامِ (Ibrahim used to see the people in a state that they were prostrating for the idols.)

<table>
<tr><td colspan="7">كَانَ إِبْرَاهِيمُ يَرَى النَّاسَ يَسْجُدُوْنَ لِلْأَصْنَامِ</td></tr>
<tr><td>الْأَصْنَامِ</td><td>لِ</td><td>يَسْجُدُوْنَ</td><td>النَّاسَ</td><td>يَرَى</td><td>إِبْرَاهِيمُ</td><td>كَانَ</td></tr>
<tr><td></td><td></td><td>فعل + فاعل (هم)</td><td rowspan="2"></td><td rowspan="2"></td><td rowspan="3"></td><td rowspan="3"></td></tr>
<tr><td colspan="3">جملة فعليّة خبريّة = حال</td></tr>
<tr><td colspan="5"></td></tr>
<tr><td colspan="7"></td></tr>
</table>

	Question	Answer
1	What is the ذو الحال in the above example?	
2	Mention the **type** and **form** (number, gender, person) of the verb يسجدون .	

<u>Line 12</u>: يَرَى النَّاسَ يَعْبُدُوْنَ الْأَصْنَامَ (He used to see the people in a state that they were worshiping idols.)

<table>
<tr><td colspan="4">يَرَى النَّاسَ يَعْبُدُوْنَ الْأَصْنَامَ</td></tr>
<tr><td>الْأَصْنَامَ</td><td>يَعْبُدُوْنَ</td><td>النَّاسَ</td><td>يَرَى</td></tr>
<tr><td></td><td></td><td rowspan="2">مفعول به</td><td rowspan="2"></td></tr>
<tr><td colspan="2"></td></tr>
<tr><td colspan="4">جملة فعليّة خبريّة</td></tr>
</table>

	Question	Answer
1	Mention the five types of مفعول with an example for each.	

<u>Line 13</u>: كَانَ إِبْرَاهِيْمُ يَعْرِفُ أَنَّ الْأَصْنَامَ حِجَارَةٌ (Ibrahim used to know that the idols were stone.)

<table>
<tr><td colspan="6">كَانَ إِبْرَاهِيْمُ يَعْرِفُ أَنَّ الْأَصْنَامَ حِجَارَةٌ</td></tr>
<tr><td>حِجَارَةٌ</td><td>الْأَصْنَامَ</td><td>أَنَّ</td><td>يَعْرِفُ</td><td>إِبْرَاهِيْمُ</td><td>كَانَ</td></tr>
<tr><td></td><td></td><td></td><td rowspan="2"></td><td rowspan="4"></td><td rowspan="4"></td></tr>
<tr><td colspan="3">مفعول به</td></tr>
<tr><td colspan="4">جملة فعليّة خبريّة</td></tr>
<tr><td colspan="4">خبر كان</td></tr>
<tr><td colspan="6"></td></tr>
</table>

	Question	Answer
1	Mention the grammatical impact of the particle أَنَّ.	
2	Why is the word إِبْرَاهِيْمُ regarded as غَيْرُ الْمُنْصَرِف ?	

Line 14: كَانَ يَعْرِفُ أَنَّ الْأَصْنَامَ لَا تَتَكَلَّمُ وَلَا تَسْمَعُ (He used to know that the idols do not speak, nor do they listen.)

<table>
<tr><td colspan="7">كَانَ يَعْرِفُ أَنَّ الْأَصْنَامَ لَا تَتَكَلَّمُ وَلَا تَسْمَعُ</td></tr>
<tr><td>لَا تَسْمَعُ</td><td>وَ</td><td>لَا تَتَكَلَّمُ</td><td>الْأَصْنَامَ</td><td>أَنَّ</td><td>يَعْرِفُ</td><td>كَانَ</td></tr>
<tr><td>فعل + فاعل (هي)</td><td rowspan="2">حرف العطف</td><td></td><td rowspan="4"></td><td rowspan="4"></td><td rowspan="5"></td><td rowspan="7"></td></tr>
<tr><td></td><td>معطوف عليه</td></tr>
<tr><td colspan="3">جملة فعليّة خبريّة</td></tr>
<tr><td colspan="3">خبر (أنّ)</td></tr>
<tr><td colspan="5">مفعول به</td></tr>
<tr><td colspan="6">جملة فعليّة خبريّة</td></tr>
<tr><td colspan="6"></td></tr>
<tr><td colspan="7"></td></tr>
</table>

	Question	Answer
1	The particle و is from the particles of عَطْف . Mention all the particles of عَطْف .	
2	Explain the terms مَعْطُوْف and مَعْطُوْف عَلَيْه .	

Line 15: كَانَ يَعْرِفُ أَنَّ الْأَصْنَامَ لَا تَضُرُّ وَلَا تَنْفَعُ (He used to know the idols do not harm, nor do they give benefit.)

<table>
<tr><td colspan="7">كَانَ يَعْرِفُ أَنَّ الْأَصْنَامَ لَا تَضُرُّ وَلَا تَنْفَعُ</td></tr>
<tr><td>لَا تَنْفَعُ</td><td>وَ</td><td>لَا تَضُرُّ</td><td>الْأَصْنَامَ</td><td>أَنَّ</td><td>يَعْرِفُ</td><td>كَانَ</td></tr>
<tr><td></td><td rowspan="2">حرف العطف</td><td></td><td rowspan="4"></td><td rowspan="4">الحروف المشبّهة بالفعل</td><td rowspan="5">فعل + فاعل (هو)</td><td rowspan="7"></td></tr>
<tr><td></td><td></td></tr>
<tr><td colspan="3"></td></tr>
<tr><td colspan="3">خبر أنّ</td></tr>
<tr><td colspan="5"></td></tr>
<tr><td colspan="6">جملة فعليّة خبريّة</td></tr>
<tr><td colspan="6">خبر "كان"</td></tr>
<tr><td colspan="7"></td></tr>
</table>

<u>Line 16</u>: كَانَ يَرَى أَنَّ الذُّبابَ يَجْلِسُ عَلَى الْأَصْنَامِ (He used to see that the fly would sit upon the idols.)

<table>
<tr><td colspan="7">كَانَ يَرَى أَنَّ الذُّبَابَ يَجْلِسُ عَلَى الْأَصْنَامِ</td></tr>
<tr><td>الْأَصْنَامِ</td><td>عَلَى</td><td>يَجْلِسُ</td><td>الذُّبَابَ</td><td>أَنَّ</td><td>يَرَى</td><td>كَانَ</td></tr>
<tr><td></td><td></td><td rowspan="2"></td><td rowspan="4"></td><td rowspan="4"></td><td rowspan="5"></td><td rowspan="7"></td></tr>
<tr><td colspan="2"></td></tr>
<tr><td colspan="3">جملة فعليّة خبريّة</td></tr>
<tr><td colspan="3">خبر (أنّ)</td></tr>
<tr><td colspan="5">مفعول به</td></tr>
<tr><td colspan="6">جملة فعليّة خبريّة</td></tr>
<tr><td colspan="6"></td></tr>
<tr><td colspan="7"></td></tr>
</table>

	Question	Answer
1	What is the فاعل of the word يَجْلِسُ?	
2	Why can't the word الذباب be the actual فاعل of the word يَجْلِسُ ?	Because, grammatically, the فاعل can **never** come before the actual verb itself.

<u>Line 17</u>: كَانَ يَرَى الْفَأْرَ يَأْكُلُ طَعَامَ الْأَصْنَامِ (He used to see the mouse eating the idols' food.)

<table>
<tr><td colspan="6">كَانَ يَرَى الْفَأْرَ يَأْكُلُ طَعَامَ الْأَصْنَامِ</td></tr>
<tr><td>الْأَصْنَامِ</td><td>طَعَامَ</td><td>يَأْكُلُ</td><td>الْفَأْرَ</td><td>يَرَى</td><td>كَانَ</td></tr>
<tr><td></td><td></td><td rowspan="2"></td><td rowspan="4">مفعول به (ذو الحال)</td><td rowspan="4">فعل + فاعل (هو)</td><td rowspan="6"></td></tr>
<tr><td colspan="2"></td></tr>
<tr><td colspan="3">جملة فعليّة خبريّة</td></tr>
<tr><td colspan="3">حال</td></tr>
<tr><td colspan="5">جملة فعليّة خبريّة</td></tr>
<tr><td colspan="5"></td></tr>
<tr><td colspan="6"></td></tr>
</table>

<u>Line 18</u>: كَانَ إِبْرَاهِيْمُ يَقُوْلُ لِوَالِدِهِ (Ibrahim used to say to his father.)

كَانَ إِبْرَاهِيْمُ يَقُوْلُ لِوَالِدِهِ					
هِ	وَالِدِ	لِ	يَقُوْلُ	إِبْرَاهِيْمُ	كَانَ
	مضاف		فعل + فاعل (هو)		
متعلّق ب(يقول)					
خبر كان					

	Question	Answer
1	Explain the term متعلّق with an example.	
2	Why does the word إِبْرَاهِيْمُ not have a *tanween?*	

<u>Line 19</u>: لِمَاذَا تَسْجُدُ لِهَذِهِ الْأَصْنَامِ (Why do you prostrate for these idols?)

لِمَاذَا تَسْجُدُ لِهَذِهِ الْأَصْنَامِ						
الْأَصْنَامِ	هَذِهِ	لِـ	تَسْجُدُ	مَاذَا	لِ	[ثَابِتٌ]
		حرف الجرّ		اسم الاستفهام	حرف الجرّ	اسم الفاعل (عامل)
مبتدأ						
جملة فعليّة خبريّة						

	Question	Answer
1	What is استفهام ?	
2	Mention 5 words used for استفهام with translation of each word.	

<u>Line 20</u>: إِنَّ هَذِهِ الْأَصْنَامَ لَا تَتَكَلَّمُ وَلَا تَسْمَعُ (Indeed, these idols do not speak nor do they hear.)

<table>
<tr><td colspan="6">إِنَّ هَذِهِ الْأَصْنَامَ لَا تَتَكَلَّمُ وَلَا تَسْمَعُ</td></tr>
<tr><td>لَا تَسْمَعُ</td><td>وَ</td><td>لَا تَتَكَلَّمُ</td><td>الْأَصْنَامَ</td><td>هَذِهِ</td><td>إِنَّ</td></tr>
<tr><td>فعل + فاعل (هي)</td><td rowspan="2"></td><td>فعل + فاعل (هي)</td><td></td><td></td><td rowspan="4"></td></tr>
<tr><td></td><td>معطوف عليه</td><td colspan="2" rowspan="3">اسم (إنّ)</td></tr>
<tr><td colspan="3"></td></tr>
<tr><td colspan="3">خبر إنّ</td></tr>
<tr><td colspan="6"></td></tr>
</table>

	Question	Answer
1	Why does the *harakah* of the word هذه not change?	
2	Why does the word تَتَكَلَّمُ have a single *dhammah?*	

<u>Line 21</u>: إِنَّ هَذِهِ الْأَصْنَامَ لَا تَأْكُلُ وَلَا تَشْرَبُ (Indeed, these idols do not eat nor do they drink.)

<table>
<tr><td colspan="6">إِنَّ هَذِهِ الْأَصْنَامَ لَا تَأْكُلُ وَلَا تَشْرَبُ</td></tr>
<tr><td>لَا تَشْرَبُ</td><td>وَ</td><td>لَا تَأْكُلُ</td><td>الْأَصْنَامَ</td><td>هَذِهِ</td><td>إِنَّ</td></tr>
<tr><td></td><td rowspan="2"></td><td></td><td></td><td></td><td rowspan="4"></td></tr>
<tr><td></td><td></td><td colspan="2" rowspan="3"></td></tr>
<tr><td colspan="3">جملة فعليّة خبريّة</td></tr>
<tr><td colspan="3"></td></tr>
<tr><td colspan="6">جملة اسميّة خبريّة</td></tr>
</table>

	Question	Answer
1	Does the *harakah* on the word لَا change? Give a reason.	
2	Why does the word تَشْرَبُ have a single *dhammah?*	

Line 22: كَانَ آزَرُ يَغْضَبُ وَلَا يَفْهَمُ (Aazar used to get angry and not understand.)

<table>
<tr><td colspan="6">كَانَ آزَرُ يَغْضَبُ وَلَا يَفْهَمُ</td></tr>
<tr><td>يَفْهَمُ</td><td>لَا</td><td>وَ</td><td>يَغْضَبُ</td><td>آزَرُ</td><td>كَانَ</td></tr>
<tr><td>فعل مضارع
فاعل (هو) +</td><td>حرف النفي</td><td rowspan="2"></td><td>فعل مضارع
فاعل (هو) +</td><td rowspan="4"></td><td rowspan="4"></td></tr>
<tr><td colspan="2">معطوف</td><td></td></tr>
<tr><td colspan="4">جملة فعليّة خبريّة</td></tr>
<tr><td colspan="4"></td></tr>
<tr><td colspan="6"></td></tr>
</table>

	Question	Answer
1	Mention the **five** different types of توابع .	
2	Mention the rules of مَعْطُوْف and مَعْطُوْف عَلَيْه .	

Line 23: كَانَ إِبْرَاهِيْمُ يَنْصَحُ لِقَوْمِهِ (Ibrahim used to advice his people.)

<table>
<tr><td colspan="6">كَانَ إِبْرَاهِيْمُ يَنْصَحُ لِقَوْمِهِ</td></tr>
<tr><td>هِ</td><td>قَوْمِ</td><td>لِ</td><td>يَنْصَحُ</td><td>إِبْرَاهِيْمُ</td><td>كَانَ</td></tr>
<tr><td></td><td></td><td rowspan="2"></td><td rowspan="3"></td><td rowspan="5"></td><td rowspan="5"></td></tr>
<tr><td colspan="2"></td></tr>
<tr><td colspan="3">متعلّق بـ(ينصح)</td></tr>
<tr><td colspan="4">جملة فعليّة خبريّة</td></tr>
<tr><td colspan="4"></td></tr>
<tr><td colspan="6"></td></tr>
</table>

	Question	Answer
1	What is لقومه *muta'alliq* (attached) to?	
2	What type of word is the هِ at the end of قَوْمِهِ and explain the reason it has a *kasrah.*	

Line 24: كَانَ النَّاسُ يَغْضَبُوْنَ وَلَا يَفْهَمُوْنَ (People used to get angry and would not understand.)

<table>
<tr><td colspan="6">كَانَ النَّاسُ يَغْضَبُوْنَ وَلَا يَفْهَمُوْنَ</td></tr>
<tr><td>يَفْهَمُوْنَ</td><td>لَا</td><td>وَ</td><td>يَغْضَبُوْنَ</td><td>النَّاسُ</td><td>كَانَ</td></tr>
<tr><td></td><td>حرف النفي</td><td rowspan="2"></td><td>فعل مضارع
فاعل (هم) +</td><td rowspan="4"></td><td rowspan="4"></td></tr>
<tr><td colspan="2"></td><td></td></tr>
<tr><td colspan="4">جملة فعليّة خبريّة</td></tr>
<tr><td colspan="4"></td></tr>
<tr><td colspan="6"></td></tr>
</table>

	Question	Answer
1	Mention the **two** different types of جملة, give an explanation and an example for each.	

Line 25: قَالَ إِبْرَاهِيْمُ: أَنَا أَكْسِرُ الْأَصْنَامَ (Ibrahim said: I will break the idols.)

<table>
<tr><td colspan="5">قَالَ إِبْرَاهِيْمُ: أَنَا أَكْسِرُ الْأَصْنَامَ</td></tr>
<tr><td>الْأَصْنَامَ</td><td>أَكْسِرُ</td><td>أَنَا</td><td>إِبْرَاهِيْمُ</td><td>قَالَ</td></tr>
<tr><td>مفعول به</td><td></td><td rowspan="3">مبتدأ</td><td rowspan="4"></td><td rowspan="4"></td></tr>
<tr><td colspan="2">جملة فعليّة خبريّة</td></tr>
<tr><td colspan="2"></td></tr>
<tr><td colspan="3">مفعول به (مَقُوْل)</td></tr>
<tr><td colspan="5"></td></tr>
</table>

	Question	Answer
1	What is the other name given to the مفعول به of قال ?	
2	What tense verb is قَالَ ? Write the Arabic name.	

Line 26: جَاءَ يَوْمُ عِيْدٍ فَفَرِحَ النَّاسُ (The day of 'Eid came, thus the people were happy.)

<table>
<tr><td colspan="6">جَاءَ يَوْمُ عِيْدٍ فَفَرِحَ النَّاسُ</td></tr>
<tr><td>النَّاسُ</td><td>فَرِحَ</td><td>فَ</td><td>عِيْدٍ</td><td>يَوْمُ</td><td>جَاءَ</td></tr>
<tr><td rowspan="2"></td><td rowspan="2"></td><td rowspan="3"></td><td></td><td></td><td rowspan="2"></td></tr>
<tr><td colspan="2">فاعل</td></tr>
<tr><td colspan="2">معطوف</td><td colspan="3">معطوف عليه</td></tr>
<tr><td colspan="6"></td></tr>
</table>

	Question	Answer
1	Why does جاءَ have a *fathah* at the end?	
2	Why type of word is فرح ?	

Line 27: قَالَ إِبْرَاهِيْمُ: أَنَا سَقِيْمٌ (Ibrahim said: I am ill.)

<table>
<tr><td colspan="4">قَالَ إِبْرَاهِيْمُ: أَنَا سَقِيْمٌ</td></tr>
<tr><td>سَقِيْمٌ</td><td>أَنَا</td><td>إِبْرَاهِيْمُ</td><td>قَالَ</td></tr>
<tr><td></td><td>مبتدأ</td><td rowspan="3"></td><td rowspan="3"></td></tr>
<tr><td colspan="2">جملة فعليّة خبريّة</td></tr>
<tr><td colspan="2">مفعول به (مقول)</td></tr>
<tr><td colspan="4"></td></tr>
</table>

	Question	Answer
1	What is the other name given to the مفعول به of قال ?	
2	Mention the difference between فاعل and نائب فاعل with examples for each.	

Line 28: ذَهَبَ النَّاسُ وَبَقِيَ إِبْرَاهِيْمُ فِيْ الْبَيْتِ (The people went and Ibrahim remained in the house.)

ذَهَبَ النَّاسُ وَبَقِيَ إِبْرَاهِيْمُ فِيْ الْبَيْتِ						
الْبَيْتِ	فِيْ	إِبْرَاهِيْمُ	بَقِيَ	وَ	النَّاسُ	ذَهَبَ

	Question	Answer
1	What is a مضاف إليه and explain any detail with an example.	
2	What is the reason of the *harakah* on the last letter of فِيْ ?	

Line 29: هَذَا طَعَامٌ وَشَرَابٌ (This is food and drink.)

هَذَا طَعَامٌ وَشَرَابٌ			
شَرَابٌ	وَ	طَعَامٌ	هَذَا
			مبتدأ
خبر			

	Question	Answer
1	Mention all the اسم الإشارة with examples.	

Line 30: سَكَتَتِ الْأَصْنَامُ وَمَا نَطَقَتْ (The idols stayed quiet and never spoke.)

سَكَتَتِ الْأَصْنَامُ وَمَا نَطَقَتْ			
مَا نَطَقَتْ	وَ	الْأَصْنَامُ	سَكَتَتِ
معطوف			

	Question	Answer
1	Look at the verb سَكَتَتْ . Mention with detail the type of verb it is (scale, number, gender).	
2	What is the particle مَا in the above example.	

Line 31: تَرَكَ إِبْرَاهِيْمُ الصَّنَمَ الْأَكْبَرَ (Ibrahim left the big idol.)

تَرَكَ إِبْرَاهِيْمُ الصَّنَمَ الْأَكْبَرَ			
الْأَكْبَرَ	الصَّنَمَ	إِبْرَاهِيْمُ	تَرَكَ
صفة			

	Question	Answer
1	What are the rules of موصوف and صفة ? Mention the detail with an example.	

<u>Line 32</u>: رَجَعَ النَّاسُ وَدَخَلُوْا فِيْ بَيْتِ الْأَصْنَامِ (The people returned and entered the idols' house.)

رَجَعَ النَّاسُ وَدَخَلُوْا فِيْ بَيْتِ الْأَصْنَامِ						
الْأَصْنَامِ	بَيْتِ	فِيْ	دَخَلُوْا	وَ	النَّاسُ	رَجَعَ

	Question	Answer
1	Why does رَجَعَ have a *fathah* at the end?	
2	Look at the verb دَخَلُوْا . Mention with detail the type of verb it is (scale, number, gender).	

<u>Line 33</u>: تَأَسَّفَ النَّاسُ وَغَضِبُوْا (The people regretted and were angry.)

تَأَسَّفَ النَّاسُ وَغَضِبُوْا			
غَضِبُوْا	وَ	النَّاسُ	تَأَسَّفَ
معطوف			

	Question	Answer
1	Mention **three** rules regarding the فاعل (doer).	
2	Look at the verb غَضِبُوْا . Mention with detail the type of verb it is (scale, number, gender).	

Line 34: قَالُوْا: مَنْ فَعَلَ هَذَا بِآلِهَتِنَا (They said: Who did this with our idols?)

<table dir="rtl">
<tr><td colspan="7">قَالُوْا: مَنْ فَعَلَ هَذَا بِآلِهَتِنَا</td></tr>
<tr><td>قَالُوْا</td><td>مَنْ</td><td>فَعَلَ</td><td>هَذَا</td><td>بِ</td><td>آلِهَتِ</td><td>نَا</td></tr>
<tr><td rowspan="7"></td><td rowspan="5">مبتدأ</td><td rowspan="3"></td><td rowspan="3"></td><td rowspan="2"></td><td></td><td></td></tr>
<tr><td colspan="2"></td></tr>
<tr><td colspan="3"></td></tr>
<tr><td colspan="5">جملة فعليّة خبريّة</td></tr>
<tr><td colspan="5">خبر</td></tr>
<tr><td colspan="6">جملة اسميّة خبريّة</td></tr>
<tr><td colspan="6"></td></tr>
<tr><td colspan="7"></td></tr>
</table>

	Question	Answer
1	What is another name for the مفعول به of قَالَ ?	
2	Where is the مشار إليه in the above example?	

Line 35: كَانُوْا يَعْرِفُوْنَ أَنَّ الْحِجَارَةَ لَا تَسْمَعُ (They used to know that stone cannot listen.)

<table dir="rtl">
<tr><td colspan="5">كَانُوْا يَعْرِفُوْنَ أَنَّ الْحِجَارَةَ لَا تَسْمَعُ</td></tr>
<tr><td>كَانُوْا</td><td>يَعْرِفُوْنَ</td><td>أَنَّ</td><td>الْحِجَارَةَ</td><td>لَا تَسْمَعُ</td></tr>
<tr><td rowspan="5"></td><td rowspan="3"></td><td rowspan="2"></td><td rowspan="2"></td><td></td></tr>
<tr><td>خبر (أنّ)</td></tr>
<tr><td colspan="3"></td></tr>
<tr><td colspan="4">جملة فعليّة خبريّة</td></tr>
<tr><td colspan="4"></td></tr>
<tr><td colspan="5"></td></tr>
</table>

	Question	Answer
1	Mention the grammatical rule of أفعال ناقصة with an example.	

Line 36: الصَّنَمُ الْأَكْبَرُ لَا يَقْدِرُ أَنْ يَمْشِيَ (The big idol does not have the ability to walk.)

<table>
<tr><td colspan="5">الصَّنَمُ الْأَكْبَرُ لَا يَقْدِرُ أَنْ يَمْشِيَ</td></tr>
<tr><td>يَمْشِيَ</td><td>أَنْ</td><td>لَا يَقْدِرُ</td><td>الْأَكْبَرُ</td><td>الصَّنَمُ</td></tr>
<tr><td></td><td>حرف ناصب</td><td rowspan="2"></td><td></td><td></td></tr>
<tr><td colspan="2">مفعول به</td><td colspan="2" rowspan="3"></td></tr>
<tr><td colspan="3"></td></tr>
<tr><td colspan="3">خبر</td></tr>
<tr><td colspan="5"></td></tr>
</table>

	Question	Answer
1	What are the حروف ناصبة ? Mention each one with an example and explain the grammatical impact it has.	

Line 37: سَكَتَ النَّاسُ وَخَجِلُوْا (People stayed quiet and were ashamed.)

<table>
<tr><td colspan="4">سَكَتَ النَّاسُ وَخَجِلُوْا</td></tr>
<tr><td>خَجِلُوْا</td><td>وَ</td><td>النَّاسُ</td><td>سَكَتَ</td></tr>
<tr><td></td><td rowspan="2"></td><td></td><td></td></tr>
<tr><td>معطوف</td><td colspan="2"></td></tr>
<tr><td colspan="4"></td></tr>
</table>

	Question	Answer
1	Mention all the **five** types of توابع with an example for each.	

Line 38: إِنَّ إِبْرَاهِيمَ كَسَرَ الْأَصْنَامَ وَأَهَانَ الآلِهَةَ (Verily Ibrahim broke the idols and disgraced the idols.)

إِنَّ إِبْرَاهِيمَ كَسَرَ الْأَصْنَامَ وَأَهَانَ الْآلِهَةَ						
الْآلِهَةَ	أَهَانَ	وَ	الْأَصْنَامَ	كَسَرَ	إِبْرَاهِيمَ	إِنَّ
جملة فعليّة خبريّة = خبر						

	Question	Answer
1	What type of word is إِنَّ and **why** does it have a *fathah* on the last letter?	
2	Look at the verb كَسَرَ. Mention with detail the type of verb it is (scale, number, gender).	

Line 39: كَانَ الْجَوَابُ: حَرِّقُوْهُ وَانْصُرُوْا آلِهَتَكُمْ (The answer was, "Burn him and help your idols.)

كَانَ الْجَوَابُ: حَرِّقُوْهُ وَانْصُرُوْا آلِهَتَكُمْ							
كُم	آلِهَةَ	انْصُرُوْا	وَ	هُ	حَرِّقُوْ	الْجَوَابُ	كَانَ

	Question	Answer
1	What type of verb is حَرِّقُوْ (based on the translation provided)?	
2	Look at the verb اُنْصُرُوْا. Mention with detail the type of verb it is (scale, number, gender).	

Line 40: رَأى النَّاسُ أَنَّ النَّارَ لَا تَضُرُّ إِبْرَاهِيْمَ (The people saw that the fire would not harm Ibrahim.)

رَأى النَّاسُ أَنَّ النَّارَ لَا تَضُرُّ إِبْرَاهِيْمَ						
إِبْرَاهِيْمَ	تَضُرُّ	لَا	النَّارَ	أَنَّ	النَّاسُ	رَأى
	فعل مضارع + فاعل	حرف النفي				
	فعل + فاعل					

	Question	Answer
1	Look at the verb تَضُرُّ . Mention with detail the type of verb it is (scale, number, gender).	
2	Why is the word تَضُرّ feminine?	

Line 41: رَأى النَّاسُ أَنَّ إِبْرَاهِيْمَ مَسْرُوْرٌ (People saw that Ibrahim was happy.)

رَأى النَّاسُ أَنَّ إِبْرَاهِيْمَ مَسْرُوْرٌ				
مَسْرُوْرٌ	إِبْرَاهِيْمَ	أَنَّ	النَّاسُ	رَأى

	Question	Answer
1	Mention all the detail of the noun مَسْرُوْر according to *sarf.*	

Line 42: دُهِشَ النَّاسُ وَتَحَيَّرُوْا (People were amazed and astonished.)

<table>
<tr><td colspan="4">دُهِشَ النَّاسُ وَتَحَيَّرُوْا</td></tr>
<tr><td>تَحَيَّرُوْا</td><td>وَ</td><td>النَّاسُ</td><td>دُهِشَ</td></tr>
<tr><td></td><td></td><td></td><td></td></tr>
<tr><td></td><td></td><td colspan="2"></td></tr>
<tr><td colspan="4"></td></tr>
</table>

	Question	Answer
1	Look at the word تَحَيَّرُوا ? Mention with detail the type of verb it is (scale, number, gender).	
2	What is the other name for نائب الفاعل ? Briefly mention the main rules for نائب الفاعل .	

Line 43: إِنَّ اللهَ حَيٌّ لَا يَمُوْتُ (Indeed, Allah is alive, he does not die.)

<table>
<tr><td colspan="4">إِنَّ اللهَ حَيٌّ لَا يَمُوْتُ</td></tr>
<tr><td>لَا يَمُوْتُ</td><td>حَيٌّ</td><td>اللهَ</td><td>إِنَّ</td></tr>
<tr><td></td><td></td><td rowspan="2"></td><td rowspan="2"></td></tr>
<tr><td colspan="2"></td></tr>
<tr><td colspan="4"></td></tr>
</table>

	Question	Answer
1	Mention the six الحروف المشبهة بالفعل with meaning.	
2	Look at the word لَا يَمُوْتُ . Mention with detail the type of verb it is (scale, number, gender).	

Line 44: إِنَّ اللهَ قَوِيٌّ لَا يَغْلِبُهُ شَيْءٌ (Indeed, Allah is powerful, nothing overpowers Him.)

إِنَّ اللهَ قَوِيٌّ لَا يَغْلِبُهُ شَيْءٌ					
شَيْءٌ	هُ	لَا يَغْلِبُ	قَوِيٌّ	اللهَ	إِنَّ

	Question	Answer
1	What type of word is a *dhameer* (pronoun)? Also mention why هُ in the above example has a *dhammah harakah.*	
2	Mention what ضمير منصوب متصل means. Give **one** example.	

Line 45: الْقَمَرُ ضَعِيْفٌ تَغْلِبُهُ الشَّمْسُ (The moon is weak, the sun overpowers it).

الْقَمَرُ ضَعِيْفٌ تَغْلِبُهُ الشَّمْسُ				
الشَّمْسُ	هُ	تَغْلِبُ	ضَعِيْفٌ	الْقَمَرُ

	Question	Answer
1	Mention what ضمير مرفوع متصل means. Give **one** example.	
2	Mention what ضمير مجرور متصل means. Give **one** example.	

Line 46: لَا يَنْصُرُنِي الْكَوْكَبُ لِأَنَّهُ ضَعِيْفٌ (The star does not help me as it is weak.)

لَا يَنْصُرُنِيَ الْكَوْكَبُ لِأَنَّهُ ضَعِيْفٌ							
ضَعِيْفٌ	هُ	أَنَّ	لِ	الْكَوْكَبُ	نِيْ	يَنْصُرُ	لَا

	Question	Answer
1	Define the terms معرب and مبني and give an example for each.	

Line 47: لَا تَنْصُرُنِي الشَّمْسُ لِأَنَّهَا ضَعِيْفَةٌ (The sun does not help me because it is weak.)

لَا تَنْصُرُنِيَ الشَّمْسُ لِأَنَّهَا ضَعِيْفَةٌ							
ضَعِيْفَةٌ	هَا	أَنَّ	لِ	الشَّمْسُ	نِيْ	تَنْصُرُ	لَا

	Question	Answer
1	Look at the verb تَنْصُرُ. Mention with detail the type of verb it is (scale, number, gender).	
2	Mention why the verb used for 'stars' was يَنْصُرُ with a *yaa,* and the verb used for 'sun' is تَنْصُرُ with a *taa.*	

Line 48: عَرَفَ إِبْرَاهِيمُ أَنَّ اللهَ رَبُّهُ (Ibrahim recognised that Allah is his Lord.)

<table>
<tr><td colspan="6">عَرَفَ إِبْرَاهِيمُ أَنَّ اللهَ رَبُّهُ</td></tr>
<tr><td>هُ</td><td>رَبُّ</td><td>اللهَ</td><td>أَنَّ</td><td>إِبْرَاهِيمُ</td><td>عَرَفَ</td></tr>
<tr><td></td><td></td><td rowspan="2"></td><td rowspan="2"></td><td rowspan="3"></td><td rowspan="3"></td></tr>
<tr><td colspan="2"></td></tr>
<tr><td colspan="4"></td></tr>
<tr><td colspan="6"></td></tr>
</table>

	Question	Answer
1	What type of word is إِبْرَاهِيمُ ? Fully explain why it has a **single *dhammah*** on the last letter.	
2	What are the **nine** causes of a word becoming غير المنصرف ?	

Line 49: إِنَّ اللهَ رَبُّ الْقَمَرِ (Verily, Allah is the lord of the moon.)

<table>
<tr><td colspan="4">إِنَّ اللهَ رَبُّ الْقَمَرِ</td></tr>
<tr><td>الْقَمَرِ</td><td>رَبُّ</td><td>اللهَ</td><td>إِنَّ</td></tr>
<tr><td></td><td></td><td rowspan="2"></td><td rowspan="2"></td></tr>
<tr><td colspan="2"></td></tr>
<tr><td colspan="4">الجملة الاسميّة الخبريّة</td></tr>
</table>

	Question	Answer
1	Mention the two cases for *majroorat* with examples.	

<u>Line 50</u>: أَنَّ اللهَ رَبُّ الْعَالَمِيْنَ (That Allah is the lord of the worlds).

أَنَّ اللهَ رَبُّ الْعَالَمِيْنَ			
الْعَالَمِيْنَ	رَبُّ	اللهَ	أَنَّ

	Question	Answer
1	Explain the terms اسم أنّ and خبر أنّ clearly, with an example.	
2	What type of word is الْعَالَمِيْنَ ? Refer to the 'magic chart' in the explanation.	

<u>Line 51</u>: هَدَى اللهُ إِبْرَاهِيْمَ (Allah guided Ibrahim.)

هَدَى اللهُ إِبْرَاهِيْمَ		
إِبْرَاهِيْمَ	اللهُ	هَدَى

	Question	Answer
1	Mention the **five** types of مفعول with an example for each.	
2	Can a مفعول come before the فاعل or before the فعل?	

Line 52: أَمَرَ اللهُ إِبْرَاهِيمَ أَنْ يَدْعُوَ قَوْمَهُ (Allah ordered Ibrahim that he calls his people).

أَمَرَ اللهُ إِبْرَاهِيمَ أَنْ يَدْعُوَ قَوْمَهُ						
هُ	قَوْمَ	يَدْعُوَ	أَنْ	إِبْرَاهِيمَ	اللهُ	أَمَرَ

	Question	Answer
1	Explain the grammatical impact of the الحروف الناصبة with an example.	
2	Can a verb have more than one مفعول به ?	

Line 53: دَعَا إِبْرَاهِيمُ قَوْمَهُ إِلَى اللهِ (Ibrahim called his people towards Allah.)

دَعَا إِبْرَاهِيمُ قَوْمَهُ إِلَى اللهِ					
اللهِ	إِلَى	هُ	قَوْمَ	إِبْرَاهِيمُ	دَعَا

	Question	Answer
1	Mention all the *harf jarr* with their meanings.	

Line 54: قَالَ إِبْرَاهِيْمُ لِقَوْمِهِ: مَا تَعْبُدُوْنَ؟ (Ibrahim said to his people: What do you worship?)

قَالَ إِبْرَاهِيْمُ لِقَوْمِهِ: مَا تَعْبُدُوْنَ؟						
تَعْبُدُوْنَ	مَا	ـهِ	قَوْمِ	لِـ	إِبْرَاهِيْمُ	قَالَ

	Question	Answer
1	Look at the word تَعْبُدُوْنَ . Mention with detail the type of verb it is (scale, number, gender).	
2	Mention the main rules of a فاعل .	

Line 55: قَالُوْا: نَعْبُدُ أَصْنَامًا (They said: We worship idols.)

قَالُوْا: نَعْبُدُ أَصْنَامًا		
أَصْنَامًا	نَعْبُدُ	قَالُوْا

	Question	Answer
1	Look at the word قَالُوْا . Mention with detail the type of verb it is (scale, number, gender).	
2	What type of word is أَصْنَام ? Refer to the 'magic chart' in the answer.	

LESSON 44: FLOWCHARTS

Alhamdulillah, with the Grace and Help from Almighty Allah, the rules for this primer have been covered. Furthermore, grammar rules have been revised and practised through the completion of many grammatical breakdowns. Now, finally, before the students continue their Arabic grammar journey by commencing more advanced grammar books, they should go over the following charts and annotate with brief definitions and examples.

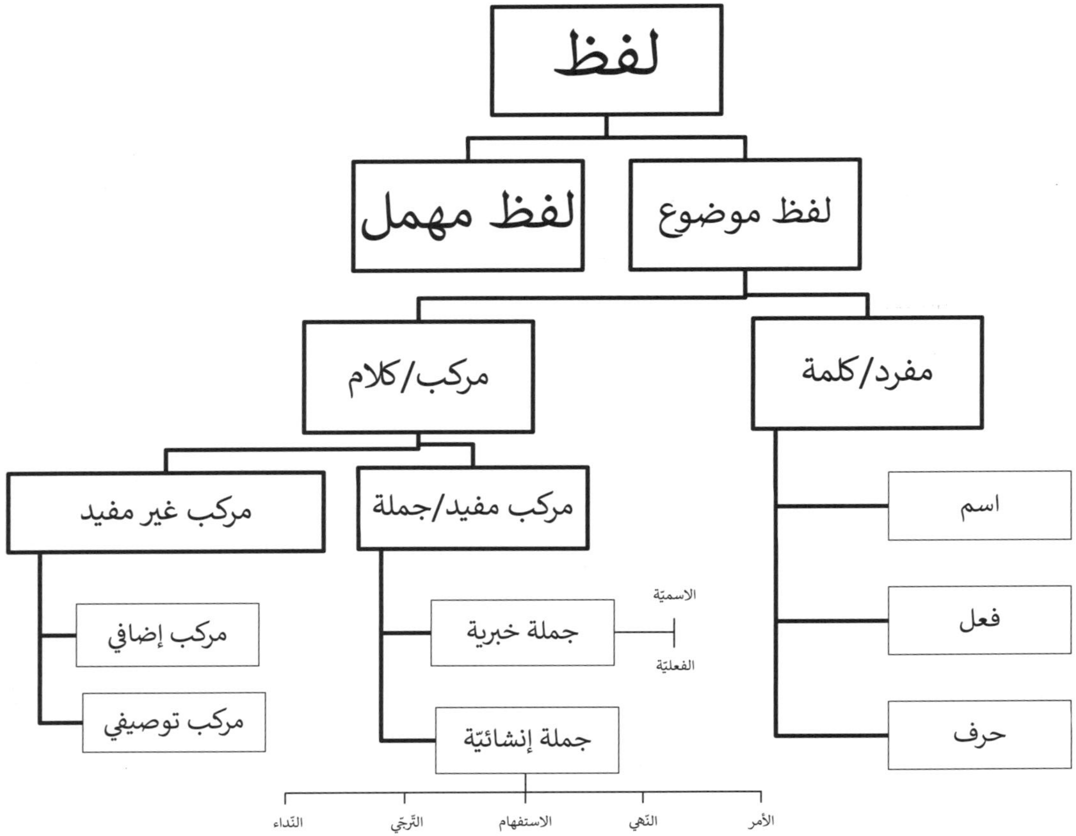
لفظ
لفظ موضوع
لفظ مهمل
مفرد/كلمة
مركب/كلام
اسم
فعل
حرف
مركب مفيد/جملة
مركب غير مفيد
جملة خبرية
الاسميّة
الفعليّة
جملة إنشائيّة
الأمر
النّهي
الاستفهام
التّرجّي
النّداء
مركب إضافي
مركب توصيفي

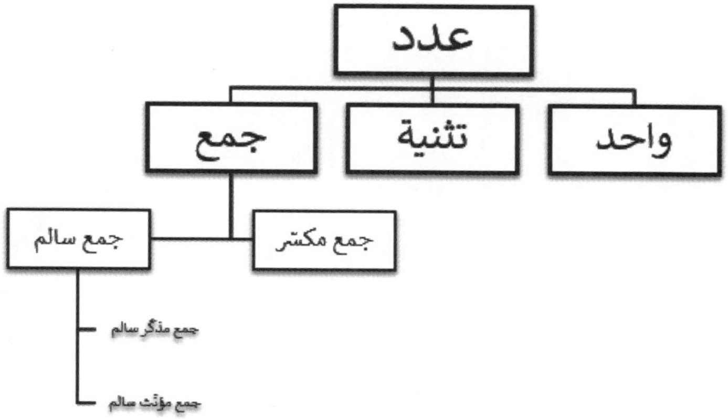
عدد
واحد
تثنية
جمع
جمع مكسّر
جمع سالم
جمع مذكّر سالم
جمع مؤنّث سالم

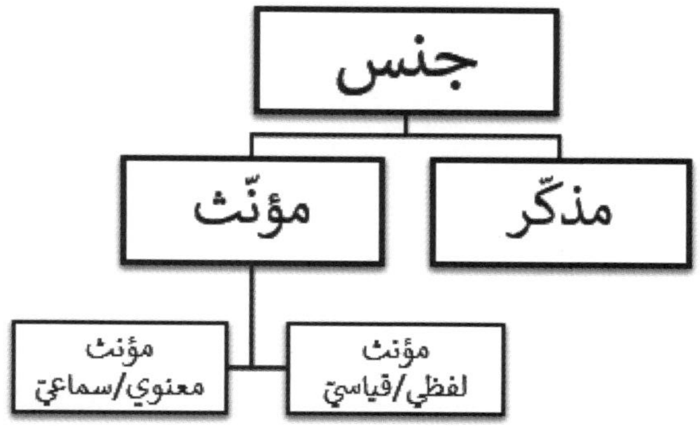
جنس
مذكّر
مؤنّث
مؤنث لفظي/قياسيّ
مؤنث معنوي/سماعيّ

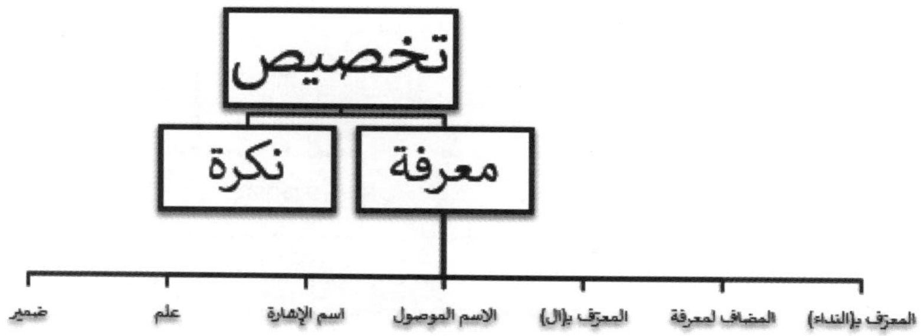
تخصيص
معرفة
نكرة
المعرّف بـ(النداء)
المضاف لمعرفة
المعرّف بـ(ال)
الاسم الموصول
اسم الإشارة
علم
ضمير

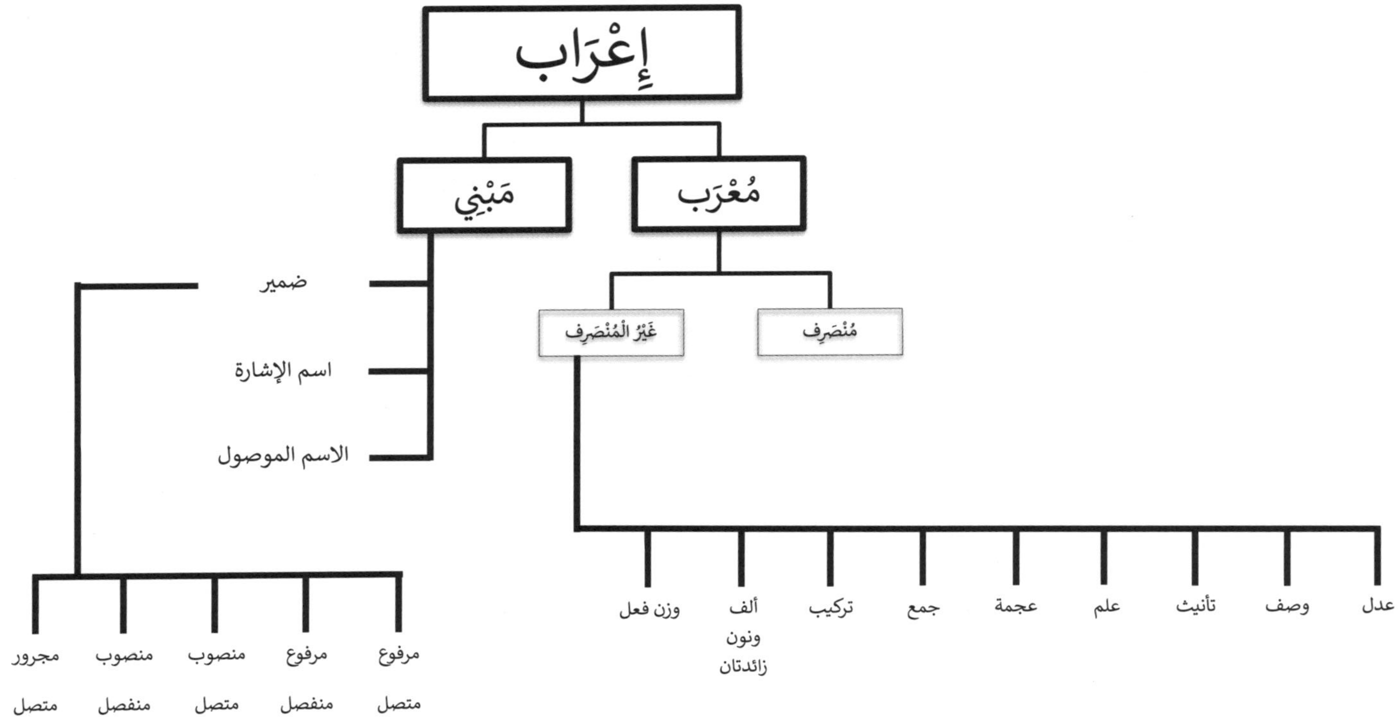
إِعْرَاب
مُعْرَب
مَبْنِي
مُنْصَرِف
غَيْرُ الْمُنْصَرِف
عدل
وصف
تأنيث
علم
عجمة
جمع
تركيب
ألف ونون زائدتان
وزن فعل
ضمير
اسم الإشارة
الاسم الموصول
مرفوع متصل
مرفوع منفصل
منصوب متصل
منصوب منفصل
مجرور متصل

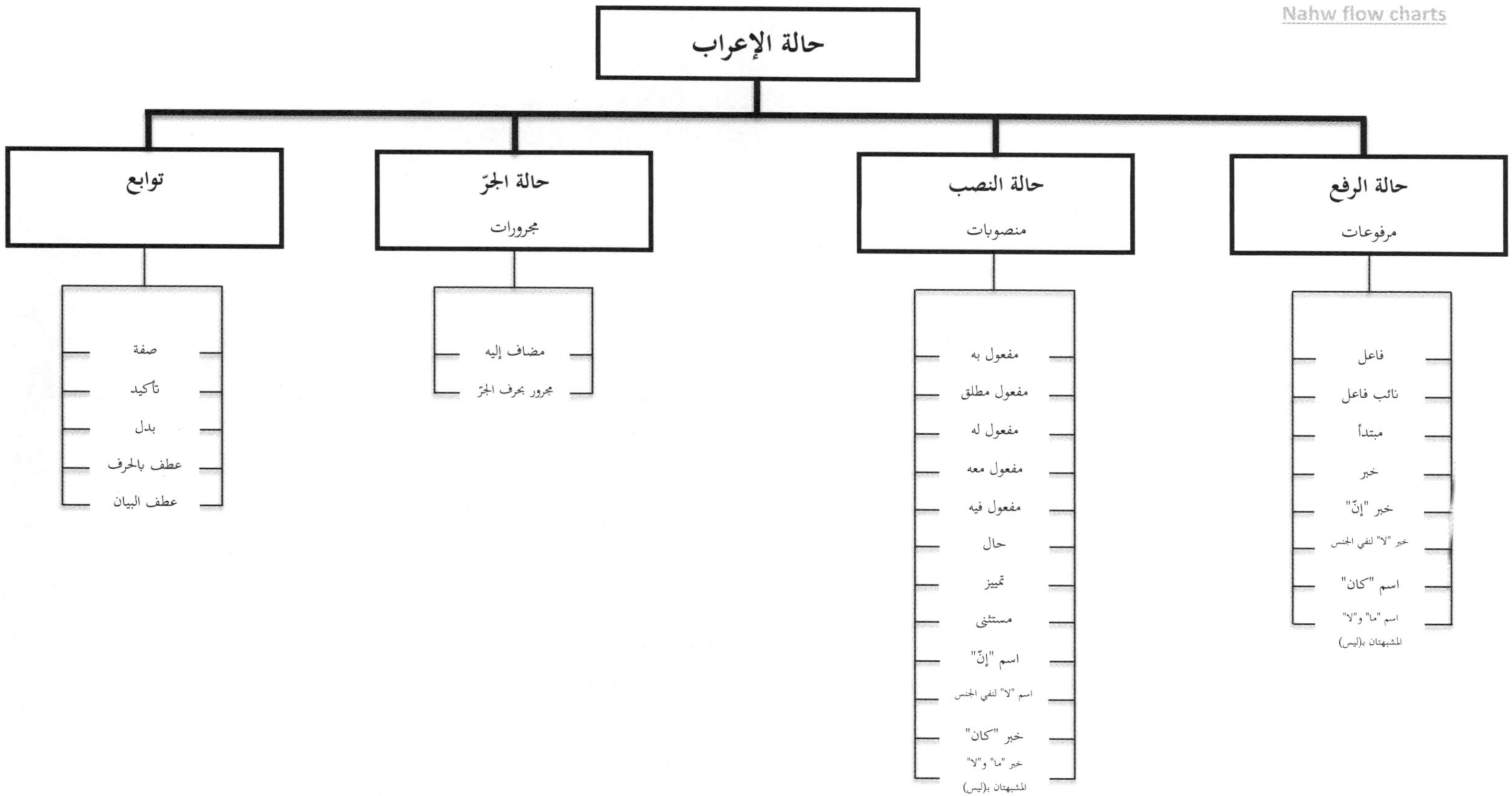
حالة الإعراب
حالة الرفع
مرفوعات
فاعل
نائب فاعل
مبتدأ
خبر
خبر "إنّ"
خبر "لا" لنفي الجنس
اسم "كان"
اسم "ما" و"لا" المشبهتان بـ(ليس)
حالة النصب
منصوبات
مفعول به
مفعول مطلق
مفعول له
مفعول معه
مفعول فيه
حال
تمييز
مستثنى
اسم "إنّ"
اسم "لا" لنفي الجنس
خبر "كان"
خبر "ما" و"لا" المشبهتان بـ(ليس)
حالة الجرّ
مجرورات
مضاف إليه
مجرور بحرف الجرّ
توابع
صفة
تأكيد
بدل
عطف بالحرف
عطف البيان

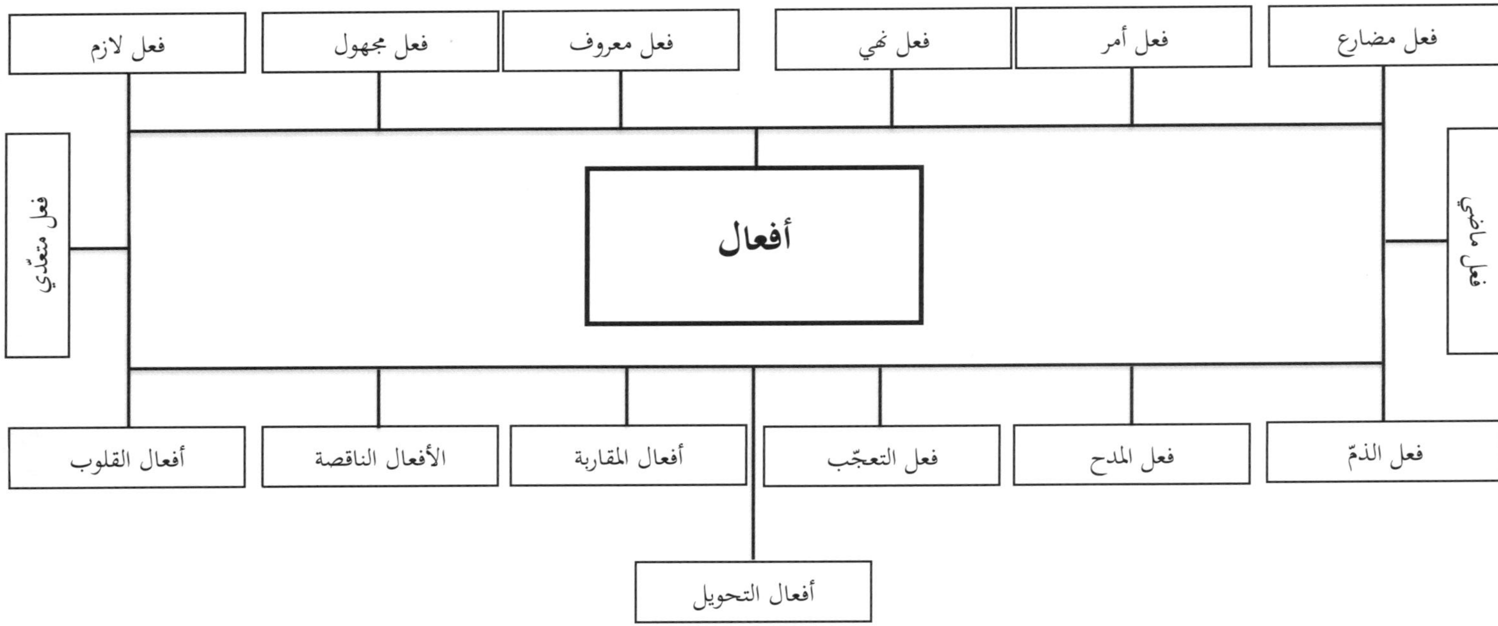
أفعال
فعل ماضي
فعل مضارع
فعل أمر
فعل نهي
فعل معروف
فعل مجهول
فعل لازم
فعل متعدّي
فعل الذمّ
فعل المدح
فعل التعجّب
أفعال المقاربة
الأفعال الناقصة
أفعال القلوب
أفعال التحويل

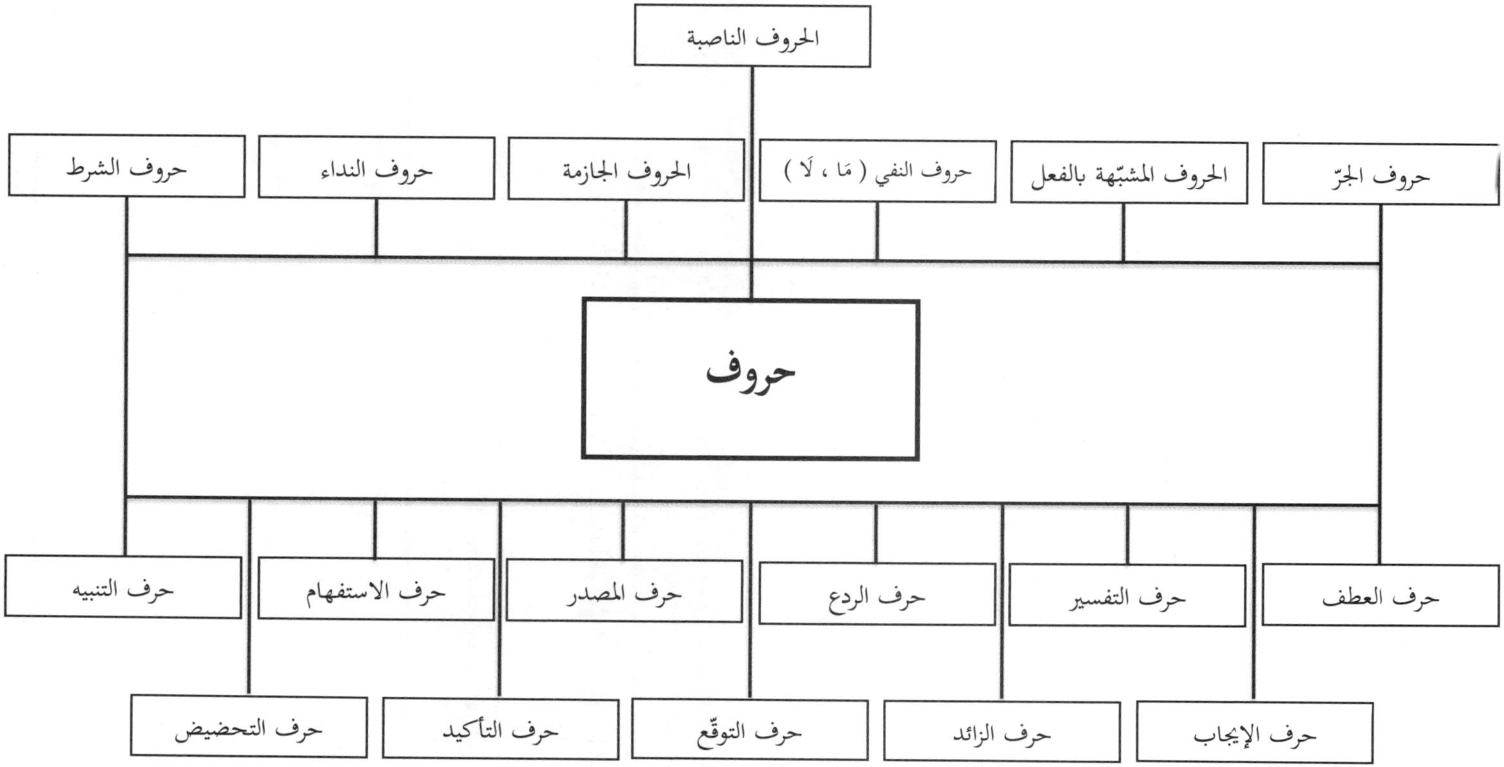
الحروف الناصبة
حروف الجرّ
الحروف المشبّهة بالفعل
حروف النفي (مَا ، لَا)
الحروف الجازمة
حروف النداء
حروف الشرط
حروف
حرف العطف
حرف التفسير
حرف الردع
حرف المصدر
حرف الاستفهام
حرف التنبيه
حرف الإيجاب
حرف الزائد
حرف التوقّع
حرف التأكيد
حرف التحضيض

Our publications

Jamiatul Ilm Wal Huda

Qur'an word list (in Arabic with Urdu and English translation)

This compilation provides the translations and definitions of over 10000 challenging words in the Holy Qur'an. It also provides the morphology of the words and its formations. The translation of the Arabic words will be of benefit to any reader, whereas, the Arabic word formations will permit the more advanced students of Arabic to engage even further with the precise and perfect word choice of the Holy Qur'an.

1000 Hadith (in Arabic with English translation)

This book is a compilation of a 1000 authentic narrations of Prophet Muhammad ﷺ from the six famous books, it is designed in chapter form. The book has originally been created for memorisation, yet it can be useful for general reading as well. The 1000 narrations have been translated into easy flowing English, easily understandable for all. A book that would not only be of great benefit in the classroom environment, rather it will be very useful for study circles and daily reminders at home as well. In sha Allah.

Usool al-Hadith (in Arabic)

This book is aimed at teaching Usool al-Hadith to an intermediate level; in an easy format. It is filled with tables and flowcharts; this style has been adopted to make the subject as easy as possible to understand. Furthermore, flowcharts have been added at the end of the book which covers majority of the subject.

Training the Students of Sacred Knowledge (in English)

This book is aimed at teaching the students of the sacred knowledge the etiquettes of studying. This book *Riyāḍat al-Muta'allimīn* is indispensable and beneficial especially for students of knowledge and teachers. Imam Ibn al-Sunnī outlines the etiquettes and guidelines for students and teachers, the methods of teaching and learning, and the different sciences that should be acquired. This compilation has translated the original work in a reader friendly manner, mentioning the approximately 300 etiquettes with proofs from narrations.

40 Hadeeth on Islamic Manners

Islam teaches us the great importance of manners and etiquettes to the extent that it has been regarded as the weightiest deed in the scale of good deeds. This compilation of 40 Hadeeth with translation and explanation of the 40 Hadeeth will, insha Allah, serve as a means of encouragement to us all; young, old, students, scholars, laity etc. The style of the explanation has been kept very simple with approximately two sides of explanation for each Hadeeth, most of the explanation are simply capturing Qur'an verses, other Prophetic narrations or sayings of the pious scholars in regards to the topic discussed. The chapters included are wide ranging, from mercy to parents, anger to jealousy, treatment towards Muslims and non-Muslims, rights of the Lord to the rights of the creation and so.

Diwan of Imam Shafe'e

The compilation includes the Arabic poetry of Imam Shafe'e with explanatory translation in English. A very simple and easy style of translation has been adopted, allowing all to benefit from the valuable advices and lessons captured by Imam Shafe'e within his poetry. It should hopefully serve beneficial for students of Arabic along with those that are unable to read or understand Arabic. Furthermore, there is a vocabulary list of the difficult words in footnotes allowing students to benefit further. Also, a treatise of Arabic poetry rules in English has been added to the beginning of the compilation for further benefit.

Dua book (with other detail regarding dua)

Sincere supplications are a fundamental facet of our religion. They are beautiful displays of our vulnerability. This compilation contains approximately 500 Prophetic supplications with English trasnaltion and brief explanations. Further, it includes other related aspects to dua including chapters on virtues, ettiquetes and 'special moments' of dua. The 99 glorious names of Almighty Allah with proof from the verses of the Holy Qur'an are also mentioned.

Sarf (volume 1)

To achieve a deep and coherent understanding of any language, it is of imperative importance that an individual grasps the fundamental and foundational rules along with working on increasing the vocabulary within that language. This volume covers the introduction of Arabic morphology (sarf), building from the basic level. It introduces all the famous nineteen scales with their past tense, present/future tense, imperative, prohibitive, emphatic forms and much more. Furthermore, it builds onto the 'small charts' *(sarf sagheer)* for these words and also provides other words for practice. The compilation also indicates to the 'special meanings' and nuances of each scale. Even though this volume does not delve into the 'advanced variations' of these nineteen scales, a small introduction to these 'advance variations' is mentioned within this volume. Finally, some words regarded difficult in the Holy Qur'an by Arabic morphology students have been mentioned and explained within this volume.

Sarf (volume 2)

To achieve a deep and coherent understanding of any language, it is of imperative importance that an individual grasps the fundamental and foundational rules along with working on increasing the vocabulary within that language. This volume covers the 'advance charts' for the subject of morphology along with the related rules. After completing the study of this compilation, the student will have covered the knowledge covered within most of the famous intermediate level morphorlogy books. Hence, the student should be able to read and analyse all the vers from the Holy Qur'an and other Arabic language books.

Nahw (beginner level)

This book is designed for teaching Nahw (Arabic syntax) for the beginner level. It has adopted a very simple style with very simple terms indicated. The depth of the subject has been avoided; aiming to consolidate the very basics of grammar for the learners. It includes many activities and also a beneficial section at the end for consolidating the 'grammatical breakdowns' of sentences.

Zahratun Nahw

This book is designed for teaching Nahw (Arabic syntax) for the beginner level. It has adopted a very simple style with very simple terms indicated. The depth of the subject has been avoided; aiming to consolidate the very basics of grammar for the learners.

Hidayatun Nahw (with Q&A in English)

The book Hidayatun Nahw is a book taught in many places for intermediate level Nahw. However, due to its complex text, many readers find many parts of the text difficult to solve. Therefore, for the English speaking readers, this book was designed with the intention of making the complex text of the book easier for understanding. Hence, the English question & answers do not go into much detail beyond the content of the book; it is more based on solving the book.

Durus al-Lughah al-Arabiyyah (part 1)

Durus al-lughah al-Arabiyyah is a book taught in many institutes as a beginners/intermediate guide for Arabic learning. Book 1 covers 23 important chapters of Arabic grammar, language and literature; allowing the students to become equipped with the foundation/intermediate before enhancing to higher level. The book was designed specifically for non-Arab students intending to learn basic writing, reading and speaking skills within modern-day Arabic. This publication explains the core lessons and meanings of each chapter in English, along with additional notes at the end of important modern-day Arabic words not covered within the original book.

Durus al-Lughah al-Arabiyyah (part 2)

Durus al-lughah al-Arabiyyah is a book taught in many institutes as a beginners/intermediate guide for Arabic learning. Book 2 covers 31 important chapters of Arabic grammar, language and literature; allowing the students to become equipped with the foundation/intermediate before enhancing to higher level. The book was designed specifically for non-Arab students intending to learn basic writing, reading and speaking skills within modern-day Arabic. This publication explains the core lessons and meanings of each chapter in English, along with additional notes at the end of important modern-day Arabic words not covered within the original book.

Das Sabak (in Urdu & English)

The book Das Sabak is a book taught in many institutes as a beginners guide for Arabic learning. The book covers ten very important topics of Arabic grammar; allowing the students to become equipped with the foundation before enhancing to intermediate level. The book was designed to make translation of the Qur'an easier for beginners; covering most words up to half of the first para. However, as the book was written in Urdu, it became hard for the English speaking audience to take benefit from the book; hence, the need arose to make a parallel English version of the book. The Urdu has been kept within the book, with explanatory English notes for each chapter.

Qisas an-Nabiyeen (part 1-4)

Qisas an-Nabiyyeen is a compilation of short and entertaining stories about some of the Messengers. It was written by Shaykh Abul Hasan Ali an-Nadwi for students starting to learn the Arabic language. The Jamiatul Ilm Wal Huda publication has the original text with an addition of over 2500 words of Arabic vocabulary with English and Urdu meanings.

Qisas an-Nabiyeen (part 5)

Qisas an-Nabiyyeen is a compilation of short and entertaining stories about some of the Messengers, part 5 is dedicated to the final Prophet, Muhammad. It was written by Shaykh Abul Hasan Ali an-Nadwi for students starting to learn the Arabic language. The Jamiatul Ilm Wal Huda publication has the original text with an addition of over 1300 words of Arabic vocabulary with English and Urdu meanings. Further, this publication has added footnotes of certain names and events and added additional Seerah information at the end of the book.

Suwar min Hayat as-Sahabiyyaat

Suwar min Hayat as-Sahabiyyat is a compilation of short and entertaining stories about eight female Companions. It was written by Shaykh Abdul Rahman Ra'fat al-Pasha for students starting to learn the Arabic language. The Jamiatul Ilm Wal Huda publication has the original text with an addition of over 1000 words of Arabic vocabulary with English and Urdu meanings; also, a brief of each female scholar in the English language.

A Comprehensive Guide To Tajweed

This book is aimed at teaching enhanced level Tajweed according to the recitation of Imam Hafs. Many simple books have been written in the English language on the subject of Tajweed; however, most were restricted to the beginner's level. Hence, the need arose to compile a book of advanced level which would enable the English speaking audience to learn detailed Tajweed directly from an English source. This book will allow the reader to straight away solve many of the detailed books of Tajweed within the Arabic language. It may even prove to be a commentary for many of the Arabic texts.

Al-Muqaddimah al-Jazariyyah

Al-Muqaddimah al-Jazariyyah is a compilation of tajweed rules by Shams al-Din al-Jazari in over 100 poems. The Jamiatul Ilm Wal Huda publication has the original text with an addition of English translation/explanation; allowing readers to easily understand the Arabic lines.

Mantiq (in Arabic)

This book is aimed at teaching the classical Mantiq (logic) terms to an intermediate level; in an easy format. It is filled with tables and flowcharts; this style has been adopted to make the subject as easy as possible to understand. Furthermore, flowcharts have been added at the end of the book which covers majority of the subject.